Extreme Poverty, Growth, and Inequality in Bangladesh

Praise for this book

'Bangladesh has moved remarkably from being a basket case to a lower middle income country. Can it eradicate the extreme poverty that still afflicts a fifth of its people? The expert team which has created this exciting book uses granular case studies to answer 'yes'. It debates the social and political costs and benefits of policy choices and pathways, comparing growth outcomes with those of distributive policy. Indispensable for anyone engaged with the character and trajectories of extreme poverty and with the world's sustainable development goals.'

Barbara Harriss-White, Emeritus Professor of Development Studies,
Wolfson College, Oxford

'Written by a group of uniquely qualified specialists, these essays offer very valuable insights into how to address extreme poverty in a country that is rapidly becoming a success story of economic and human development. The editors make a strong case for a universal basic income to address extreme poverty that deserves the attention of policy-makers. This book will remain required reading for social scientists interested in studying extreme poverty for a long time.'

Santosh Mehrotra, Professor of Economics, School of Social Sciences,
Jawaharlal Nehru University, New Delhi

Extreme Poverty, Growth, and Inequality in Bangladesh

Edited by
Joe Devine, Geof D. Wood,
Zulfiqar Ali, and Shamsul Alam

PRACTICAL ACTION
Publishing

Practical Action Publishing Ltd
The Schumacher Centre, Bourton on Dunsmore, Rugby, Warwickshire, CV23 9QZ, UK
www.practicalactionpublishing.org

A catalogue record for this book is available from the British Library.

A catalogue record for this book has been requested from the Library of Congress.

ISBN 9781853399466 Hardback
ISBN 9781853399473 Paperback
ISBN 9781780449470 eBook
ISBN 9781780449463 Library PDF

Citation: Devine, J., Wood, G.D., Ali, Z., and Aslam, S., *Extreme Poverty, Growth, and Inequality in Bangladesh*, Rugby, UK: Practical Action Publishing, <http://dx.doi.org/10.3362/9781780449463>

Since 1974, Practical Action Publishing has published and disseminated books and information in support of international development work throughout the world. Practical Action Publishing is a trading name of Practical Action Publishing Ltd (Company Reg. No. 1159018), the wholly owned publishing company of Practical Action. Practical Action Publishing trades only in support of its parent charity objectives and any profits are covenanted back to Practical Action (Charity Reg. No. 247257, Group VAT Registration No. 880 9924 76).

Cover photo: Slum dweller in Faridpur, Bangladesh
Credit: Matt Wenham, Practical Action
Cover design by Andrew Corbett
Typeset by vPrompt eServices, India
Indexed by Elizabeth Ball
Printed by Replika Press Pvt, India.

Contents

List of figures and tables   vi
Acronyms   viii
Bengali terms   xi
Acknowledgements   xii

1. Sharing the well: towards sustained eradication
   of extreme poverty in Bangladesh   1
   Geof D. Wood and Joe Devine

2. Ending extreme poverty in Bangladesh:
   trends, drivers, and policies   11
   Binayak Sen and Zulfiqar Ali

3. Leaving no one behind in Bangladesh:
   the case for a new political settlement   31
   Joe Devine and Geof D. Wood

4. Guardianship and processes of change:
   the feminization of extreme poverty in Bangladesh   51
   Mathilde Maîtrot

5. Financial exclusion and extreme poverty in Bangladesh   71
   Mustafa K. Mujeri

6. Dynamics of regional poverty and real wages:
   policy implications for development interventions   89
   Shamsul Alam and Kazi Iqbal

7. Agricultural commercialization and employment generation:
   implications for the extreme poor   109
   K.A.S. Murshid

8. Urbanization and extreme poverty   125
   Nazrul Islam

9. Reforming the social security system for poverty reduction   141
   Sadiq Ahmed

10. Conclusion: sharing the well   161
    Zulfiqar Ali and Geof D. Wood

Index   181

List of figures and tables

Figures

2.1	Trends in national extreme poverty	14
3.1	Model for well-being regimes	34
4.1	Fahmida's life trajectory	59
4.2	Jalmai's life trajectory	60
6.1	Trends in real wages in agriculture	93
6.2	Trends in nominal wages and rice prices	95
6.3	Change in poverty rates by sub-district (UPL)	96
6.4	Change in poverty rates (LPL)	98
6.5	Real wages by region	100
6.6	Relationship between poverty (UPL) and real wages	102
6.7	Relationship between poverty (LPL) and real wages	102
6.8	Relationship between poverty (UPL) and real wages	103
6.9	Relationship between poverty (LPL) and real wages	103
7.1	Typical value chain for agriculture in Bangladesh	111
8.1	Annual growth rates of population (1974–2011)	127
8.2	Projected rural and urban population in Bangladesh (2011–51)	127
8.3	The distribution and size of urban centres in Bangladesh	130
9.1	Lifecycle risks	146
9.2	Cumulative distribution of per capita consumption	153

Tables

2.1	Poverty headcount rates (%)	14
2.2	Growth elasticity estimates	20
2.3	Extreme poverty headcount projections for 2011–21	21
2.4	Costs of supporting extreme poor beneficiaries	23
5.1	Overall state of financial inclusion in Bangladesh (2014)	73

5.2 Characteristics of households with access to
     financial services (2009–10)   74

5.3 Transaction costs of borrowing from different
     markets (2009–10)   76

6.1 Association between poverty and real wages   104

7.1 Potato production (2013–14 and 2007) by land size group
     (*maunds*/household)   116

7.2 Storage of table and seed potatoes by land size group (*maunds*) 117

7.3 Agricultural input costs (BDT/household)   118

9.1 Poverty impact of current SSP spending   147

9.2 Poverty impact of the redefined lifecycle programmes   158

10.1 Resource requirements for UBI and other alternative
      social protection measures: option 1   177

10.2 Resource requirements for UBI and other alternative
      social protection measures: option 2   177

Acronyms

ADP	Annual Development Programme
BBS	Bangladesh Bureau of Statistics
BBS-WFP	Bangladesh Bureau of Statistics and the World Food Programme
BDT	Bangladeshi Taka
BHH	Beneficiary Household
BIDS	Bangladesh Institute of Development Studies
BIG	Basic Income Grant
BNPL	Bangladesh National Poverty Line
BPD	Bangladesh Poverty Database
BRAC	Bangladesh Rural Advancement Committee
CBN	Cost of Basic Needs
CBO	Community-Based Organization
CFPR-TUP	BRAC's Challenging the Frontiers of Poverty Reduction – Targeting the Ultra Poor
CIDA	Canadian International Development Agency
CLP	Char Livelihoods Programme
CPRC	Chronic Poverty Research Centre
CSR	Corporate Social Responsibility
CUS	Centre for Urban Studies
DFAT	Department of Foreign Affairs and Trade
DFID	Department for International Development
DSS	Department of Social Services
EEP	Economic Empowerment of the Poorest
FYP	Five Year Plan
G2P	Government to Person
GDP	Gross Domestic Product

GED	General Economics Division
GMIE	Group Mobilization and Individual Entrepreneurship
GNP	Gross National Product
GoB	Government of Bangladesh
HDI	Human Development Index
HIES	Household Income and Expenditure Survey
HYV	High-yielding Variety
ICT	Information and Communications Technology
IDPM	Institute for Development Policy and Management
ILO	International Labour Organization
IRM	Institutional Responsibility Matrix
ISIS	Islamic State of Iraq and Syria
KYC	Know Your Customer
LGI	Local Government Institution
LPL	Lower Poverty Line
M&E	Monitoring and Evaluation
MDG	Millennium Development Goals
MFI	Microfinance Institution
MFS	Mobile Financial Services
MHVS	Maternal Health Voucher Scheme
MIC	Middle-income Country
MIS	Management Information System
MNC	Multinational Corporation
MNO	Mobile Network Operator
MSD	Ministry of Social Development
NDBOSS	Nagor Doridro Bastibashi Odhikar Suroksha Samiti
NDBUS	Nagar Daridra Basteebashir Unnayan Sangstha
NEP	New or Emerging Entry Point
NFA	No-frills Account
NGO	Non-Governmental Organization
NSIS	National Social Insurance Scheme
NSPS	National Social Protection Strategy

NSSA	National Social Security Agency
NSSS	National Social Security Strategy
OECD	Organisation for Economic Co-operation and Development
OLS	Ordinary Least Squares
OMS	Open Market Sales
PMT	Proxy Means Test
PoS	Point of Sale
PPP	Purchasing Power Parity
PVP	Private Voluntary Pension
REOPA	Rural Employment Generation for Public Assets
RMG	Ready-made Garment
SDG	Sustainable Development Goal
SHOUHARDO	Strengthening Household Abilities for Responding to Development Opportunities
SSP	Social Security Programme
SSS	Shidhulai Swanirvar Sangstha
TEP	Traditional Entry Point
TUP	Targeting the Ultra Poor Programme
UBI	Universal Basic Income
UPL	Upper Poverty Line
UPPR	Urban Partnerships for Poverty Reduction Programme
VGD	Vulnerable Group Development
VWB	Vulnerable Women's Benefit
WFP	World Food Programme

Bengali terms

Adivasi	Indigenous person
Aman	A type of paddy typically harvested in November/December
Aratdars	Commission agents, wholesalers
Aus	A type of paddy typically harvested in July/August
Beel	Body of water
Char	River island
Durnam	Disrepute, bad reputation
Haor	Large seasonal waterbody in north-east Bangladesh
IRRI-boro	A high-yielding paddy typically harvested in April/May
Khas	Government-owned land
Maund	Unit of measurement in South Asia, approximately 37 kg
Monga	Chronic seasonal distress
Pourashavas	Municipalities
Purdah	Social or religious practice that involves the seclusion of women by means of concealing clothing, enclosures, curtains, and so forth
Samiti	Association, savings group
Ummah	An Arabic term used to refer to human community or society – in the context of Islam, it refers to the community of believers
Upazila/thana	Local administrative unit below districts
Union Parishad	An administrative unit below *upazilas*
Zamindari	The estate of a zamindar, a large landlord

Acknowledgements

The origins of this book lie in an international conference entitled 'Towards Sustained Eradication of Extreme Poverty in Bangladesh' held in Dhaka in April 2015, and co-organized by the General Economics Division of the Planning Commission of Bangladesh, the Bangladesh Bank, and the Bangladesh Institute of Development Studies. The role of the General Economics Division of the Planning Commission in supporting the publication of the book has been particularly important.

The conference was supported by UK aid from the UK government, and the EEP/Shiree project. The editors gratefully acknowledge funding from UK aid and support from ECORYS UK Ltd, which allowed us to spend time working on the book.

The findings, interpretations, and conclusions expressed in the book are those of the authors and do not necessarily reflect the views of any of the co-organizers or supporters mentioned above.

The editors would like to thank David Jackman for invaluable help in preparing the final text.

CHAPTER 1

Sharing the well: towards sustained eradication of extreme poverty in Bangladesh

Geof D. Wood and Joe Devine

This chapter uses two metaphors to explore the moral and practical dimensions of extreme poverty eradication. The first metaphor, 'leaving no one behind', currently dominates policy discussions and broadly sees the eradication of extreme poverty as the consequence of economic growth and prosperity. In contrast, the chapter outlines an alternative approach, captured in the 'sharing the well' metaphor, which focuses much more on redistribution and rights. The chapter argues that, although both approaches are laudable, their differences are important. Crucially, the 'sharing the well' approach, although politically challenging, has roots in values shared by the people of Bangladesh. This argument helps contextualize the different chapters of the book.

Keywords: extreme poverty, redistribution, political settlement, sharing the well, leaving no one behind

Introduction

This volume examines evidence of the links between extreme poverty, growth, and inequality in contemporary Bangladesh. It brings together contributions from academics, practitioners, and policy leaders who, over the course of the past two to three years, have been working closely to inform policy debates in Bangladesh about extreme poverty. One of the highlights of this collaboration was a conference held in April 2015 and organized under the auspices of the General Economic Division (GED) of the Planning Commission of Bangladesh, the Bangladesh Bank, and the Bangladesh Institute of Development Studies (BIDS).[1] One of the aims of the conference was to explore the policy challenges of eradicating extreme poverty in Bangladesh in the context of the government deciding on the strategic priorities for its seventh Five Year Plan. The original concept note for the conference promoted the metaphor of 'sharing the well', while other voices were keen to connect to the global language of 'leaving no one behind'. While both terms are appropriate,

http://dx.doi.org/10.3362/9781780449463.001

they hide subtle differences of meaning about settlements and processes, and crucially about core values in a society. This contestation of language is the starting point of our initial reflections on the relationship between extreme poverty, growth, and inequality.

While the focus of this volume is one country, Bangladesh, the issues posed by this contestation apply more globally to many countries faced with large-scale poverty, including extreme poverty. Indeed, we might well argue that they apply with equal force to poverty eradication in rich countries such as the UK, which retain significant levels of poverty that have particular implications for the life chances of their child populations. So, although Bangladesh represents a case of recent transition from a low-technology, agrarian-based society to a differentiated and increasingly urban-oriented one, the core issues raised by the contestation of language are more generalized. To put the point bluntly, does poverty eradication require a rights-based, value commitment to the sharing of existing levels of wealth plus whatever is accumulated in the future? Or will it happen in the future only as a function of trickle-down inclusion from economic growth? 'Leaving no one behind' reflects the logic of the latter question, and refers to a society where most people will move forward and there is some need to purposefully include those who may be struggling. For neoliberals, this is best achieved by growth and the expansion of employment – any kind of employment. However, extreme poverty poses a particular challenge to that formula when the assumption of a capacity to work (to sustain individual or family livelihoods) cannot be applied due to old age; morbidity; mental health; disabilities; effects of chronic malnutrition, often arising from early stunting; gender discrimination; ethnic minority exclusion, and so forth. Societies faced with any aspects of this challenge (i.e. all societies) then have to think about trying to pass the more challenging test of sharing present resources more inclusively, thus addressing core issues of morality, fairness, and inequality. Evidence of increased inequalities within rich societies suggests that they are not so good at passing this test. What hope, then, for a society such as Bangladesh which faces large-scale moderate poverty alongside significant absolute numbers in extreme poverty? This volume, in effect, examines Bangladesh as a tough test case where, despite all kinds of political instabilities and profound contestation (Devine et al., 2017), there have been remarkable successes in poverty and extreme poverty reduction over the last three decades, and especially over the last 15 years. Moreover, the country now has a very explicit public discourse about the removal of extreme poverty by 2021, with the Government of Bangladesh's Planning Commission taking the lead. So, there is not just NGO and civil society pressure. And not just donor pressure. Thus the contributors to this volume invite the reader to witness and reflect on an explicit wrestling with moral, strategic, and pragmatic dimensions of extreme poverty eradication in a society more superficially noted for its poverty, violence, and floods.

Although the volume has an explicit focus on the challenges of extreme poverty eradication, its spotlight falls not just upon the fortunes of the extreme poor, but upon society as a whole, specifically its core morality. This is what lies at the heart of the 'sharing the well' metaphor. Today, Bangladesh retains large-scale poverty challenges alongside its many positive development achievements and signs of progress. But it is also a country that, since its inception four decades ago, has faced significant problems of identity and cohesion – challenges that have been sadly exposed by recent high-profile campaigns of targeted killings allegedly credited to Al-Qaeda and the Islamic State of Iraq and Greater Syria (ISIS).[2] There is an ongoing contestation for the soul of Bangladesh and what it means to be Bengali in a country that combines strong traditions of folk cultures and Islamic beliefs with significant minorities of Hindu and Adivasi populations. This is the context within which the society searches for a settlement or an agreed position on the distribution of life chances and well-being among its people.

The subtle differences between the 'leaving no one behind' and 'sharing the well' metaphors highlight the significance of inequality, rights, and community or *ummah*. 'Leaving no one behind' is clearly laudable, but it implies an acceptance of inequality, a policy agreement on absolute rather than relative poverty, and an acknowledgement that there will always be 'stragglers'. Such a notion is akin to the adage that 'the poor will always be with us', inviting at best the idea of policy as charity welfare for (deserving) victims rather than the removal of victimhood – that is, the condition of being a victim. Unfortunately this is a widespread understanding of social policy, combined with a power-holder's instinct for narrowing the criteria of entitlement to reduce the redistributive burden upon the more self-sufficient, 'hardworking' others. There is much labelling at work in such an approach (Wood, 2007). It is also a reflection of the limited-access state (North et al., 2009).

'Leaving no one behind' implies a growing economy, one moving forward, in which some people could get left behind unless they are held in by Pareto-optimizing assumptions. This frames the analysis in terms of the 'poverty elasticity response' to economic growth. 'Sharing the well', instead, allows for the possibility that growth is not inevitable, and questions assumptions made about adequate trickle-down. It thus asks the harder political economy question of redistribution and sharing under conditions of inequality reproduced by elite powerholders. In the context of a fragile political economy, potentially made worse by climate change, are the social and cultural forces in Bangladesh able to compensate by acting out the values of solidarity and gendered fairness? Can the well – and the well-being that goes with it – be shared? Or at least shared to the extent that no one is left behind?

Part of the understanding of this question lies in the fact that Bangladesh is changing in its structure and values. While there has never been a golden age when the 'well' was 'well shared', Bangladesh's pre-capitalist, agrarian quasi-feudal society did contain some safety nets at the local level across the *zamindari* estates. If labour is the relatively scarce factor of production under low technological conditions, then those classes that need agricultural labour have to ensure the basic terms of its reproduction. So, alongside exploitation, there has to be a sufficient condition of multi-period redistribution to cope with both perennial seasonal fluctuations in food availability and the years between droughts and floods. This was therefore not a golden age, but there was some social and cultural capacity within an unequal political economy to share, even if unevenly and only under extreme conditions. The Mughal and colonial states added some elements of state-led relief to this welfare mix through public works, while continuing to preside over pre-capitalist arrangements. Perhaps the early signs of change occurred through the partial monetization of the rural economy through the use of jute as a cash crop for peasant production (there had previously been plantation-led indigo production), adding little security to livelihoods while partially exposing those livelihoods to the volatility of commodity markets and monopoly farm gate pricing. Indeed, East Pakistan, and East Bengal before it, provided this commodity at the expense of its own food security, classically under-developing as a result.

The liberation struggle also intensified a sense of unity among Bengalis against a common enemy – an enemy that was increasingly perceived as responsible for the immanent nation's underdevelopment. Despite ideological efforts to the contrary, that spirit eroded in the years after liberation. The removal of the external threat, at great cost to public infrastructure and public goods, led to an internal scramble for rents under conditions of post-liberation scarcity, posing a serious socio-cultural threat to a collective sharing of the well. The inheritance of widespread poverty morphed into a problematic for the internal political economy; close to 90 per cent of the population at liberation was rural, and approximately 50 per cent of them were effectively landless and reliant upon an uncertain monsoon rice crop. The nation was significantly dependent on food imports, with only jute to pay for them. If the cake was fixed in size, then survival became an internal zero-sum game, comprising a powerful threat to any concept of Bengali solidarity as the basis for sharing.

Change has certainly occurred since those early, post-liberation days. But the story is complex and mixed. The major contribution to food security has been the widespread introduction of the Green Revolution *IRRI-boro* rice crop in the dry season – supported, ironically, by irrigation from both surface and groundwater sources. Jute, a declining international commodity, has largely given way to this innovation. The overall decline in poverty in the country can be attributed partly to a rise in real agricultural wages, while the differentiated story is also a function of a more idiosyncratic and cyclical divergence of dependency ratios. Wage rates are rising, and in some areas, in some seasons, labour can now even be scarce. This shift is partly a function of greater diversification in the economy, which has accompanied the rise of urbanization, the commercialization of agriculture as a result, and an increase in internal trade, facilitated by enhanced road networks.

Agriculture, now less cereally homogeneous, has therefore shifted as a socio-economic phenomenon towards a greater emphasis on contract farming and absentee landowners, entailing more rurbanization as well as the growth of large urban centres, not just confined to Dhaka. The structure of employment and thus the labour force has changed, and, as a result, so have the explanations of persistent, extreme poverty. Many credit–labour exchanges have given way to cash wages and cash-fixed rents that are market sensitive rather than a function of social reproduction imperatives. Security may have been achieved in a Faustian pact, but at least it was more predictable and morally instanced, a function of intimate asymmetric transactions between people and families who were not, nevertheless, strangers. Those in the West, witnessing the rise of zero-hour contracts, will acutely recognize this point. Relying for sustained poverty reduction on rising real wages without any safety nets replaces socially sanctioned forms of insurance with nothing.

While there are many ways to characterize change in the country, in the context of a discussion about sharing the well, the key point to emphasize is that society has become more differentiated due to the diversification of the economy. The solidaristic liberation idea of Bangladesh comprising a homogeneous society of small, subsistence peasants (never strictly true; see Wood, 1981) has to give way to much greater complexity as the society interacts with globalization, pulling livelihood options apart and segmenting life chances. Both economic and social transactions become more contractual and instrumental, and risk becoming devoid of any moral dimension.

In 2021, Bangladesh will have been liberated for 50 years. It will probably then be classified as a middle-income country. Although there have been many transformations since 1971 and although the country has in many ways been a beacon of development success, there is still significant extreme poverty, much of it chronic. Approximately 17.6 per cent or 25 million are extreme poor according to the lower poverty threshold (BBS, 2011), and a large number of the population is moderately poor by the upper poverty threshold. On top of this, we already know that there is a churning of fortunes between extreme and moderate poverty, and that the thresholds themselves do not fully capture the real number of people living in poverty or vulnerability. Despite very realistic ambitions to be a middle-income country, therefore, Bangladesh still faces core problems of poverty in a context of climate vulnerability, inequality, and regional disparities.

Bangladesh has entered a further plan period with the launch of its seventh Five Year Plan, which lists the eradication of extreme poverty much more explicitly among its priorities. There have been a number of important government-supported initiatives that, accumulatively, offer optimism in relation to this priority. These include: significant success in addressing the challenges of eradicating extreme and moderate poverty; commitment to reforming its social protection policies; investment via infrastructure in labour mobility and market expansion, especially in the agricultural sector, which results in increases in agricultural wage rates; an improved environment for foreign direct investment and local collaboration, especially in the garments sector; an increase in budgetary commitments to the education and health sectors; and collaborative arrangements with donors and NGOs to extend targeted asset transfer programmes beyond its own direct interventions. For good reasons, therefore, the commitment to 'leave no one behind' has been ratcheted up by both political and policy leaders in Bangladesh. But will this vision require a fairer sharing of the well – that is, of present and predicted wealth? And how might that revised settlement in the political economy come about? And how might it be monitored and maintained?

In effect, this volume convenes a dialogue between applied academics contributing research analysis and policy leaders providing technical and political insights to influence the formation and formulation of that settlement. The driving focus of the dialogue takes the form of a core question: as Bangladesh moves towards middle-income status, implying stronger domestic revenues, how should its social policy evolve to eradicate extreme poverty? This implies a paradigm shift away from a reliance on mostly donor-supported, discrete development projects towards more domestically supported, mainstreamed policy across a range of sectors. Such a paradigm shift requires serious thought about the institutional challenges of leading, coordinating, and monitoring progress towards the eradication of extreme poverty when duty-bearers are spread across so many government and non-government organizations, as well as other parts of civil society and donors.

Volume contributions

Turning to the volume itself, our first empirical chapter is written by Binayek Sen and Zulfiqar Ali and builds on a background paper on extreme poverty commissioned by the Planning Commission as part of its preparatory work for the seventh Five Year Plan. The chapter offers a comprehensive overview of poverty reduction trends in Bangladesh, as well as an analysis of extreme poverty characteristics and dynamics. It then addresses the twin themes of responsiveness to growth and enduring inequality. In so doing, the authors embrace respectively the two perspectives of 'leaving no one behind' and 'sharing the well'. In relation to growth, they develop an analysis of poverty elasticity, and offer statistically informed projections of responses to different growth scenarios. This allows them to calculate the projected costs of eradicating extreme poverty in the future. In terms of inequality as an enduring cause of extreme poverty, they note that Bangladesh, like other countries in South Asia and indeed globally, remains a deeply differentiated society in terms of class relations and other stratification indicators. Although the population is mainly ethnically homogeneous, there are significant ethnic and religious minorities who experience deep discrimination. Inequalities also manifest themselves spatially, in urban and rural locations but also in significant regional variations. The significance of these inequalities is that they frame opportunities and capabilities and contribute to the sustained reproduction of poverty.

In arguing for a new political settlement more aligned to 'sharing the well', Devine and Wood's chapter points out that extreme poverty can be both socially and economically contrasted with moderate poverty in terms of marginalization, social isolation, and intensity, as well as the prevalence of ethnic minorities, feminization, the elderly and the disabled. The poverty of the extreme poor is more idiosyncratic than the systemic poverty of the moderate poor. Thus, the political economy analysis of extreme poverty needs to be modified and more onus placed on duty-bearers, because the extreme poor have less of a voice and have less capacity for counterpart social action. This modification requires a deliberate dialogue with the middle classes to re-set the *de facto* welfare regime of the country. The chapter uses a well-being regime model to illustrate the challenge of agency between the poor themselves and other duty-bearers in society, and to indicate the structural limitations of agency and well-being outcomes for the majority of the population as offered by an institutional landscape, comprising the four domains of state, market, community, and household. The chapter concludes by reflecting on drivers and key dimensions of a future political resettlement.

It is abundantly clear across all the data arising from poverty research and programme interventions that poverty is significantly feminized. This is all the more evident in cases of extreme poverty. Drawing upon that research plus life history narratives generated through the EEP/Shiree programme, Maîtrot discusses the significance of female-headed and female-managed households within the extreme poverty category. Focusing on the significance of marriage for both a woman's well-being and household security and stability, Maîtrot asks the direct question of what happens when 'male guardianship' is removed, forcibly or otherwise, from a household, and how women, left with responsibility for those households, cope and survive. The chapter highlights the plurality of women's experiences at different life stages, influenced by, *inter alia*, class, marital status, and social marginalization. However, what remains common is the existence and influence of gendered inequalities. The chapter offers insights into different coping strategies and also highlights attempts by female-headed or female-managed households to try to rebuild forms of male guardianship through family or community members.

Mustafa Mujeri's chapter offers an in-depth analysis of the need for and challenges of extending financial inclusion to the extreme poor. There are numerous price and non-price barriers, grounded in complex local political economy conditions, that prevent the extreme poor from accessing formal and quasi-formal financial services. As a result, the extreme poor turn to informal services, which, although crucial for liquidity management and consumption smoothing, often come with unfavourable terms and conditions. Mujeri's analysis offers some optimism. The current policy landscape for financial services includes a number of inclusive and progressive initiatives; Bangladesh has a strong track record of opening up access to the poor, especially to microcredit; and the country has witnessed a proliferation of mobile technologies that can facilitate access to financial services. Mujeri examines options that might lead to greater access to and adoption of financial services, including investments in electronic infrastructure for financial services, linking microfinance institutions to formal financial service providers, building partnerships with the private sector, and incentivizing the inclusion of the 'hard to reach'. All of this, Mujeri argues, will help Bangladesh move towards establishing itself as a cashless society.

All of the chapters in this volume build their analyses on the successful track record of Bangladesh in reducing national levels of poverty and extreme poverty. Globally, these are very impressive achievements. Shamsul Alam and Kazi Iqbal's chapter breaks new empirical ground and for the first time explores poverty reduction performance at sub-district levels. This disaggregated analysis provides a far more complex overview of extreme poverty in Bangladesh and identifies geographical concentrations of extreme poverty that intersect with key covariates including seasonality, local political economy conditions of marginalization, climate vulnerability, and migration. Importantly, some of these areas of concentration have witnessed an increase in extreme poverty levels. What, then, best explains the variation in poverty rates (and the relatively poor poverty reduction record) at the sub-district level? The quantitative analysis offered by the authors shows a clear association between variations in real wages and variations in poverty levels. The chapter makes a forceful argument that future poverty reduction will require policy leaders to look beyond national aggregate data and focus more on local, specific conditions.

Above, we refer to some of the major socio-economic changes that have taken place in Bangladesh. Primary among these is the transformation of the agricultural sector as evidenced in increased contract farming, absentee landowners, more rurbanization, and the expansion of large urban centres. All of this has radically changed the structure of employment in rural areas and thus the labour force. K.A.S. Murshid addresses this directly in his chapter, which examines non-farm employment opportunities for the extreme poor. Using the case of potato value chains, he shows how non-farm opportunities stimulate labour demand, particularly among casual and temporary workers. Many of these workers are extreme poor. However, this more positive note needs to be treated with some caution, because Murshid also warns that those taking on these new employment opportunities will find themselves with insecure and temporary contracts, will receive lower wages that increase only marginally over time, and will find it difficult to move up into higher value forms of employment. While employment creation may be pivotal for future extreme poverty eradication, this chapter asks more profound questions about the quality of any new employment opportunity.

Murshid's focus on rural contexts is followed by an analysis of the relation between urbanization and extreme poverty. Bangladesh is urbanizing at a relentless pace, reflecting changes in the economy and signalling a more mobile and connected population at both national and international levels. These changes offer both challenges and opportunities for extreme poverty eradication. In his chapter, Nazrul Islam examines Bangladesh's past and current urban profile, noting the speed and intensity of urbanization throughout the country – a process that seems to continue unabated. He then maps the links between urban growth and the prevalence of extreme poverty. The result is a complex picture that highlights the distinctive features of 'urban' extreme poverty and the specific challenges they pose. These challenges include the enforcement of core citizen rights, as identified in the Constitution, around movement, housing and shelter, employment, and associational life. They also include access to basic services such as safe transport, good quality water and sanitation, effective education, and responsive health services. The future of extreme poverty eradication in Bangladesh will undoubtedly be a significantly urban challenge, and addressing these issues needs to move centre stage in policy deliberations and actions.

There is no doubt that Bangladesh's social security system can play an important role in reducing extreme poverty further and, crucially, in ensuring that any progress is sustainable over time. However, it is widely recognized that to be effective, the country s social security system needs to be reviewed. It needs to be robust and agile enough to deal simultaneously with long-term support needs for the chronic extreme poor and with time-bound support needs for those affected by crises arising from shocks, hazards, and impacts resulting from seasonality. It also needs to increase the effectiveness of social security interventions. These challenges are rehearsed in the chapter written by Sadiq Ahmed, in which he also provides insights into the logic underpinning the government's decision to reform the social security system around the lifecycle approach. He then examines some of the policy options stemming from this approach, especially in relation to children, those of working age, the elderly, and the disabled. The challenge of increasing investments in and reforming the social security system in Bangladesh is urgent, and it is likely to be urgent for many years to come as the demographic profile of the country's population changes and increased demands are placed on the state to address the needs of its citizens.

Our final chapter acts as a conclusion but extends beyond this. It revisits the 'sharing the well' and 'leaving no one behind' discussion, and reinforces arguments for a political resettlement with more distributive welfare commitments. Building on a critique of neoliberal analyses of extreme poverty and the policies they support, Ali and Wood warn against simply 'parachuting in' social policy solutions, especially when these solutions are found to be wanting. Instead, they offer an optimistic scenario for a future welfare strategy built around core values of solidarity that were deployed even before the country became independent. These values acknowledge all citizens' rightful share of Bangladesh's current and future prosperity and the collective good. In terms of eradicating extreme poverty, this rightful share can be translated into a form of basic income for all citizens. The authors test and cost this welfare strategy against two other current strategies: more rigorous targeting to determine resource distribution and the lifecycle approach underpinning the country's social protection strategy. The three strategies are found to be affordable, but they reflect different articulations of the political resettlement challenge.

Notes

1. The conference was supported by the UK's Department for International Development in Bangladesh and the Economic Empowerment of the Poorest (EEP) programme (see <www.shiree.org>).
2. The most recent attacks resulted in the death of 20 mostly foreign hostages on 1 July 2016, and the death of three people on 7 July when gunmen carrying bombs launched an attack at the country's largest gathering of Muslims celebrating the Eid holiday.

References

BBS (2011) *Report of the Household Income & Expenditure Survey 2010*, Dhaka: Bangladesh Bureau of Statistics (BBS), Government of Bangladesh.

Devine, J., Basu, I. and Wood, G.D. (2017) 'Governance challenges in Bangladesh: old wine in not so new bottles', in I. Basu, J. Devine, G.D. Wood, and R. Khair (eds), *Politics and Governance in Bangladesh: Uncertain Landscapes*, Abingdon: Routledge.

North, D., Wallis, J. and Weingast, B.R. (2009) *Violence and Social Order: A Conceptual Framework for Interpreting Recorded Human History*, New York: Cambridge University Press.

Wood, G.D. (1981) 'Rural class formation in Bangladesh 1940–1980', *Bulletin of Concerned Asian Scholars* 13(4): 2–15.

Wood, G.D. (2007) 'Labels, welfare regimes and intermediation: contesting formal power', in J. Moncrieffe and R. Eyben (eds), *The Power of Labelling: Why It Matters*, pp. 17–32, London: Earthscan.

About the authors

Geof D. Wood is Emeritus Professor at the University of Bath. A sociologist by training, he has over 40 years of research experience in South Asia, particularly Bangladesh, working on issues ranging from agrarian change, extreme poverty, and social mobilization to urban livelihoods, governance, and political settlements. He is also interested in and has written on the application of social policy concepts to thinking about welfare and development in poorer countries.

Dr Joe Devine is Head of the Department of Social and Policy Sciences at the University of Bath, and a Senior Lecturer in International Development. His main research interests lie in poverty, vulnerability, inequality, and governance, and in how these have an impact on the well-being of citizens and are addressed through policy interventions. He has collaborated over many years with government, NGOs and other civil society groups in Bangladesh.

CHAPTER 2

Ending extreme poverty in Bangladesh: trends, drivers, and policies

Binayak Sen and Zulfiqar Ali

Recent decades have seen significant progress in reducing extreme poverty, and this is due to a range of factors including improved education, urbanization, and higher agricultural wages. Despite this, pockets of extreme poverty persist, and these relate particularly to ecological differences. This chapter examines how to continue reducing extreme poverty in Bangladesh, arguing for a 'mini big push'. This would require significant investment in targeted programmes, and a range of previous interventions seen in the country serve as cost-effective examples of these.

Keywords: 'mini big push', pro-poorest interventions, drivers of improvement extreme poverty, growth elasticity

Introduction: growth and extreme poverty

Can growth alone overcome the poverty trap?

We live in a non-linear world where economic realities are punctuated by broken lines, twists and turns, sudden slippages, breaks, and traps. The persistence of poverty, especially in its extreme forms, is both a testimony to and reminder of this. In a linear and abstract world marked by economics of constant return to scale, it is assumed that the disappearance of extreme poverty is only a matter of time. Or at least this is what the theory says. In reality, of course, reducing extreme poverty has proved to be a far more stubborn challenge. We want to highlight three main reasons why extreme poverty is so persistent.

First, extreme poverty is difficult to tackle because the extreme poor do not stand in the same queue as the moderate poor or the non-poor. They are not part of the same single micro-economy, or even part of the single society, as envisaged by linear conceptions of development. In other words, the extreme poor are far more likely to be excluded from opportunities enjoyed by other citizens, including poor ones; and they are governed by different rules and institutions.

Second, the trap-centric view of extreme poverty implies that certain threshold levels of assets are needed to overcome the extreme poverty trap. Without these assets, the poorest cannot participate effectively in labour and product markets in the same way as other members of society. However, while the transfer of assets can help the extreme poor, on their own they cannot eradicate extreme poverty. This is the central notion underlying the idea of a 'mini big push' highlighted in this chapter.[1] The focus, therefore, is not only on assets, but also on the return of assets (Sen and Hulme, 2006), as well as on the ability of the extreme poor to retain any gains from their assets and to overcome their social exclusion and isolation.

Third, the real economic world of the extreme poor resembles more a game of 'snakes and ladders' in which successful climbs in the income ladder can be followed by setbacks and declines triggered by various shocks, such as poor health, natural disasters, and personal insecurities (Rahman and Hossain, 1995; Sen, 2003; Krishna, 2010). This implies the need to support the extreme poor so that they can become more resilient in material asset terms but also in social, political, and cultural terms.

Zeroing in on 'zero extreme poverty'

Official statistics for Bangladesh indicate that a significant number of the extreme poor have managed to escape the aforementioned poverty trap. Yet extreme poverty is far from being eradicated. In light of this, it is legitimate to ask if the aim for a total eradication or near-total eradication of extreme poverty is realistic. We would argue that such a goal is both a desirable and achievable objective for three main reasons. First, Bangladesh has set itself the goal of extreme poverty eradication by 2021, the year when the country will celebrate the fiftieth anniversary of its independence. This goal aligns well with the other overarching macro-economic targets set by the government in 2009 so that the country can achieve middle-income status by 2021. By keeping the agenda of securing middle-income status linked to the aim of eradicating extreme poverty, Bangladesh finds itself in a position to once again demonstrate a model of national development that can provide important lessons to others. Second, it is possible to finance a 'zero extreme poverty' strategy without jeopardizing high growth. This is because Bangladesh is in a position to mobilize the necessary resources, estimated to be in the order of 3 per cent of gross domestic product (GDP), to eradicate extreme poverty.[2] Indirect estimates suggest that an allocation of not more than 0.5 per cent of GDP annually over a period of six years (2015–21), together with perfect targeting, is sufficient to eradicate extreme poverty (Shiree, 2013). Even if we include an allowance of deliberate leakage to mobilize the much needed buy-in of the non-poor (Gelbach and Pritchett, 1995), additional resources would not exceed 1 per cent of GDP annually. The country's seventh Five Year Plan[3] offers an excellent opportunity to deliver on all of the above; indeed, we would argue that the eradication of extreme poverty should be achieved by the end of the Five Year Plan.

Third, now is the time for Bangladesh to commit to zero extreme poverty because we already know a great deal about what works best for the extreme poor; the government is committed to the sustainable development goals (SDGs) and can build on its significant success with millennium development goals (MDGs); development partners are interested; and market conditions are also favourable for the extreme poor, as evidenced in the rising real wage incomes for manual wage workers (Zhang et al., 2013).

The changing face of extreme poverty: cause for optimism

The plea for ending extreme poverty by the end of the seventh Five Year Plan period is motivated by the country's successful track record in reducing poverty. Diverse definitions of extreme poverty are found in the literature and it is important to clarify the way in which we use and measure the term here. First, our understanding of the term 'extreme poverty' reflects the national extreme poverty line in Bangladesh, which corresponds to the monetary 'lower poverty line' estimated for the country (Ravallion, 1998).[4] Second, the national extreme poverty line is considerably lower than the US$1.25/day poverty line using the 2005 purchasing power parity or the $1.90/day line proposed in 2011. In adopting a monetary line and restricting ourselves to the poorest segment of the poor, we want to highlight the policy need to serve the poorest first before serving other poor groups.

Trends in extreme poverty

The most remarkable aspect of poverty reduction in Bangladesh over the past two and a half decades is the significant drop in the incidence of extreme income poverty:[5]

- First, extreme poverty has decreased dramatically (see Figure 2.1), with the proportion of the rural population living in extreme poverty dropping from 44 per cent in 1991–2 to 21 per cent in 2010, and the proportion of the urban population living in extreme poverty dropping from 24 per cent to 7 per cent over the same period (see Table 2.1).
- Second, the rate of extreme poverty reduction has been faster in the decade of the 2000s compared with the 1990s in both rural and urban areas. In the 1990s, the annual reduction rate of extreme poverty was 1.8 per cent, compared with 4.8 per cent in the 2000s.
- Third, data shows that, over the 2000–10 period, the incidence of extreme poverty dropped for all educational, land-ownership, and occupational categories. In other words, we see significant improvements also among those with no schooling and no land and classified as having no job.
- Fourth, not only has there been a decline in extreme poverty but the 'structure of poverty' has also changed, with the proportion of extreme poor among the total population of poor declining, especially in the second half of the 2000s.

Besides the reduction in extreme poverty, we also know that the poorest are now better equipped in human development terms. There are many examples that could be cited here. For example, the level of illiteracy

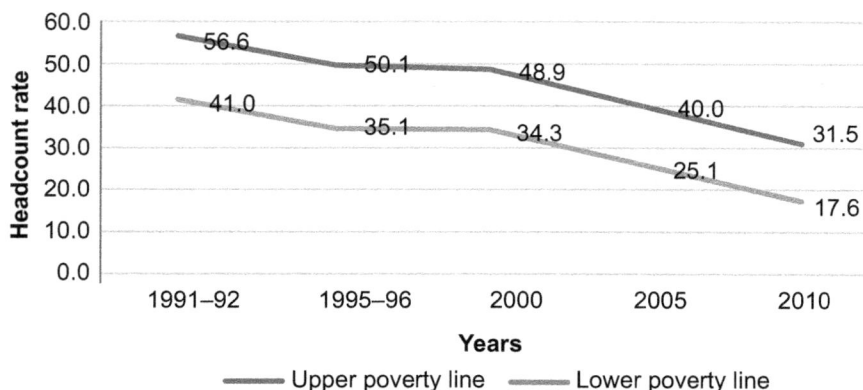

Figure 2.1 Trends in national extreme poverty

Table 2.1 Poverty headcount rates (%)

	Upper poverty line					Lower poverty line				
	1991–2	1995	2000	2005	2010	1991–2	1995	2000	2005	2010
National	56.8	53.1	49.8	40	31.5	41.3	34.4	33.7	25.1	17.6
Urban	42.6	35	36.6	28.4	21.3	23.6	13.7	19.1	14.6	7.7
Rural	58.7	56.7	53.1	43.8	35.2	43.7	38.5	37.4	28.6	21.1

Source: HIES, various years, Bangladesh Bureau of Statistics (BBS).

among the poor has declined from 64 per cent in 2004 to 46 per cent 2011; the under-five mortality rate for the lowest asset quintile in the country has dropped impressively from 121 to 64 per 1,000 live births over the same seven-year period; and the proportion of poor women with access to antenatal care has increased from 33 per cent to 48 per cent, again over the 2004–11 period. These human development indicators are important in their own right, but, when considered with real reductions in income poverty, they signal a more robust or holistic approach to tackling extreme poverty.

Profile of the contemporary extreme poor

The extreme poor experience poverty through multiple deprivations manifested in having little or no income or employment, little or no education, poor housing, ill health, malnutrition, social marginalization, and lack of voice and power (Sen and Hulme, 2006; Ali and Devine, 2011). In what follows, we use Household Income and Expenditure Survey (HIES) data to give a brief overview of three well-known indicators of poverty: occupation status, education levels, and land ownership. We then move on to note the significance of specific conditions of extreme poverty, including social marginality.

First, in Bangladesh there is considerable discussion about the poverty reduction potential of shifting labour from agricultural to rural non-farm sectors. While this is a justified discussion, it is important not to forget that agriculture still has a significant role to play. This is borne out in the data. Thus, in 2000, the incidence of rural extreme poverty was similar (i.e. approximately 41 per cent) across household heads engaged in agriculture, service, and transport/production sectors. However, by 2010, the incidence of rural extreme poverty was lower in cases where household heads were engaged in agricultural sectors compared with service and transport/production sectors (23 per cent as opposed to 29 and 31 per cent respectively). The only rural non-farm sector that fared better in terms of extreme poverty reduction was rural trade, where the incidence of extreme poverty was 15 per cent.

Second, in contrast, the importance of non-rural sectors in reducing rural extreme poverty cannot be overemphasized, especially through the channel of rural–urban migration. The argument is that rural to urban *inter-sectoral* migration results in a substantial lowering of rural extreme poverty. This can be indirectly judged by comparing the 2010 HIES results for rural extreme poverty to those of urban extreme poverty across the economic sectors. Thus, the incidence of extreme poverty in 2010 was 23 per cent in agriculture in rural areas whereas it was 17 per cent in urban services and 11 per cent in urban production sectors.

Third, access to educational human capital seems to be an important driver of extreme poverty reduction. In 2010, the incidence of extreme poverty was 17 per cent nationally. However, the incidence of extreme poverty was highest among those with no formal education (25 per cent), lower for those who had completed primary school education (16 per cent), and even lower for those considered literate (6 per cent). This is indirect evidence and suggestive of a 'threshold effect' in the distribution of extreme poverty.

Fourth, land is still the single most important asset, especially in the agrarian context. In 2010, 21 per cent of the rural population lived in extreme poverty. The equivalent figure rises sharply to 36 per cent for households owning less than 5 decimals of land, but falls equally sharply to 22 per cent for those owning between 5 and 49 decimals. Again, this is suggestive of a 'threshold effect' in the distribution of extreme poverty. This also suggests that the policy of *khas* (land owned or vested with the government) land distribution to the landless and near-landless is still relevant and impactful.

While profiling the extreme poor along the lines of occupation, education, and land brings out important broad patterns, more micro-level evidence allows us to focus on the specific dimensions or situations of vulnerability of the extreme poor. These include households where the head is female, where there are no savings or regular income, where sanitation and water conditions are poor or non-existent, where children go without schooling, and where food poverty exists (Sen and Ali, 2015). All this evidence points to the fact that income and non-income deprivations are closely linked when it comes to extreme poverty.

The social face of marginality is often ignored in economic policy discourse, reflecting the weak influence of marginal groups over the policy process. The adverse nexus of power and knowledge is strongly revealed in the case of socially marginal groups. These groups tend to be relatively small and hence remain obscured from the gaze of the policymakers and the elites in general.

In Bangladesh, marginalized communities can be defined by religion, ethnicity, physical condition, remoteness, ecological vulnerability, and occupation. These communities may not always be extreme income-poor but they suffer extreme forms of exclusion and discrimination. The latter has a huge impact on people's ability to negotiate secure livelihood options.

To sum up the discussion so far on the profile of the extreme poor, we highlight two main messages. First, there seem to be important 'threshold effects' (or non-linearity) in the distribution of extreme poverty: the incidence of poverty sharply rises in the lowest asset (both land and human) categories compared with the second lowest asset group. Second, threshold effects tell only part of the story, however. It is impossible to understand extreme poverty dynamics in Bangladesh without considering micro-conditions and situations as well as the impact of social marginalization, stigma, and exclusion. While the threshold effects can in principle be addressed via policy investments in initiatives to enhance income, employment, and human development, there may be extreme poverty conditions for which these initiatives are not so relevant and there are other conditions (marginality) for which additional measures, such as those building social cohesion, will be required.

Spatial dimensions of extreme poverty: the interface between ecology, deprivation, and income poverty

In Bangladesh, extreme poverty is also expressed spatially, with the most remote and ecologically vulnerable areas inhabited by socially marginalized and extreme poor groups. In policy terms, these areas also tend to be neglected or bypassed. Here we wish to focus on three aspects of this spatial dimension of extreme poverty, drawing on our more detailed and extensive research into spatial poverty patterns in Bangladesh (Sen and Ali, 2015).

First, we discern an indirect interface between adverse ecology and extreme income poverty. This relationship is more pronounced in the case of extreme poverty (i.e. for the lower poverty line) than it is overall. Relatively high extreme poverty appears to be spread throughout the four distinct zones most prone to adverse ecology, encompassing the north-west and north-east, south-west and south-central areas of Bangladesh.

Second, from the above it is clear that extreme income poverty is not always a good predictor of areas with high levels of social deprivation. In some geographic terrains we find a distinct overlap between the two, but in others a separate, divergent dynamic seems to be at work. For example, the north-eastern parts of the country are marked by relatively low extreme poverty but relatively high non-income poverty. If, for example, we decided to use poverty criteria other than income (such as education and health indicators), we would then prioritize these areas from a spatial targeting point of view. We find something similar in three districts of the Chittagong Hill Tracts lying in the south-east, as well as in the areas susceptible to flooding for a considerable part of the year (known as *haor* areas). These areas also exhibit lower levels of extreme income poverty but higher levels of non-income poverty. In contrast, areas in the south-east and south-central parts of the country, with the exception of the coastal areas of Patuakhali, Bhola, and Lakshmipur, have relatively lower incidences of non-income poverty, as measured by the synthetic social deprivation index, but higher incidences of extreme income poverty.

Third, when considering the interface between ecological vulnerability and social deprivation, we found that it was not so much the extent of ecological vulnerability per se that causes slow progress in fighting non-income poverty, but geographical remoteness. Chapter 6 offers insights and more detailed analysis of the significance of geographical remoteness and physical connectivity.

From an economic perspective, spatial disadvantage increases transaction costs, reduces incentives for private investment, and generates negative spatial externalities, all of which make the reduction of extreme poverty even more challenging. It is important, therefore, to assess what happens to the extreme poor in these areas over time. Two aspects are worth bearing in mind. First, the spatially poorest areas have also exhibited important progress in socio-economic terms. The bottom 50 *upazilas* (sub-districts), for example, have made progress in most human development education and health indicators, while real wages have increased even in areas of chronic seasonal distress (locally known as *monga*). Some of this success reflects the fact that NGOs have recently targeted some of these more remote areas. Second, since the transition to electoral democracy in 1991, a number of important political representatives have been elected from constituencies that include these spatial poverty pockets. The list includes former speakers of parliament, cabinet ministers, and presidents – all of whom have successfully lobbied for greater public resource allocation to these poorer areas.

Drivers of improvements in extreme poverty

In what follows we examine four key factors that have made a significant contribution to the reduction of poverty and extreme poverty in Bangladesh.

The first factor has been a rise in rural wages (Hossain et al., 2013). A significant share of extreme poor households depends on agricultural work for their livelihoods. Consequently, they benefit when real agricultural wage rates increase. In Bangladesh, the agricultural labour market has been tightening since the early 2000s and this has led to an increase in real agricultural wage rates. So, for example, the rice wage per day was stagnant for most of the 1980s, increased marginally in the 1990s, and then almost doubled in the second half of the 2000s. This pattern is borne out by real wage trends using the general consumer price index in both rural and urban areas.

The second factor is related to the first. The tightening of the agricultural wage labour market witnessed in the 2000s was triggered by three important changes: 1) the relocation of farm labour to rural non-farm sectors; 2) the relocation of rural labour to urban activities, in particular to labour-intensive construction and transport activities; and 3) the creation of jobs for the poor and the extreme poor in the manufacturing sector. The significance of increased urban employment opportunities for the rural poor is highlighted in a recent study on 1,600 female ready-made garment (RMG) workers drawn from 13 areas of greater Dhaka city (Sen, 2014). The workers had been employed in the RMG sector for about four years on average. Before joining the RMG sector, the economic situation of the workers' households was precarious: 17 per cent of households lived in extreme food poverty and a further 63 per cent lived in moderate food poverty. Over the period of their employment, the poverty status of the household changed significantly, with the proportion living below the food-poverty line dropping to 43 per cent from 80 per cent, and the proportion in a 'breakeven' status (i.e. neither in deficit nor surplus) increasing from 19 per cent to 36 per cent.

The third factor relates to the impact of migration on the wages of those who remain in the rural areas. It is worth looking separately at the impact of domestic and international migration. Most domestic migrants come from landless and functionally landless households, with the latter's share increasing from 51 per cent to 57 per cent during 2000–8.[6] This suggests that domestic migration for seasonal or temporary work mostly helps the poorest groups. While, in most cases, extreme poor households do not have the resources to support international migration, there is strong evidence that the indirect effects of international migration through the labour market are of greater significance for this group. Thus, for example, households residing in villages with high remittance levels also report higher agricultural wage growth (Hossain et al., 2013). Wage growth also tends to be faster in villages experiencing high growth in overseas remittances.

Finally, one of the characteristics of recent growth in Bangladesh is that it has been institutionally transformative. By this we mean that it has not only accelerated per capita GDP or gross national product (GNP) growth, but it has also brought about institutional changes that magnify the poverty-reducing effects of economic growth. The first and most significant growth-induced transformation in Bangladesh to take place in the countryside is the emergence of pro-poor and pro-poorest land tenancy institutions.[7] For example, the Green Revolution in the crop sector has also led to pro-poor shifts in rural factor markets such as the land tenancy market. We thus observe that the amount of land under tenancy has increased, accompanied by shifts from share tenancy to fixed rent, leasehold tenancy, and 'pure tenancy' arrangements. Evidence suggests that the landless and marginal farmers have been the major beneficiaries of these changes. For instance, the share of leased-in land held by rural households increased from 23 per cent in 1988 (i.e. 23 per cent leased-in versus 77 per cent 'owned') to 33 per cent in 2000, rising further to 40 per cent in 2004 (Hossain and Bayes, 2009). The second most significant growth-induced transformation relates to the emergence of credit market institutions for the rural poor and the poorest. Evidence suggests that the landless and near landless groups account for the bulk of institutional credit in Bangladesh, increasing from 21 per cent in 1988 to 43 per cent in 2008 (Hossain and Bayes, 2009). The third – and most significant – transformation relates to the emergence of labour market institutions for the rural poor and the poorest. Thus, the share of casual wage-dependent agricultural labour has gradually decreased and given way to contractual labour in farm activities.

Growth elasticity of extreme poverty

Although poverty projections have been carried out in the past (Gimenez et al., 2014), they have not been done for extreme poverty. This section analyses the role of economic growth and inequality on poverty reduction in the 2000s and then projects future poverty rates until 2021 based on the lower poverty line. In estimating extreme poverty projections, it is important to keep in mind three caveats. First, the net growth elasticities are based on past trends on inequality of consumption expenditure, which were largely favourable. There is no guarantee that this favourable trend will continue in the future. Second, net growth elasticities also assume that extreme poverty trends will not deteriorate over the next decade. Bangladesh is susceptible to shocks, especially those induced by climate change, and these impact on poverty reduction efforts. Third, growth elasticities statistically treat all groups equally. In the context of extreme poverty, we already know that in Bangladesh there are diverse groups that experience different forms of extreme poverty.

Table 2.2 presents the elasticity of both moderate poverty and extreme poverty with respect to the per capita consumption growth and to the growth of the Gini coefficient of inequality for national, rural, and urban areas. According to our calculations, a 1 percentage point increase in per capita consumption would have resulted in a 1.77 percentage point decline in the national headcount ratio of extreme poverty. With a headcount of about 34.3 per cent, this represents a 0.61 percentage point decline in the population below the lower poverty line. Table 2.2 also shows that declining inequality results in declining extreme poverty: that is, a 1 percentage point decrease in the Gini coefficient of inequality decreases the headcount index for the extreme poor by 0.28 percentage points. The net elasticity of poverty with respect to growth is thus –2.05 compared with the gross elasticity of –1.77. About 14 per cent ($\beta \times \delta$ as a percentage of λ) of the extreme poverty decline would have come from the decrease in inequality over the period reviewed.

We then project poverty estimates to 2021 by applying the net elasticity of poverty to growth estimated above and by using the baseline 2010 extreme poverty rates at national, rural, and urban levels (Table 2.3). Projections are made using four real GDP growth scenarios (5.5, 6, 7, and 8 per cent).

Table 2.2 Growth elasticity estimates[8]

Parameter	Upper poverty line (adept based)			Lower poverty line (adept based)		
	National	Rural	Urban	National	Rural	Urban
γ	−1.55	−1.84	−0.78	−1.77	−2.52	−0.59
$\beta \times \delta$	−0.09	0.13	−0.69	−0.28	0.27	−1.25
λ	−1.64	−1.71	−1.47	−2.05	−2.24	−1.84

Notes: λ represents the net elasticity of poverty with respect to consumption growth.
γ is the gross elasticity of poverty to growth, implying the percentage change in poverty due to the percentage change in consumption expenditure holding the level of distribution of per-capita real expenditure constant.
β is the elasticity of inequality to consumption growth, and δ is the elasticity of poverty to inequality (holding real consumption expenditure constant).
The indirect effect, $\beta \times \delta$, captures the percentage change in poverty due to the percentage change in inequality, keeping the level of per-capita real consumption expenditure constant
While γ is expected to be negative, $\beta \times \delta$ could be either positive or negative depending on the role of consumption growth to the inequality.

The projected figures suggest that Bangladesh would reduce its extreme poverty level to below 8.8 per cent with the current growth scenario of 5.5 per cent. More importantly, under a constant real GDP growth scenario of 7 per cent per year, the extreme poverty level would decline to 7.2 per cent. The significance of this calculation is that 7 per cent growth is the target set out in the government's current seventh Five Year Plan. In this scenario, there would still be around 11.92 million people living in extreme poverty. If Bangladesh wishes to achieve zero extreme poverty by 2021, it therefore has three choices: 1) achieve growth rates in excess of 7 per cent; 2) implement a more equitable and inclusive pattern of growth; or 3) achieve a 7 per cent growth rate in the medium term and supplement this with more direct interventions to eradicate extreme poverty. Some of these options are discussed in the subsequent sections.

Scaling up successful pro-poorest interventions

'Big-push' approaches to reduce poverty demand a substantial injection of resources. This was at the heart of the gap between savings and investment that drove the aid debate in the 1950s and 1960s. As indicated earlier, in a scenario of 'perfect targeting', extreme poverty eradication does not require aggregate lump-sum transfers of more than an additional 0.5 per cent of GDP annually to be spent over the next six years. This is a realistic fiscal plan requiring some modest resource mobilization effort. The strategy of raising the additional fiscal resources to be targeted to the extreme poor is called the 'mini big push'. It is important to note that not all the resources need to be spent through the public expenditure channel. Some pilot interventions conceived outside the traditional rubric of public anti-poverty programmes are already under way, and it might be possible simply to scale up the successful ones. In what

Table 2.3 Extreme poverty headcount projections (2011–21)

Assumed GDP growth rates	National					Rural					Urban				
	5.5	6.0	6.5	7.0	8.0	5.5	6.0	6.5	7.0	8.0	5.5	6.0	6.5	7.0	8.0
Net elasticity	−2.05	−2.05	−2.05	−2.05	−2.05	−2.24	−2.24	−2.24	−2.24	−2.24	−1.84	−1.84	−1.84	−1.84	−1.84
2010	17.6	17.6	17.6	17.6	17.6	21.1	21.1	21.1	21.1	21.1	7.7	7.7	7.7	7.7	7.7
2011	16.52	16.42	16.33	16.23	16.03	19.69	19.56	19.43	19.30	19.05	7.28	7.24	7.20	7.16	7.08
2012	15.51	15.33	15.14	14.96	14.60	18.37	18.13	17.89	17.66	17.19	6.88	6.80	6.73	6.66	6.52
2013	14.56	14.30	14.05	13.79	13.30	17.14	16.81	16.48	16.15	15.52	6.50	6.40	6.29	6.19	6.00
2014	13.67	13.35	13.03	12.72	12.12	15.99	15.58	15.17	14.78	14.00	6.14	6.01	5.88	5.76	5.52
2015	12.83	12.45	12.09	11.73	11.04	14.92	14.44	13.97	13.52	12.64	5.80	5.65	5.50	5.36	5.07
2016	12.04	11.62	11.21	10.81	10.05	13.92	13.39	12.87	12.36	11.41	5.48	5.31	5.14	4.98	4.67
2017	11.31	10.84	10.40	9.97	9.16	12.99	12.41	11.85	11.31	10.30	5.18	4.99	4.81	4.63	4.30
2018	10.61	10.12	9.65	9.19	8.34	12.12	11.50	10.91	10.35	9.30	4.90	4.69	4.50	4.31	3.95
2019	9.96	9.44	8.95	8.47	7.60	11.31	10.66	10.05	9.47	8.39	4.63	4.41	4.21	4.01	3.64
2020	9.35	8.81	8.30	7.81	6.92	10.55	9.88	9.25	8.66	7.57	4.37	4.15	3.93	3.73	3.34
2021	8.78	8.22	7.70	7.20	6.30	9.84	9.16	8.52	7.92	6.84	4.13	3.90	3.68	3.47	3.08

follows, we first examine some successful programmes, then attempt to offer a cost analysis of reducing extreme poverty, and finally we reflect on the overall success of the interventions. We have identified six successful programmes that are relatively large-scale; involve significant resource transfers; are graduation-oriented; promote the accumulation of livelihood assets; and have been subjected to third-party evaluations.

First, the Char Livelihoods Programme (CLP) seeks to improve the livelihoods of extreme poor households living in *chars* in the north-west of Bangladesh. The first phase of the programme targeted 55,000 of the poorest households while the second, starting in April 2010, targeted 67,000 extreme poor households. Beneficiary households choose an income-generating asset of their own choice up to the value of 16,000 Bangladeshi Taka (BDT). Access to clean water and sanitary latrines is ensured through services and training. Over a period of 18 months, households are also given stipend payments, access to village savings and loans, and in some cases training and vouchers to access health services.

Second, the Rural Employment Opportunities for Public Assets (REOPA) supports female-headed households by providing two years of employment for destitute women and employment for casual labourers during lean periods. Women are also provided with training sessions on social and legal issues, gender equity, human rights, primary healthcare, nutrition, and income generation. The project has been implemented in six vulnerable districts and employs 60 destitute women per union[9] in two two-year cycles to maintain 30 km of earthen roads in that union. Beneficiaries tend to be widowed, divorced, and abandoned women.

Third, CARE Bangladesh established its Strengthening Household Abilities for Responding to Development Opportunities (SHOUHARDO) programme to reduce chronic and transitory food insecurity. SHOUHARDO addresses not only the availability, access, and utilization of food and food services, but also key determinants of vulnerability such as lack of participation, social injustice, and discrimination. In its second phase, the programme added a component aimed at strengthening local governance and improving adaptation to climate change.

Fourth, in 2002 BRAC[10] initiated a programme called 'Challenging the Frontiers of Poverty Reduction' (CFPR), later renamed 'Targeting the Ultra-Poor' (TUP). The main objective of the programme is to help the ultra-poor graduate from extreme poverty, secure access to mainstream development programmes, and establish sustainable livelihood improvements. TUP incorporates both livelihood protection and advancement components. It seeks to build social capital for the extreme poor by building village support networks and securing the sponsorship of community leaders. It also emphasizes the development of human and physical capital (such as asset transfers) for its female beneficiaries.

Fifth, the Urban Partnerships for Poverty Reduction programme (UPPR) works in slums and informal settlements in 23 cities and towns, and seeks to improve the livelihoods and living conditions of 3 million urban poor and extremely poor people, especially women and girls. It works directly with communities so that people can flourish and improve their own lives, and demand better services from the government.

Sixth, the Economic Empowerment of the Poorest/Stimulation Household Improvement Resulting in Economic Empowerment (EEP/Shiree) is an extreme poverty-focused programme that was established to enable over 1 million people to lift themselves out of extreme poverty and achieve sustainable livelihoods. The programme also seeks to reduce the vulnerability of the extreme poor to natural disasters, economic shocks, social exclusion, and malnutrition. EEP/Shiree is also committed to addressing the needs of extremely poor women, children, the elderly, and ethnic minorities and marginalized groups. The programme supports the transfer of assets to the extreme poor with partner NGOs working locally to identify and support the most appropriate asset package to be transferred.[11]

The costs of reaching the extreme poor in Bangladesh

Here we attempt to estimate the cost per beneficiary household of each of the programmes mentioned above. The aim is not to compare programmes nor assess their relative effectiveness or 'value for money'. Instead, the estimations are useful because they provide an idea of the likely cost if Bangladesh were to adopt similar programmes in the future.

Table 2.4 sets out the estimates of total and annual costs per beneficiary household. Not surprisingly, there are variations in both cost estimates: for example, the total cost per beneficiary household ranges from BDT21,643 ($271) to BDT125,692 ($1,571). These differences, however, capture important factors such as working in different areas (rural, urban, and more remote regions), in adverse geographic locations (island *chars*, *haors*, coastal

Table 2.4 Costs of supporting extreme poor beneficiaries

Programmes	Total cost (million BDT)	Duration under consideration (years)	No. of beneficiary households (BHHs)	Total cost per BHH (BDT)	Total cost per BHH ($)	Annual cost per BHH ($)
CLP-II	9,804	6	78,000	125,692	1,571	262
CFPR-TUP-III	16,240	5	400,000	40,600	508	102
UPPR	7,680	5	326,995	23,487	294	59
SHOUHARDO	10,400	5	370,000	28,908	361	72
REOPA	3,030	4	140,000	21,643	271	68[12]
EEP/Shiree	10,080	8	309,000	32,621	408	51
Weighted average	–	–	–	35,425	443	82

Source: Data taken from financial reports of the implementing organizations.

areas, hill tracts, etc.), and with ethnic and marginalized communities (ethnic minorities, people with disabilities, the elderly, etc.). For this reason, we prefer to take the average cost per beneficiary household of all six programmes as a guide for future planning. Looking at all six programmes, therefore, we see that the average total cost per beneficiary household is BDT35,425 or $443. This means that it would cost an average of not more than $500 per household to help lift them out of extreme poverty. Given that programmes tend to run over a five-year period, we estimate that in order to achieve its desired target of 'zero extreme poverty' by 2021, Bangladesh would need to spend no more than $100 per beneficiary extreme poor household each year.

Effectiveness of the programmes: experiences from TUP, CLP, and EEP/Shiree

Bangladesh has a global reputation for establishing innovative and effective anti-poverty programmes. Can this success be replicated with anti-extreme-poverty programmes? An overview of different evaluations of the programmes highlighted above would indicate that it is possible to achieve the same level of success. A micro-simulation of TUP, for example, estimated that while about 89 per cent of the beneficiary group achieved graduation from poverty, only about 40 per cent of the control group achieved the same. Similarly, it has been calculated that, two years after recruitment onto the programme, the real value of non-land productive assets owned by TUP participants had increased by BDT11,829 over their control counterparts (DFID, 2012). A similar level of success is reported for the CLP programme: it has been found that the income of 24 per cent of the beneficiary households has been raised significantly, thus taking the households over the extreme poverty threshold. Also, the value of productive assets among sampled households from all cohorts appreciated significantly from a maximum of BDT5,000 to an overall average of just over BDT34,000 (DFID, 2011). Finally, difference-in-difference analysis of EEP/Shiree's panel data shows that beneficiary households have made improvements in all the programme's selected indicators. Large improvements can be seen in access to and accumulation of assets; movement from wage labour to self-employed activities; earning incomes and savings; food security; and women's empowerment. Graduation analysis also reveals that beneficiary households have been able to make significant improvements in all livelihood criteria except nutrition (Sen and Ali, 2015).

Eradication of extreme poverty: implications for policy

Success has many claimants and, like all stories of success, the narrative set out above could be presented in many different ways. However, we would argue that the true measure of a success story lies in its sustainability (internally) and replicability (externally). We would suggest that five ingredients are required for a successful strategy to end extreme poverty by 2021.

First, we cannot overlook the overall importance of the favourable macro context that has underpinned the decline in extreme poverty and poverty so far. Put simply, it is easier to pull a boat when the wind is in your favour. For the past two decades, many growth-related factors have been very favourable: per capita growth has increased; the volatility of annual growth has been minimal; inflation has remained in single-digit figures; domestic industrial entrepreneurship has developed beyond expectations; exports and remittances have increased, and so forth. It is crucial to maintain this favourable macro-economic context to sustain the progress made in reducing extreme poverty in the next decade. This means sustaining the five major drivers of growth in Bangladesh: agriculture, the rural non-farm sector, exports, remittances, and urbanization. At the moment, the prospects are bright in relation to these drivers, provided measures are taken in advance to prevent slippages.

Second, Bangladesh has witnessed numerous examples of successful poverty eradication programmes, each adopting different approaches. These need to be replicated on a larger scale. Some programmes have been successful in reducing poverty, others in improving human development. More recently we have also seen the emergence of innovative programmes focusing on extreme and chronic poverty. A defining marker of many of these programmes is that they transfer resources (assets or financial savings) to their extreme poor clients. We calculated above, in quite crude terms, that the average amount needed to support beneficiaries in extreme poverty was around $100 per year. Will the simple transfer of cash help a beneficiary out of extreme poverty? No. The success of programmes designed for the extreme poor is as much about the support given to beneficiaries as the transfer of assets. Examples of such support include developing savings practices, financial and marketing skills relating to assets, and literacy and management skills. All of these are 'non-tradable' and cannot be developed by the transfer of money alone.

Third, shocks play a decisive role in shaping the pace of extreme poverty reduction. As Krishna (2010) has forcibly argued, the search for a grand or mono-causal theory of poverty reduction is misplaced. We have to give equal emphasis to asset generation as well as to preventing asset erosion. Shocks make poor people poorer, and turn the extreme poor into the destitute. The new panel analysis of rural households in 62 villages over the 1988–2008 period is revealing in this respect. Out of 684 non-split matched households tracked in both 1988 and 2008, 15 per cent fell into poverty, 37 per cent moved out of poverty, 27 per cent were 'never poor', and 21 per cent remained in poverty.[13] Since health shocks are found to be the single most important explanatory factor underlying falls into extreme poverty, effective health protection for the poor and the poorest should be prioritized in any national effort to eradicate extreme poverty.

Governance shocks need also to be prioritized. While it is true that most if not all citizens in Bangladesh suffer from poor governance, the poor and the poorest are affected most by protracted periods of political instability marked by blockades and strikes, since these have an immediate impact on basic livelihood activities. The poorest are also greatly affected by corruption in service delivery, poor performance of duty-bearers, and any deterioration in the law and order situation.

Fourth, tackling extreme poverty needs to be part of a broad agenda that includes addressing inequality in human development and responding to new challenges that particularly affect the poorest. First, there are geographical areas of deprivation where overall progress in human development terms has not been great. Inevitably, these areas have larger extreme poor populations. Second, as the income levels of the extreme poor grow, their demands for services that improve human development will also increase. This is especially the case for quality education and healthcare. Third, some of the human development targets that affect the extreme poor very directly require social actions that cannot be addressed by policy alone. Making breakthroughs in areas such as dowry demands, early marriages, and so forth, requires longer-term interventions and the creation of innovative, norm-changing approaches.

Finally, there are about 100 social protection schemes currently running in Bangladesh. These range from large to very small programmes, and together they have a budgetary envelope equivalent to 2.2 per cent of GDP. Not all of these programmes are strictly 'core social protection programmes', and for this reason Kidd and Khondker (2013) have suggested that as little as 0.77 per cent of GDP is currently spent on core programmes. Moreover, we know that an even smaller fraction of social protection funds actually go to the extreme poor since the programmes have significant leakage, corruption, and poor targeting. Renewed emphasis on social protection is a welcome move, but it should not distract from or displace the extreme and chronic poverty agenda. The two approaches can analytically complement each other provided the reform of social protection to address lifecycle challenges prioritizes the needs of the extreme and chronic poor.

Conclusion: the need for a 'mini big push'

Bangladesh seems to present an 'alternative narrative' in which the extreme poor have escaped the poverty trap in large numbers over the last two and a half decades. The present chapter examines this positive poverty reduction experience and points to the need to undertake further action to end extreme poverty. It acknowledges that accelerated economic growth over the past two and a half decades has been a powerful tool for extreme poverty reduction. However, it argues that growth alone will not automatically lead to extreme poverty eradication. A specific policy package of support is required – and we have called this the 'mini big push' package. This chapter highlights three key messages with supporting evidence and analysis.

First, growth in Bangladesh has been transformative, and has generated structural change that has benefited the economic mobility of the extreme poor. This transformative role needs to be strengthened further because we cannot assume that the trade-off between rising inequality and extreme poverty reduction will follow the same path as it has over the past 15 years. A number of factors can alter future trade-offs, including greater rewards being given to skilled workers in non-agricultural sectors; bad or poor governance; the impacts of rising affluence, including the potential to generate more greed than charity, especially in a context of low accountability, and so forth. It is therefore imperative in the future that growth itself becomes more transformative in both rural and urban areas.

Second, the 'mini big push' package includes strong livelihood interventions. In contrast to tokenistic interventions that offer conventional and very limited income transfers and stipends, what is needed is a substantive resource allocation to the extreme poor over a period of at least one and a half to two years. We have calculated this to be in the region of $500 per beneficiary spread over such a period.

Third, measures for shock prevention (where shocks can be prevented) and shock mitigation (where they occur) should be simultaneously put in place in order to address the risks of falling into extreme poverty. This requires reorienting social protection and human development schemes to the needs of the extreme poor in general. Resilience against shocks needs to be viewed as a central pillar of the strategy to end extreme poverty. These measures need to be targeted, have bespoke and appropriate financing, and be made part of the government's policy commitment. Such policies will have beneficial effects for non-poor households as well.

As argued in the chapter, now is a very favourable time to attack the remaining vestiges of extreme poverty in Bangladesh. The government is committed to extreme poverty eradication; market conditions are also favourable, with signs of rising wages and employment; development partners are interested in pursuing this social goal; and both NGOs and the private sector are playing important supporting roles in social development. Rarely have the interests of all these actors converged in such a way on a single issue. As Bangladesh approaches 50 years of independence, it is in a strong position to remove the most stubborn face of poverty and to become a proud example to other countries throughout the world.

Notes

1. This is inspired by the theme of 'increasing returns and economic progress' articulated first by Allyn Young and later found in the idea of the 'big push' articulated first by Paul Rosenstein-Rodan in the context of industrialization in Eastern and South-eastern Europe. More recently, there has been a resurgence of interest in the idea of the 'big push' (Murphy et al., 1989; Ray, 1998).
2. This is implied by the value of the 'poverty gap index' calculated for the extreme poverty line for the 2010 HIES.

3. In October 2015, the government of Bangladesh approved the country's seventh Five Year Plan, which began in 2016. The Five Year Plans are centralized national economic programmes, designed, executed, and monitored by the Planning Commission.

4. The monetary poverty line deviates from the extreme poverty line used by the Bangladesh Bureau of Statistics (BBS) in the 1980s and 1990s. The latter was based on the 'cost of basic needs' approach and calculated the explicit bundle of foods typically consumed by the poor at local prices. We adopt a monetary line as opposed to the calorie line because the latter is not an appropriate measure for capturing trends in extreme poverty (on this methodological issue in determining poverty lines, see Ravallion and Sen, 1996).

5. Strictly speaking, the term 'income poverty' refers to consumption poverty, as the income status is typically measured by the BBS through the lens of consumption expenditure.

6. This, however, does not take adequate account of the seasonal migration of labour for the construction sector in urban areas.

7. For initial attempts at these interpretations, see Hossain et al. (2013).

8. The results represent the 'decomposition of the overall poverty reduction into growth and redistribution components' as observed between 2000 and 2010 and have been derived according to the Datt–Ravallion (1992) method. The national poverty line for 2005 has been used as the 'reference' poverty line for this exercise since it is the mid-point between 2000 and 2010. The authors are indebted to Mansur Ahmed for deriving these 'decomposition' results based on HIES unit-record data.

9. A union is the smallest rural administrative and local government unit in Bangladesh.

10. BRAC is one of the most famous NGOs in Bangladesh and is also referred to as the largest in the world. Over time, the organization has changed its name from the Bangladesh Rehabilitation Assistance Committee to the Bangladesh Rural Advancement Committee to Building Resources Across Communities. For more information see <www. brac.net>.

11. For more information on CLP, see <www.clp-bangladesh.org>; on REOPA, see <www.lgd.gov.bd/projects/45/>. We have also considered unpublished survey results derived by Binayak Sen who conducted an evaluation of REOPA for the United Nations Development Programme in 2011. On SHOUHARDO, see <www.carebangladesh.org/shouhardoII/abt_shouhardo. php>; on TUP, see <www.brac.net/tup>; on UPPR, see <www.upprbd.org>; on EEP/Shiree, see <www.shiree.org>.

12. However, in REOPA, the 24,444 women were the core beneficiaries, and excluding costs (as well as the target beneficiaries) for short-term employment and service delivery, the total cost of the road maintenance plus graduation component was $34,350,000, which means a cost of $1,400 or BDT112,000 per BHH.

13. This is based on the ongoing analysis of the 62-village panel data carried out by Binayak Sen and Mansur Ahmed. Their results are reported in Gautam and Faruqee (2016). For an earlier account on the methodology based on the same set of data, see Sen (2003) and Hossain and Bayes (2009).

References

Ali, Z. and Devine, J. (2011) *Poverty Thresholds Analysis: Reassessing and Revalidating Quantitative Indicators*, EEP/Shiree Working Paper 10, Dhaka: Shiree <www.shiree.org/wp-content/uploads/2012/02/Poverty-Thresholds-Analysis-Zulfiqar-Ali.pdf> [accessed 1 January 2016].

Datt, G. and Ravallion, M. (1992) 'Growth and redistribution components of changes in poverty measures: a decomposition with applications to Brazil and India in the 1980s', *Journal of Development Economics* 38: 275–96.

DFID (2011) *Independent Impact Assessment of Chars Livelihoods Programme – Phase 1. Final Report. August 2011*, Dhaka: Department for International Development (DFID) Bangladesh.

DFID (2012) *Joint End of Project Review: Challenging the Frontiers of Poverty Reduction (CFPR) Phase II. Final Report: June 2012*, Dhaka: Department for International Development (DFID) Bangladesh.

Gautam, M. and Faruqee, R. (2016) *Dynamics of Rural Growth in Bangladesh: Sustaining Poverty Reduction*, 'Directions in Development' series, Washington, DC: World Bank.

Gelbach, J.B. and Pritchett, L. (1995) *Does More for the Poor Mean Less for the Poor: The Politics of Tagging*, Policy Research Discussion Paper, Washington, DC: World Bank.

Gimenez, L., Jolliffe, D. and Sharif, I. (2014) 'Bangladesh, a middle income country by 2021: what will it take in terms of poverty reduction?', *Bangladesh Development Studies* 37(1&2): 1–20.

Hossain, M. and Bayes, A. (2009) *Rural Economy & Livelihoods: Insights from Bangladesh*, Dhaka: A.H. Development Publishing House.

Hossain, M., Sen, B. and Sawada, Y. (2013) 'Jobs, growth and development: the making of "other" Bangladesh', background paper prepared for *World Development Report 2013: Jobs*, Washington, DC: World Bank.

Kidd, S. and Khondker, B. (2013) 'Scoping report on poverty and social protection in Bangladesh', background paper prepared for the National Social Protection Strategy (NSPS), AusAID, Dhaka: Department of Foreign Affairs and Trade (DFAT), March (mimeo).

Krishna, A. (2010) *One Illness Away: Why People Become Poor and How They Escape Poverty*, Oxford: Oxford University Press.

Murphy, K.M., Shleifer, A. and Vishny, R.W. (1989) 'Industrialization and the big push', *Journal of Political Economy* 97(5): 1003–26.

Rahman, H.Z. and Hossain, M. (eds) (1995) *Rethinking Rural Poverty: Bangladesh as a Case Study*, New Delhi: Sage Publishers.

Ravallion, M. (1998) *Poverty Lines in Theory and Practice, Living Standards Measurement Study*, Working Paper 133, Washington, DC: World Bank.

Ravallion, M. and Sen, B. (1996) 'When method matters: monitoring poverty in Bangladesh', *Economic Development and Cultural Change* 44(4): 761–92.

Ray, D. (1998) *Development Economics*, Princeton, NJ: Princeton University Press.

Sen, B. (2003) 'Drivers of escape and descent: changing household fortunes in rural Bangladesh', *World Development* 31(3): 513–34.

Sen, B. (2014) 'Opportunity, agency, and well-being: economic lives of the female workers in the readymade garments sector in Bangladesh', a study for 'Policy review on garment workers' rights and thematic study on the approaches along with the strategies of SEEMA project of CARE Bangladesh', Dhaka, October (mimeo).

Sen, B. and Ali, Z. (2015) 'Ending extreme poverty in Bangladesh during the seventh Five Year Plan: trends, drivers and policies', background paper for the seventh Five Year Plan, prepared for the General Economics Division (GED), Planning Commission, Government of Bangladesh, January.

Sen, B. and Hulme, D. (eds) (2006) *Chronic Poverty in Bangladesh: Tales of Ascent, Descent, Marginality and Persistence*, Dhaka and Manchester: Bangladesh Institute of Development Studies (BIDS) and Chronic Poverty Research Centre (CPRC), Institute for Development Policy and Management (IDPM), University of Manchester.

Shiree (2013) *Manifesto for the Extreme Poor*, Dhaka: Shiree.

Zhang, X., Rashid, S., Ahmad, K., Mueller, V., Lee, H.L., Lemma, S., Belal, S. and Ahmed, A.U. (2013) *Rising Wages in Bangladesh*, Washington, DC: International Food Policy Research Institute.

About the authors

Dr Binayak Sen joined the Bangladesh Institute of Development Studies (BIDS) in 1986 and is now one of its Research Directors. He is one of the country's leading experts on poverty, income inequality, and human development and has extensive experience in engaging with policymakers at national and international levels. He recently co-authored a study on poverty dynamics that is forthcoming as a World Bank Policy Research Working Paper.

Dr Zulfiqar Ali is a Senior Research Fellow at the Bangladesh Institute of Development Studies (BIDS). From July 2014 to September 2016, he was seconded to EEP/Shiree as Head of Research and Advocacy. Dr Ali's expertise lies in the economics of inequality and poverty; human and social development; food security; natural resources and environmental economics. He recently co-authored the background paper on extreme poverty for the seventh Five Year Plan of Bangladesh.

CHAPTER 3

Leaving no one behind in Bangladesh: the case for a new political settlement

Joe Devine and Geof D. Wood

With Bangladesh now moving towards middle-income country status, the dynamics of its policy response to extreme poverty will inevitably change. This chapter directly addresses this challenge by highlighting the need for a new inclusive political settlement that realigns the distribution of responsibility for poverty reduction action and resource mobilization between the extreme poor themselves and other duty-bearers in society. Behind this simple formulation, however, lies much complexity. The chapter introduces and examines this complexity, to arrive at some more simple propositions conducive to policy and practice.

Keywords: extreme poverty, well-being regimes, social agency, middle classes, political settlement

Introduction: the significance of middle-income status

As the fiftieth anniversary of Bangladesh's independence approaches in 2021, the prospects of it achieving middle-income country (MIC) status are very real. The country took an important step towards this goal in July 2015 when the World Bank officially classified it as a lower MIC. This achievement triggered a renewed commitment on the part of government officials and policymakers to attain full middle-income status before the target date of 2021. In economic terms at least, Bangladesh inspires confidence and few would bet against the country achieving MIC status. However, the challenge of doing so is complex and should not be underestimated. Future growth will depend on a number of factors, including increased investment from the private sector; increased productivity and a move towards higher-value products; diversification of exports; employment creation; infrastructure development; improvements in human resources; and improved governance. Future growth will also have to be broad-based, inclusive, and able to reduce levels of extreme poverty in society. These are arguably the two most important political economy challenges facing Bangladesh at the moment. If left unaddressed, they will jeopardize the country's MIC ambitions.

One aspect of the extreme poverty challenge is a prospective paradigm shift in the way that development, and with it poverty reduction, is conceived

http://dx.doi.org/10.3362/9781780449463.003

in Bangladesh. We know from Kanbur and Sumner (2012) that the majority of the world's poor is now concentrated in MICs such as India and China, with countries including Pakistan and Bangladesh soon to contribute to that number. It is assumed that MICs possess the resources themselves to remove poverty through a combination of growth and revenue-based welfare redistribution. However, MIC status carries with it a potentially dangerous 'trap' (Felipe, 2012): the poorest make far less progress in human development terms than other wealth groups (Lenhardt and Shepherd, 2013) and, as a result, inequality increases (OECD, 2011). As Bangladesh moves towards MIC status, therefore, it faces a new policy landscape underpinned by a paradigm shift that entails thinking more deliberately about forms of growth that will produce a greater elasticity of poverty response, about the quality of institutions through which people can act successfully for themselves, and about the broad concept of social policy. What is required in this new landscape is not a continuation of 'development business as usual' but a deliberate policy focus, supported and driven internally, that will deliver more conducive and inclusive conditions of well-being.

From development state to social policy regime

Social policy in Organisation for Economic Co-operation and Development (OECD) countries is usually associated with state support for livelihoods that cannot otherwise be sustained via markets, employment, savings, capital acquisition, self-funded pensions, or residual family relationships. A Polanyian principle is at work in which the labour market is partially de-commodified by public intervention to insulate individuals and their families from market volatility. As Gough et al. (2004) have argued, this de-commodification reflects a political settlement between labour and capital under conditions of pervasive formal labour and financial markets, accompanied by highly legitimate states arising from democratic processes and possessing the ingredients of accountability and transparency as features of good governance. This combination of conditions provides for a wide range of rights-based entitlements in return for high rates of taxation with redistributive, flat-rate, and regressive elements. Thus, in principle, both taxation and benefits operate within strong legal frameworks based on equity and precedent case law.

However, even under the more robust versions of this ideal welfare model, neither state nor the market have a monopoly on support for people's livelihoods. And even where state support has theoretically been available, quality and adequacy continuously fall short of needs, and the support that exists can be highly variable in 'postcode terms'. Furthermore, even within a broad political settlement, the quality, comprehensiveness, and adequacy of state support have been a function of both the ideological complexion of ruling parties, which affects provision and entitlements at the margin, and, as the recent global financial crises demonstrated, policy responses to broader global trends and priorities. Thus, even for OECD societies, the search for welfare security extends well beyond the state. The same is true for lower- and middle-income countries.

In order to engage with the state and with market conditions of lower- and middle-income countries, Gough et al. (2004) extended the focus of Esping-Andersen's welfare state regimes (1991) to countries with diverse and different institutional landscapes. Amid this comparative complexity, they found two prominent 'condition' variables: states that are problematic with respect to their legitimacy to uphold rights and effect de-commodification; and highly imperfect, non-pervasive labour and finance markets, inhibiting employment-related forms of universal social insurance. The main conclusion – especially for South Asia – was that, in terms of institutional choice, people are obliged to rely more heavily on community and family or household arenas. Thus, their livelihoods are much more a function of personalized social embeddedness than of impersonal rights, which are not sensitive to the preferentialism of powerholders. This reliance highlights a key feature of poverty in Bangladesh: namely the contrast between dependent and autonomous security and agency. The argument in social policy terms is that, while the normative goal may be towards autonomous (in the sense of rights-based) security, what people actually experience is dependent security at best (dependent upon local patrons, other family members, or the informalized state). In other words, the social policy regime retains a hybridity of partial formal provision alongside the continuation of partial but significant informal provision. This is certainly the case for Bangladesh but it may also be a relevant observation for many other societies, including richer ones. We therefore need to be aware of the different types of non-state welfare and their significance for both the continuation of dependent security and the receding goal of autonomous security. The concern is not just to identify and describe forms of non-state welfare but to assess their social and institutional implications for ongoing political settlements with regard to responsibility for poverty reduction and support for livelihoods.

Figure 3.1 sets out the basic inclusive model of a well-being regime, proposed as a conceptual advance on Esping-Andersen's model of welfare state regimes. The focus on well-being as opposed to welfare captures greater ultimate outcome value, embracing both objective (how people are doing) and subjective (people's experience and aspirations) dimensions (White and Abeyasekera, 2014). Thus, well-being and ill-being incorporate Rawlsian ideas about citizenship and belonging (Rawls, 1970), and Sen's ideas about capabilities (Sen, 1999); and, in capturing cognitive and perceptual dimensions, they help pursue a more inclusive policy agenda.

Beginning at the bottom right-hand corner, the well-being outcomes of the population represent the classic objectives that social policy and social development aim to meet through social protection and social investment in human resources and agency. These can include satisfaction of basic and intermediate needs, reduction of poverty and vulnerability, and other measures of low or inadequate resources. In moving from welfare to well-being, outcomes

INSTITUTIONAL RESPONSIBILITY MATRIX

RESOURCE PROFILES ◄──► ALLIANCE BUILDING

	Domestic	Supra-national
State	Domestic governance	International Organizations, national donors
Market	Domestic markets	Global markets, MNCs
Community	Civil Society, NGOs	International NGOs
Household	Households	International Household strategies

POLICY intervention: improve resource, profile enable alliance building and sharing of well-being agenda amongst different actors within IRM

WELL-BEING OUTCOMES
- HDI
- MDGs
- Need satisfactions
- Subjective well-being
- Security of Agency (avoidance of alienation)
- **Freedom to + freedom from:** i.e. capabilities, rights and citizenship
- Universal sense of well-being to overcome negative diversity but allow local conceptions of well-being

CONDITIONING FACTORS
- Societal integration and cohesion (identity, social closure, adverse incorporation)
- Differentiation in cultures and values
- Location in global political economy (influence of globalization)
- Framing of policy agendas and priorities (universal vs. local)
- State form: legitimacy & competences
- Labour markets
- Financial markets

REPRODUCTION CONSEQUENCES

(−) **Simple reproduction:** Reproduction or reinforcement of stratification outcomes (inequality, exclusion, exploitation, domination). Mobilizations of elites to maintain status quo to buttress own power resources

(+) **Extended/expanded reproduction:**
New alliances established between poor and different actors within IRM (e.g. middle class) to enhance agency to negotiate IRM and manage resource profiles, starts a virtuous circle to improve well-being outcomes and mobilize the poor

Mobilization of elites and poor to reinforce or change reproduction consequences

Stratification

+/−

+/−

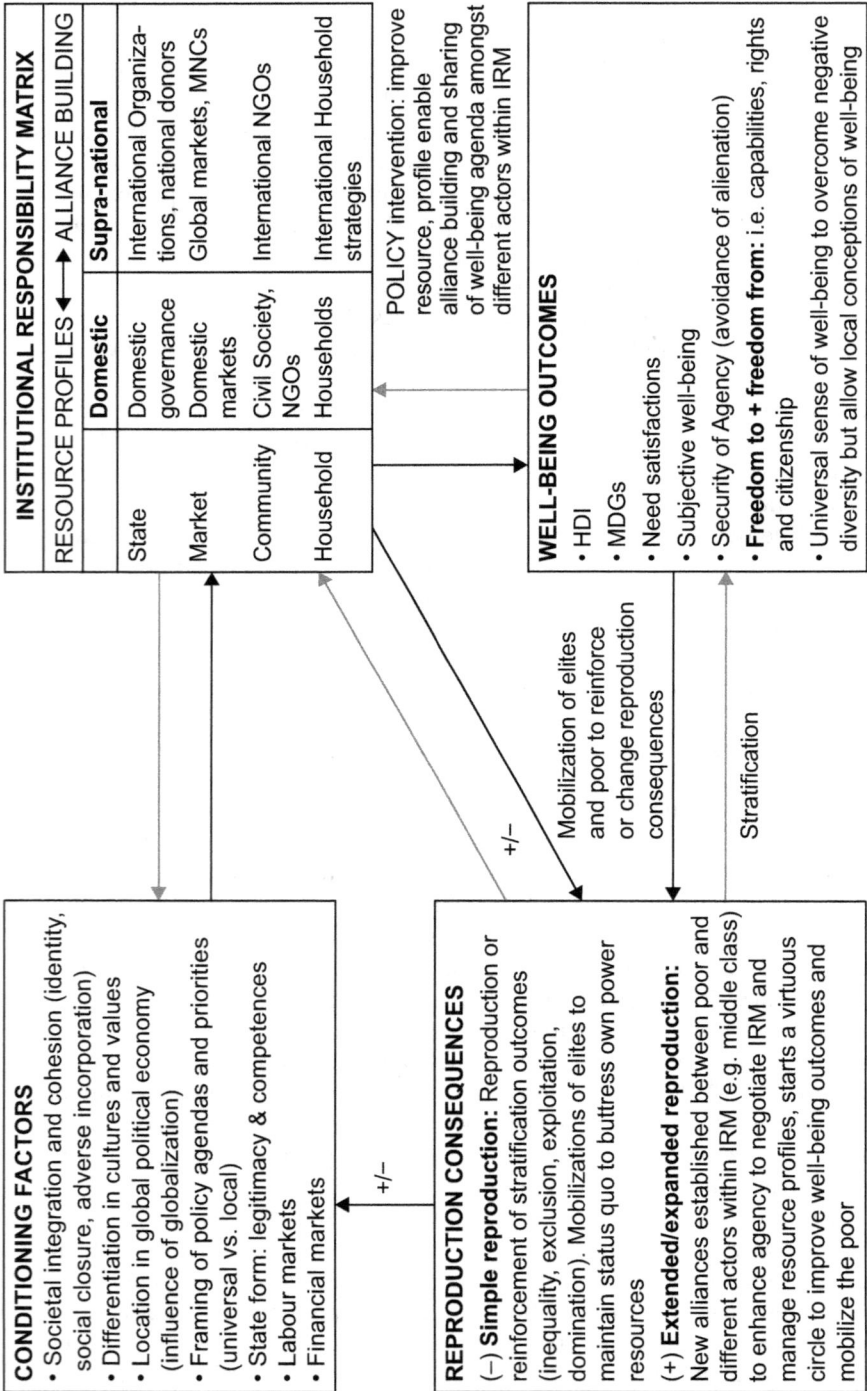

Figure 3.1 Model for well-being regimes

are extended to include social identity, citizenship, participation, reduced alienation, and freedom from fear. Moving to the top right of Figure 3.1, well-being outcomes are not explained simply by the presence and practice of policy, but most immediately by agency–structure interaction within an institutional responsibility matrix (IRM) or welfare mix. This is the institutional landscape within which people pursue their livelihoods and welfare objectives, and it embraces the role of government, the community, private-sector market activity, and the household in mitigating insecurity and ill-being, alongside the role of matching international actors and processes. The welfare mix in turn is shaped by the conditioning factors of a country (top left): the pervasiveness and character of markets, the legitimacy of the state, the extent of societal integration, cultural values, and the position of the country in the global system. Finally, under 'reproduction consequences' we consider social stratification and patterns of political mobilization by elites and other groups (bottom left of Figure 3.1) as both the cause and the consequence of the other factors. Social stratification refers to both the existing distribution of power in society and the extent and nature of societal inequalities. These and the related mobilizations of different groups and coalitions reproduce or change the institutional conditions of society, and thus reproduce or change the country's welfare mix and patterns of welfare. These processes can reproduce a stable political settlement (in more settled societies) or be a driver for fundamental change.

One way to understand this policy agenda is to make a distinction between 'freedom from' and 'freedom to'. Thus, welfare policy in richer societies has been able to focus more upon the principle of 'freedom from', leaving 'freedom to' agendas to other social policy domains, such as education and health. By contrast, any welfare policy agenda in poorer societies – while not deserting the 'freedom from' and human security agenda – has to embrace a stronger social development agenda that places more emphasis on 'freedom to' and human development objectives, in a way that goes beyond investment in individual human capital, competences, and skills. This is more than merely a semantic point about the labelling of what goes under the heading of welfare policy in richer and poorer societies. It is crucially about where the responsibility lies for addressing the fuller capabilities and universal human needs agendas between individual agency and collective institutions.

The permeability problem

Let us take the general argument about well-being regimes one step further. A crucial feature of the IRM is that the main institutions do not operate independently from each other in terms of rules and pervading moralities. In other words, there is 'permeability' between the institutional domains of the matrix as a function of the overall conditioning factors. This in turn sets limits on the possibility of one set of institutions counteracting or compensating for the shortcomings or dysfunctional effects of another.

It has been common to assert that, under welfare state conditions, the state can compensate, in distributional terms, for the market. While there is some truth to this assumption, it reaffirms rather than challenges the permeability problem. So, in richer societies, we might acknowledge a consistency between the publicly espoused principles of fairness, equity, and transparency as they operate in all domestic institutions of the IRM. It is as if people accept the obligations of citizenship enacted through the state domain because they acknowledge their own propensity, along with that of others, to free-ride otherwise. However, a different problem arises when, in lower- and middle-income societies, this permeability functions with the opposite effect and when alternative principles prevail; these could include privilege, the acceptance of socially exclusive rights and entitlements, and the pursuit of private, short-term gains. Here, all the domestic components of the IRM exhibit 'failures': markets are imperfect, communities clientelist, households patriarchal, and states patrimonial. Under such conditions, how does it make sense to expect the state to disentangle itself from deep social and political structures and function to compensate for them? As Poulantzas once put it:

> the state should not be regarded as an intrinsic entity: like 'capital', it is rather a relationship of forces, or more precisely the material condensation of such a relationship among classes and class fractions, such as this is expressed within the State in a necessarily specific form. (Poulantzas, 1978: 128–9)

Although, heuristically, a sharp contrast has been made between positive and negative permeability, it would be wrong to assume an equally sharp contrast between the absence and presence of non-state forms of welfare. Clearly, under conditions of positive permeability, there are numerous forms of charitable, NGO, and not-for-profit interventions in welfare. But they can be seen as (usually regulated) supplements to state provision. There are also non-state forms of 'for-profit' private provision contracted by the state in various forms of public–private partnership. However, the general conclusion remains: under conditions of negative permeability, we can expect more institutional choice in the direction of non-state forms of welfare. And while we might expect public–private partnerships, they will be more opaque. The social significance and meaning of this non-state space in regime terms has profound implications for rights, entitlements, and the security of livelihoods.

Positive and negative permeability is a way of expressing a contrast between social capital and more personalized social resources. A well-functioning state and near-perfect markets are consistent with the principles found in North's contract society (North, 1990); in such a society, implicit as well as explicit contracts are possible, based on trust, transparency, and accountability. This underpins an institutional setting for rights, including rights to welfare and well-being. However, such forms of social capital should, in our view, be distinguished from the idea of social networks or resources that are more personalized and sensitive to the principle of subtractability – that is, they do not continue in an institutionalized form independently of their composition in terms of personnel. Thus, under conditions of positive permeability, non-state forms of welfare may operate within a recognized framework of social capital: for example, charities and other forms of collective behaviour buttressed by the state via regulation or partnership. However, under conditions of negative permeability, they are much more likely to operate outside such institutionalized protection and contract assumptions, and be far more dependent upon the quality of more immediate personalized loyalties and obligations (Wood, 2015).

The significance of a contrast between extreme poor and moderate poor

Having established the theoretical distinctiveness of well-being regimes under lower- and middle-income country conditions, we should consider whether the circumstances of extreme poverty present distinct challenges for agency when compared with the potential for agency among the moderate poor. The contrast matters if the imperfections of the state place a stronger imperative upon successful agency in a 'freedom to' sense. Other chapters in this volume show the differences between the poor and the extreme poor by primarily analysing official poverty line measurements (see Sen and Ali, 2017 in particular). In this chapter, we want to complement this work by focusing on the agency of the extreme poor. To do so, we want to deconstruct the 'extreme poverty' term for its broader socio-economic and behavioural meanings, since these also provide important insights to help us understand how distinctive the condition of extreme poverty is.

The extreme poverty category

It is not uncommon to see 'extreme poverty' and 'chronic poverty' being used interchangeably. We believe, however, that it is useful to distinguish the terms because they indicate qualitatively different conditions and experiences of poverty. Thus, individuals or households can be chronically moderate poor: that is, having some productive assets and social networks and only occasionally running short of food. Extreme poor households, on the other hand, have far fewer assets; rely only on their labour power if they are able-bodied; have weak social and political support; 'inherit' their poverty from previous generations; and have very limited, if any, real prospects for socio-economic mobility. It is important, however, not to treat the extreme poor as a homogeneous group. Kabeer (2009), for example, compares the 'chronically income poor' and the 'chronically food poor' and finds that the former are far more likely to be upwardly mobile. The chronically income poor are, she argues, 'like the poor but just poorer'. The chronically food poor, however, are far more vulnerable and less able to survive and meet basic needs. Mobility for this group is far more difficult.

A second way of thinking about the category of extreme poverty rests on the distinction between forms of poverty that can be described as systemic and those that result more from chance or random occurrence (i.e. idiosyncratic). This kind of distinction is not without its difficulties. For example, among the extreme poor, there is a very high percentage of female-headed households (see Maîtrot, 2017). Is this the result of random or systemic determinants? While the absence of adult male members in the household may not be systemic, not being able to access particular employment opportunities and external services because you are a female heading a household is instead the result of wider relations and norms. Notwithstanding this, the distinction between idiosyncratic and non-idiosyncratic forms of poverty raises significantly different policy challenges. Cases where the condition of extreme poverty is tied to idiosyncratic characteristics – disability, age, mental health, and so forth – require different policy responses from cases of extreme poverty that are linked to more systemic processes, such as expropriation of productive assets, restricted market opportunities, infra-subsistence wages, lack of access to adequate healthcare, and so on.

Extreme poverty: assets and liabilities

By definition, the extreme poor have to deal with multidimensional and interlocked deprivations. In his research into poverty dynamics in Bangladesh, Davis (2010) asked respondents to list the reasons why people remained in poverty. The main reasons identified are broadly familiar and include: illness and injury; dowry and marriage; death of family member; household or property division; theft or cheating; and litigation. Davis also reminds us of the weight that needs to be given to the fact that the extreme poor are also 'rich in liabilities'. Often these liabilities are by-products of the actions taken to deal with the causes of poverty and include loans from moneylenders and relatives, unpaid dowry commitments, exorbitant medical payments for chronic illness, and so forth.

To say that the extreme poor possess fewer resources and assets and have more liabilities is, of course, stating the obvious. It reinforces the risk, identified by Green and Hulme (2005), of focusing on 'poverty effects' and ignoring the underlying contexts or causes of those effects (Banks, 2016). Policy discussions about enhancing the asset portfolio of the extreme poor are intuitively appealing but they must not be divorced from an examination of the contextual conditions in which the extreme poor have to live. These conditions are not only unfavourable but hostile and deeply exploitative. Hence the policy imperative, articulated in our well-being regime model, is to support the agency of the extreme poor as well as to increase the assets they own or can access.

The intensity of extreme poverty

> 'We are caught up in a complex knot ... other poor people also get caught up from time to time in a knot, but their knots are simpler ... you can easily detect the source and do something about it ... our knots have many sources ... often pulling on one carelessly only makes the knot more complex.' (Matin et al., 2008)

Extreme poverty entails a form of vulnerability that is extended in time and transmitted across generations (Scott, 2015). We would take this further by arguing that what characterizes extreme poverty is its persistent intensity. This highlights the duration of extreme poverty over time, but also the way in which it penetrates and affects all aspects of life on a day-to-day basis. This sense of intensity is captured well in the quote cited above. There are two key aspects to be considered here. First of all, extreme poverty entails an interlocking of disadvantages that affect each other and evolve into something which, like a knot, is not easy to subsequently disentangle or separate out. 'Poverty effects' accumulate more rapidly if you are extremely poor but also combine to form different (usually more negative) 'knots'. Second, because the severity and accumulation of poverty effects are greater among the extreme poor, their impacts will be felt more keenly in both the short and the longer term. Thus, it is fairly well established that illness is one of the most powerful poverty determinants (Chowdhury et al., 2013). When members of an extreme poor household fall ill, the consequences for the entire household manifest themselves quickly. This is clearly evident in many, if not all, of the life histories of extreme poor households collected by the Economic Empowerment of the Poorest programme.[1] The 'knot effect' of illness starts to take shape almost immediately, with days off work resulting in reduced income and quite quickly reduced food intake. Over a relatively short period of time, some of the scarce household resources may have to be sold. Then, not long afterwards, other decisions are taken that reproduce the effects of the illness across generations: children are removed from school and sent to work instead; households are split up as part of a survival strategy; daughters are married off. The imperative to meet short-term survival goals therefore undermines longer-term resilience – an illustration of Wood's Faustian bargain (Wood, 2003).

Extreme poverty and social isolation

As mentioned above, one of the aims of the well-being regime model is to highlight the social, political, and economic contexts that converge to determine the survival and livelihood options open to poor households. This draws attention to the structural or relational determinants of poverty and contrasts with discussions on poverty reduction that focus only on the resource or asset deficits (i.e. the 'poverty effects') of the poor. This is an important approach because, again as highlighted earlier, one of the key differences between the moderate poor and the extreme poor is that the former have more prospects of accessing both formal and informal forms of support (family, neighbours, friends, and local elites), even if these might come with unfavourable conditions. The moderate poor are also more likely to be included in mainstream development programmes run by NGOs or the state (Emran et al., 2014). All of these 'resources' give the moderate poor more prospects of accessing services and opportunities that in turn strengthen their livelihood options and offer a platform from which more substantive entitlement or rights-based claims can be made.

The extreme poor do not have the relative luxury of being able to call on these support networks, and have little value in the eyes of political leaders – or, indeed, to the modern political economy (Harriss-White, 2002). This was clearly demonstrated recently when one of the authors witnessed the eviction of a young mother with three children from a slum in Dhaka. When we asked about the reason for the eviction, we were told that she had not paid her rent. During discussions, it became clear that many in the slum were equally indebted and yet they were not under threat of eviction. The decision to evict the young mother came almost immediately after her husband had abandoned her. She had no job and, more importantly, no one to protect her or to 'speak on her behalf'. The significance of her immediate financial debt was overshadowed by her social isolation (see Maîtrot, 2017).

The significance of the isolation and social vulnerability of the extreme poor is further highlighted when we consider the relation between space, geography, and poverty. Perhaps not surprisingly, the majority of extreme poor households are concentrated in the most adverse and remote areas of the country (BBS, 2011). The remoteness means that the extreme poor are the last to benefit from the country's increased infrastructural connectivity; the adversity means that they are the most exposed to all forms of natural disaster and calamity. Spatial considerations of poverty are not restricted to geographical variables; for example, some areas of low productive land have attracted rural-to-rural migration with incoming migrants having to take on more informal and insecure land titles because of the dominance of coercive landlords and local social and political leaders. Arriving in new areas of settlement, they find that they have only each other to rely upon, and, crucially, no supportive networks to link them to employment and credit. The same can be seen in urban slum settlements when poorer households with no existing networks are forced to reside in areas that are less well protected and serviced but are controlled by equally exploitative leaders.

Navigating the IRM

As indicated earlier, the core proposition prompted by the IRM is the distribution of responsibility for action and resource mobilization between the extreme poor themselves and other duty-bearers in society. In the model (see Figure 3.1), the crucial immediate element is the relationship between the bottom and top right-hand quadrants, specified as 'Policy intervention: improve resource profile to enable alliance building and sharing of well-being agenda amongst different actors within IRM'. Thus, policy intervention is premised upon improving the resource profiles of the extreme poor so that they can better negotiate the complex landscape that determines their well-being outcomes. This is the 'freedom to' agenda. There are two important assumptions to consider here. First, the extreme poor may be able to achieve only limited outcomes, more likely of the Faustian kind. This includes a concern that any improved outcome does not jeopardize their current scarce resource portfolio. Second, the extreme poor have a bundle of fragile resources to deploy that include material, human, social, cultural, and political resources. Asset transfer programmes – arguably the dominant strategy employed to reduce extreme poverty – concentrate mostly on the material dimensions of the resource portfolio and are thus limited and probably transient in effect. Once we consider a broader capabilities agenda (Sen, 1999) or a citizenship rights agenda (Rawls, 1970), then the policy imperative is to support agency through the two main windows: 'freedom to' and 'freedom from'. In so doing, more of the resource bundle is supported and the underlying contextual conditions within which the extreme poor operate are also addressed. However, neither of these windows can be mobilized without the support of other, non-poor actors in society. This leads us to consider the need for a new political settlement.

Shifting the paradigm for a new political settlement

The main policy paradigm of poverty reduction over the last three to four decades in Bangladesh can be summarized as 'group mobilization and individual entrepreneurship' (GMIE), driven by a curious alliance between the principles of socialist advocacy and collective action on the one hand, and capitalist neoliberalism on the other. This paradigm was especially pursued by NGOs, supported by overseas donors and lubricated by microcredit, but also by the Government of Bangladesh through its Comilla legacies.[2] In either case, it was assumed that the 'beneficiaries' had capacity (material, human, and social) to follow GMIE. This is not necessarily the case for all extreme poor. There is therefore a contestation between the GMIE hegemony and those who recognize the case for distinguishing between types of poverty, and who thus accept that GMIE may not be appropriate for all those living in extreme poverty. At the heart of this contestation is a drive for alternative, more appropriate forms of support for the extreme poor, such as social protection programmes and safety nets. In terms of a political settlement between the middle and other classes in society, the stark choice seems to have been between a neoliberal avoidance of direct responsibility by relying upon growth and market expansion for 'graduation', and forms of social protection that confirm the subaltern condition of being poor in Bangladesh and consolidate the privileged position of the middle class as elite patrons with a monopoly in deciding the terms of such transfers.

In supporting the extreme poor to negotiate the IRM, and in trying to make the IRM more institutionally and structurally conducive for the extreme poor, that stark choice has to be replaced. Sen and Ali's chapter in this volume (Sen and Ali, 2017) shows that there is an elasticity of extreme poverty response to growth in terms of living standards, security of agency, and capabilities. However, this assumes that future growth trends will be similar to past ones, and that there will be no further reversals or falls into extreme poverty. Furthermore, the calculations also treat the extreme poor as a single homogeneous group. We know that these are unrealistic assumptions. At the same time, there is an important intergenerational dimension to the elastic proposition. Thus, the response of extreme poor adults (especially women) to growth may be inelastic, but the younger generation has the potential for a more elastic response via investment in the 'freedom to' window, assisted by 'freedom from' support both for their parents and for themselves. The 'starkness' of the choice between GMIE and paternalistic social protection can thus be replaced by greater investment in medium-term human capital focused on the youth among the extreme poor, while pursuing stronger rights-based forms of social protection and clever safety nets for the adult extreme poor.

The 'freedom to' driver is usually associated with the capability arguments of Amartya Sen. But do his arguments apply with equally realistic force to the extreme poor? We argue that the characteristics of extreme poverty include forms of both exclusion and dependency that disable the extreme poor economically and politically, thus requiring forms of intermediation and representation from other parts of society. Even the moderate poor and not-so-poor engaging in collective action rarely represent themselves directly. Instead, they are represented by political party representatives, NGOs, local leaders, or kinship heads – all via their patron–client hierarchies (Devine, 2002; Wood, 2000). The poor are therefore de facto co-opted into extant forms of powerholding. Their interests are mediated via representatives, 'elected' or self-appointed, exposing them in the process to elements of uncertainty and in some cases violence (Devine, 2007). What realistic prospects therefore are there for the extreme poor to exercise their voice independently? Once the capability test is applied, more sociologically than Sen does, we start to inject a note of realism into the capability jargon. We find that the emperor has no clothes.

With such caveats about the theoretical and empirical comprehensiveness of 'capabilities', though not a rejection of their ultimate normative value, a broader approach to social policy is required, one that embraces the realism of the political and economic weakness of the extreme poor. This requires a deliberate political debate about the intersections between poverty, growth, rights, responsibility, and redistribution; about what it means to be a citizen in Bangladesh, especially with respect to widening the tax base for social policy; and about what it means to be an effective state, especially with respect to policy priorities and commitments. Such a debate will bring the state into play in terms of its legitimacy, capacity, competences, and framework of governance. It will also open up a discussion about setting limits on the commodity fetishism of free-market, unregulated capitalism as well as aspects of its de- or pre-commodified imperfections, which systemically discriminate against the poorly networked poor. This latter reflection reminds us that any such debate will also have to consider the impact of globalization and international forces on domestic political settlements.

Some might argue that Bangladesh is not yet ready for this debate. We disagree. We are now 45 years beyond the country's independence. The country has experienced steady growth, low inflation, significant inward remittance flows, and expansion of its infrastructure, and has achieved significantly higher progress across a range of human development indicators than other economies with similar levels of income (Asadullah et al., 2014). It is a dynamic society despite the many challenges it still faces, including persistent large-scale poverty. However, the latter has been persistently deployed as an alibi by successive governments to maintain the country's dependency on aid, thus avoiding or postponing an internal debate about the formation of a fundamental political settlement. This settlement, as our colleague Professor Rehman Sobhan has repeatedly and correctly reminded us, should reflect the values of Bengali society.

Drivers and dimensions of a settlement debate

So, in a soon-to-be MIC with an expanding middle class alongside inequality and persistent large-scale poverty, what are the imperatives for an internal debate? As social analysts, we start by looking at self-interested motives rather than altruistic ones. The former can be divided into fears about security and necessary conditions for overall well-being. The first category of self-interest depicts a scenario in which highly unequal or divided societies with weak government capacity to maintain order are continuously or periodically unstable. This poses a threat to the welfare of all: the identities of the excluded and the weakest increasingly move away from the narrative of the state, and the threatened middle classes resort to strong-arm or even fascist state preferences, which rarely deliver over the longer term. The history of social policy in richer societies has involved a combination of early, self-interested philanthropy increasingly codified and aggregated into state-led infrastructural investment and services. Thus voluntarism is quickly replaced with tax-based duty-bearing to avoid free-riding.

The second category of self-interest (necessary conditions for well-being) refers to the difficulty of enjoying one's own well-being when others nearby cannot, as well as conceding that order is best maintained when others have some meaningful stake in society through employment, identity, and livelihoods. A further condition is that economic growth relies on an expansion of 'freedom to' agency, crucially underpinned by wider education access. Again, in the early modern era of social policy in OECD country contexts, these 'freedom to' public goods were initially provided through an element of enlightened philanthropy but also by large capitalist investment derived from charitable foundations (especially in the USA).

So what will drive a progressive internal debate about social policy that will benefit the extreme poor in a society on the cusp of becoming an MIC? The socio-political structure of Bangladesh, derived from the post-agrarian nature of its political economy, clearly contains the potential for constructive contestation. The interests of the poor are partially represented by institutionalized intermediaries in civil society – especially, but not exclusively, by development NGOs. This kind of advocacy has had some cumulative effect on the discourse among the political class and its supporting technocracy. However, under 'limited access conditions' (North et al., 2009), such lobbying is not a sufficient guarantee of pro-poor policy or budgetary allocation. Thus, we have to ask the question: what is or could be the policy effect of the self-interested motivations (fears about security and necessary conditions for well-being) among the middle classes exercising power over the four meta domains of the IRM described earlier in this chapter? And can these move us on from limited to more open access conditions?

We believe the answer lies in a 'new political settlement' articulated around the common public goods interest between the elite and the poorer classes. A common interest in 'sharing the well', in other words. The term 'political settlement' refers to the de facto agreements that have evolved between different classes, groups, and interests over time regarding the ways in which the society is run, de facto rights are distributed, and resources are allocated. Such settlements can perpetuate welfare inequalities but can also enshrine concessions to politically weaker groups. The stability or regime characteristics of such settlements become hegemonic in that no one can imagine meaningful policy negotiation occurring outside of these accumulated agreements.

So what kind of policies might be conceded by the middle classes that both support their self-interests and move society towards a more inclusive well-being regime? The answer to this falls beyond the scope of this chapter and will require a longer and well-informed dialogue involving different duty-bearers and stakeholders. Here we offer a very brief outline of what we consider to be relevant propositions rooted in the analysis presented in the chapter.

First, efforts to strengthen the asset base of the extreme poor need to be increased. However, here we understand assets in their wider sense; in other words, not just as material resources but as constitutive of enhanced capability or agency. Second, it is important to enhance entitlement to social transfers that make stable and predictable contributions to the livelihoods of extreme poor households. On their own, neither of these two steps is likely to eradicate extreme poverty. However, if properly resourced and allocated, they can help protect other economic gains; increase resilience; mitigate risks; and hopefully also ensure that benefits are better distributed within households.

A key third strategy in moving towards a more inclusive well-being regime is to expand the revenue base for public investment as well as targeted interventions to support the extreme poor. The most obvious way to achieve this in Bangladesh would be to increase revenues from tax. This reinforces the need for a careful and informed dialogue including the middle and upper classes. However, part of this dialogue will have to clearly show that benefits from increased tax revenues will result in policies that are relevant to all classes in society, including the upper and middle classes. There are obvious illustrative examples. For example, there is no doubt that the economic growth of the last two decades has resulted in the creation of new jobs. However, the terms and conditions of employment – including pay, health and safety, sickness and maternity support, and retirement packages – all need to be improved urgently. These 'employment challenges' are of interest to all classes in society. It is ironic, for example, that those facing greater employment uncertainty in Bangladesh are the youth, including those from the middle and upper classes who have benefited from significant investments in education. Another area where concessionary policies can be constructed is education. If Bangladesh is to compete and benefit in a globalized economy, it will need a skilled and educated labour force. Such an investment will also help raise the relative surplus value of labour.

Ways forward?

At the beginning of the chapter, we wanted to offer a set of reflections and ideas that would be relevant for policy and practice. This is a real challenge. The more ambitious agenda of resetting the well-being regime in Bangladesh from its present path dependency of inequality, rent-seeking limited access state (North et al., 2009), and limited poverty reduction through a combination of growth elasticity and enclave projects cannot be achieved at the stroke of a pen or through government budgetary reallocations. The idea of policy planning itself has to be more ambitious, embracing structural reform rather than just shifting deckchairs. For this reason, we argue for a purposeful dialogue involving a broad range of duty-bearers and stakeholders.

In planning for this dialogue, Bangladesh has four clear resources. First, there are leaders from political parties, media, academia, professional organizations, and NGOs who have demonstrated a desire to change the status quo and eradicate poverty. These include the Prime Minister's office, members of the Cabinet, the Bangladesh Bank, and the Planning Commission. The same could not be said about many other societies. Second, the legacy of liberation, which celebrates the unity of the Bengali tradition, gives Bangladesh a unique heritage that marries values with inclusive material outcomes conducive to the removal of poverty. However the window of opportunity for that marriage is limited and, some might argue, disappearing quickly. Third, Bangladesh has considerable experience of successfully implementing programmes tailored specifically to the extreme poor. Examples include the Economic

Empowerment of the Poorest (Shiree) programme, the Char Livelihoods Programme, BRAC's Challenging the Frontiers of Poverty Reduction, and Urban Partnerships for Poverty Reduction. And fourth, relatively successful macro-economic management has so far successfully reduced the sensitivity of the economy to the volatility of global financial markets.

The task of building a national consensus around a more inclusive extreme poverty agenda also brings many challenges. Here we want to focus on two initial challenges that flow from our arguments above. First, there is a vast range of stakeholders involved in poverty reduction in Bangladesh, and more has to be done to coordinate efforts that help support the dialogue between duty-bearers and other interest groups in society, and to construct a more inclusive policy agenda. This raises the prospect of a deliberately created national entity – a national commission, perhaps – established with a time-bound mandate to coordinate across the political and policy spectrums and help reset the well-being regime in Bangladesh. Second, any discussion of a new political settlement needs to be anchored in reflections of broader governance concerns. Here, the prognosis in Bangladesh is less positive. The country is currently experiencing a deep political crisis that has also allowed, inter alia, the increased use of state-sponsored violence (Devine et al., 2017). If we take North and colleagues' analysis, the increased use of violence as a way of controlling social order and determining the allocation of resources signals a situation of elite failure (North et al., 2009). The current elite settlement in Bangladesh is uncertain, nervous, and defensive, creating a perverse incentive for elites to protect and perhaps further invest in imperfect institutions that are functional for them even if they may be dysfunctional for everyone else.

Conclusion

This chapter is intended to provoke a deliberate policy discussion around the political economy of extreme poverty eradication in Bangladesh. It is prompted by an admiration of the country's exceptional progress to date in terms of growth, human development, and poverty reduction, as well as a conviction that the prospects for future extreme poverty eradication will require radical and ambitious policy reform. Growth alone will not eradicate extreme poverty nor will attaining MIC status. At the heart of more radical reform is a commitment to a new political settlement that reflects the inclusive values of Bengali society and is responsible not just for the redistribution of resources to the extreme poor but also for altering the political economy conditions that are so unfavourable to the extreme poor. This is a significant challenge, but, as various chapters in this volume show, it is achievable. Therefore, as the global community moves to embrace the 'leave no one behind' agenda, Bangladesh is once again in a position to show the world how to create the kind of political settlements that can turn this 'agenda' into a reality.

Notes

1. See <www.shiree.org/>.
2. The Comilla Model was a rural development programme launched in 1959 by the Pakistan Academy for Rural Development. In 1971, it was renamed the Bangladesh Academy for Rural Development. The leader of the Academy was Akhter Hameed Khan, a pioneer of grassroots cooperative and participatory development.

References

Asadullah, N., Savoia, A. and Wahiddudin, M. (2014) 'Paths to development: is there a Bangladesh surprise?', *World Development* 62: 138–54.

Chowdhury, A.M.R., Bhuiya, A., Chowdhury E.M., Rasheed, S., Hussain, Z. and Chen, L.C. (2013) 'Bangladesh: innovation for universal health coverage. 1. The Bangladesh paradox: exceptional health achievement despite economic poverty', *The Lancet* 382: 1734–45.

Banks, N. (2016) 'Livelihoods limitations: the political economy of urban poverty in Dhaka, Bangladesh' *Development and Change* 7(2): 266–92.

BBS (2011) *Report of the Household Income & Expenditure Survey 2010*, Dhaka: Bangladesh Bureau of Statistics (BBS), Government of Bangladesh.

Davis, P. (2010) 'Exploring the long-term impact of development interventions within life-history narratives in rural Bangladesh', IFPRI Discussion Paper 991, Washington, DC: International Food Policy Research Institute (IFPRI).

Devine, J. (2002) 'Ethnography of the policy process: a case study of land redistribution in Bangladesh', *Pubic Administration and Development* 22: 403–14.

Devine, J. (2007) 'Doing things differently? The everyday politics of membership based organisations', in M. Chen, R. Jhabvala, R. Kanbur, and C. Richards (eds), *Membership Based Organizations of the Poor*, pp. 297–312, London: Routledge.

Devine, J., Basu, I. and Wood, G.D. (2017) 'Governance challenges in Bangladesh: old wine in not so new bottles', I. Basu, J. Devine, G.D. Wood, and R. Khair (eds), *Politics and Governance in Bangladesh: Uncertain Landscapes*, Abingdon: Routledge.

Emran, M.S., Robano, V. and Smith, S.C. (2014) 'Assessing the frontiers of ultra-poverty reduction: evidence from Challenging the Frontiers of Poverty Reduction/Targeting the Ultra Poor, an innovative program in Bangladesh', *Economic Development and Cultural Change* 62(2): 339–80.

Esping-Andersen, G. (1991) *The Three Worlds of Welfare Capitalism*, Cambridge: Polity Press.

Felipe, J. (2012) 'Tracking the middle-income trap: what is it, who is in it, and why? Part 1', ADB Economics Working Paper Series 306, Manila, Philippines: Asian Development Bank (ADB).

Gough I., Wood, G., et al. (2004) *Insecurity and Welfare Regimes in Asia, Africa and Latin America: Social Policy in Development Contexts*, Cambridge: Cambridge University Press.

Green, M. and Hulme, D. (2005) 'From correlates and characteristics to causes: thinking about poverty from a chronic poverty perspective', *World Development* 33(6): 867–79.

Harriss-White, B. (2002) 'A note on destitution', QEH Working Paper 86, Oxford: Queen Elizabeth House (QEH), University of Oxford.

Kabeer, N. (2009) 'Alternative accounts of chronic disadvantage: income deficits versus food security', in D. Lawson, D. Hulme, I. Matin, and K. Moore (eds), *What Works for the Poorest: Poverty Reduction Programmes for the World's Extreme Poor*, Rugby: Practical Action Publishing.

Kanbur, R. and Sumner, A. (2012) 'Poor countries or poor people? Development assistance and the new geography of global poverty', *Journal of International Development* 24(6): 686–95.

Lenhardt, A. and Shepherd, A. (2013) 'What has happened to the poorest 50%?', BWPI Working Paper 184, London: Overseas Development Institute, Chronic Poverty Advisory Network (CPAN).

Maître, M. (2017) 'Guardianship and processes of change: the feminization of extreme poverty in Bangladesh', in J. Devine, G. Wood, Z. Ali, and S. Alam (eds), *Extreme Poverty, Growth, and Inequality in Bangladesh*, Rugby: Practical Action Publishing.

Matin, I., Sulaian, M. and Rabbani, M. (2008) 'Crafting a graduation pathway for the ultra poor: lessons and evidence from a BRAC programme', CPRC Working Paper 109, Manchester: Chronic Poverty Research Centre (CPRC).

North, D. (1990) *Institutions, Institutional Change and Economic Performance*, Cambridge: Cambridge University Press.

North, D., Wallis, J.J. and Weingast, B.R. (2009) *Violence and Social Orders*, Cambridge: Cambridge University Press.

OECD (2011) *Divided We Stand: Why Inequality Keeps Rising*, Paris: Organisation for Economic Co-operation and Development (OECD), <www.oecd.org/els/socialpoliciesanddata/dividedwestandwhyinequalitykeepsrising.htm> [accessed 10 January 2016].

Poulantzas, N. (1978) *State, Power, Socialism*, London: NLB.

Rawls, J. (1970) *Theory of Justice*, Cambridge: Cambridge University Press.

Scott, L. (2015) 'Raising voice or giving assets? Reducing extreme poverty in an uncertain environment: a case study from Bangladesh', BWPI Working Paper 213, Manchester: Brooks World Poverty Institute (BWPI), University of Manchester.

Sen, A. (1999) *Development as Freedom*, Oxford: Oxford University Press.

Sen, B. and Ali, Z. (2017) 'Ending extreme poverty in Bangladesh: trends, drivers, and policies', in J. Devine, G. Wood, Z. Ali, and S. Alam (eds), *Extreme Poverty, Growth, and Inequality in Bangladesh*, Rugby: Practical Action Publishing.

White, S.C. and Abeyasekera, A. (eds) (2014) *Wellbeing and Quality of Life Assessment*, Rugby: Practical Action Publishing.

Wood, G. (2000) 'Prisoners and escapees: improving the institutional responsibility square in Bangladesh', *Public Administration and Development* 20: 221–37.

Wood, G. (2003) 'Staying secure, staying poor: the Faustian bargain', *World Development* 31(3): 455–71.

Wood, G. (2015) 'Situating informal welfare within imperfect wellbeing regimes', *Journal of Comparative Social Policy* 31(2): 132–50.

About the authors

Dr Joe Devine is Head of the Department of Social and Policy Sciences at the University of Bath, and a Senior Lecturer in International Development. His main research interests lie in poverty, vulnerability, inequality, and governance, and in how these have an impact on the well-being of citizens and are addressed through policy interventions. He has collaborated over many years with government, NGOs and other civil society groups in Bangladesh.

Geof D. Wood is Emeritus Professor at the University of Bath. A sociologist by training, he has over 40 years of research experience in South Asia, particularly Bangladesh, working on issues ranging from agrarian change, extreme poverty, and social mobilization to urban livelihoods, governance, and political settlements. He is also interested in and has written on the application of social policy concepts to thinking about welfare and development in poorer countries.

CHAPTER 4

Guardianship and processes of change: the feminization of extreme poverty in Bangladesh

Mathilde Maîtrot

This chapter presents an original approach to studying the feminization of poverty. The intersection between gender and poverty is often analysed through quantitative approaches, focusing on the female-headedness of households as a condition. By contrast, this chapter focuses on the dynamic processes in which being a woman and being poor interact. This interaction can be framed through the notion of 'guardianship', and it is within this that we can understand how and why women descend into extreme poverty, and how that poverty is exacerbated. Marriage represents the key institution in which women experience guardianship, conditioning their relationships to assets and the labour market, and determining well-being and security. A male guardianship deficit makes female-headed households experience severe and sometimes violent forms of destitution. The coping strategies extreme poor women employ often deepen experiences of marginalization and poverty.

Keywords: feminization, extreme poverty, guardianship, destitution, gender

Introduction

On the verge of becoming a middle-income country (MIC), the Government of Bangladesh (GoB) has set its own poverty reduction objectives as part of its development strategy for Vision 2021. A recent World Bank report (2013) shows a significant decline in the national poverty headcount rates by 17.4 percentage points between 2000 and 2010, with a greater drop in rural areas, where around 70 per cent of the population resides (BBS, 2011). There is some consensus that poverty reduction success in Bangladesh reflects a pattern of steady and strong growth rather than a process of redistribution (see Chapter 2). While economic growth may be necessary for poverty reduction, it is not sufficient to eradicate all forms of extreme poverty (Rahman and Islam, 2013). So even if poverty levels in Bangladesh have decreased, addressing inequalities and targeting the under-pinning drivers of extreme poverty will be essential to achieve the GoB's targeted poverty headcount rate of 14 per cent by 2021 (Gimenez et al., 2014).

There is growing evidence that, among the poor, the nature and severity of poverty experienced are diverse and therefore the speed of poverty reduction

http://dx.doi.org/10.3362/9781780449463.004

will vary across populations. Women are often considered to be among the most vulnerable populations. The 'feminization of poverty' thesis, made popular in policy circles in the late 1970s and 1980s, argued that women represented the majority of the poor population and that they were more likely to live in extreme poverty than men. A general consensus emerged across a wide range of international development agencies that gender equality unequivocally contributes to poverty reduction (Moser, 2005). Gender equality implies that, although men and women have different needs and priorities, they should have equal access to opportunities to realize 'their full human rights, and have the opportunity to contribute to and benefit from national, political, economic, social and cultural development' (CIDA, 1999).

In Bangladesh, women's limited market access, participation, and capital accumulation are often identified as primary factors behind their vulnerability and poverty. A few quantitative studies have found that Bengali female-headed households are more likely to be poorer (Quisumbing and Maluccio, 2003) and less able to invest in children's health and education than their male-headed counterparts (Goto et al., 2012). The picture, however, is not uniform. A study by Mallick and Rafi (2010) conducted in the Chittagong Hill Tracts concluded, for example, that female-headed households' well-being was a function of their 'greater freedom to participate in the labour force'. This participation is itself then partly a function of other non-economic, socio-cultural norms and values that determine the capacity of a household to meet its basic needs.

To understand what is unique about women's experiences in Bangladesh, this chapter proposes a qualitative exploration of the 'feminization of poverty' that is not limited to studying female-headedness. It differentiates between understanding poverty as a *condition* and understanding it as a *process*, and will focus on the latter, emphasizing the dynamic reproduction of conditions that create and perpetuate poverty. To do this, it shifts the focus of attention from the perspective of 'being a woman' and concentrates instead on analysing how power relations affect women, and how they affect different women in different ways. Following sections that outline the emergence of the feminization of poverty discourse and lay the conceptual framework underpinning my subsequent arguments, I then introduce the concept of guardianship in Bangladesh. I argue that it is the nature of male guardianship that significantly determines women's experiences of extreme poverty. Inevitably, this requires an analysis of marriage, since this is a key event through which the terms of male guardianship are negotiated.

Feminization of poverty

The 'women problem'

The phrase 'feminization of poverty' was coined by Pearce (1978) to raise awareness of the vulnerability of female-headed households, understanding them as 'under-resourced' compared with male-headed households

(Chant, 2004). Many socio-demographic studies have since observed the phenomenon in a range of countries including the US (Fuchs, 1986; Peterson, 1987), Ireland (Byrne, 1988), Great Britain (Wright, 1992), and Latin America (Medeiros and Costa, 2008). Collectively these studies highlight that poverty is a particularly 'female problem' in developed and middle-income countries (Pearce, 1978: 28). Although there was broad acceptance of the feminization of poverty hypothesis, we can question the ways in which it has been studied and the theory on which it is grounded.

The feminization of poverty thesis marks an important moment in the study of poverty and economic inequalities for social policy. Relationships between women and poverty are often conceptualized through the prism of 'institutional voids' (Mair et al., 2012), the idea that women's disadvantage is due to the lack of functioning formal institutions or women's unequal access to any institutions that do exist. Thus, for example, many authors consider unfavourable access to markets and weaker property rights as determining factors that make and keep women poorer than men (Grichting, 1986), causing an increase in the proportion of female-headed households among the poor population (Gallagher Robbins and Morrison, 2014). During the 1980s, the term was used to stress the negative impact that structural adjustment programmes had on poor women. Differential and gendered access to state and non-state institutions and entitlements laid the institutional bases for other economic and social inequalities between men and women. These included access to justice, participation in the labour force, occupational segregation, information access and use, and political representation and voice (Kodras and Jones, 1991). Although gender practices and institutions vary significantly across and within countries, policy and practice on gender seek to address the fact that a large proportion of women are engaged in unpaid domestic duties and excluded from commercial labour markets, and have limited ability to control or own resources and accumulate capital.

In studying the feminization of poverty, researchers and policymakers have focused on household or individual income deficits, examined principally through quantitative studies, and some variant of the 'institutional void' argument. This approach carries important weaknesses. First, important and often informal processes and institutions underpinning poverty and its reproduction are neglected. Second, the ways in which women are both subject to these processes and active agents in relation to them are left unanalysed. Third, the use of the household as a 'unit of analysis' has been fiercely criticized because it overlooks important gendered intra-household inequalities (Agee and Walker, 1990). Finally, the tendency of the feminization of poverty focus to look exclusively at female-headed households discounts the significance of experiences of poverty of women within male-headed households.

The 'women project'

Historically, in many societies women were considered 'natural resources' that assist male wage workers in their quest for capital accumulation (Agee and

Walker, 1990). As a result, women's paid labour was excluded from economic analyses. However, discourse around the role of women in international development emerged through the convergence of 'institutional voids' analysis with 'smart economics', portraying women as agents for social development and institutional transformation.

Scholarship on institutions (Agarwal, 1994; Quisumbing and Maluccio, 2003) points to the role of formal institutions – or their absence – in shaping the informal economy and order in society. This stream of research typically presents institutional voids as inhibitors to establishing effective property rights, for example. A legacy of this strand of the literature can be seen in poverty reduction policies and projects that instrumentalize markets as intermediaries to compensate for institutional voids (Mies et al., 1988). The emergence of 'smart economics' promulgates the principle that women-focused development projects generate large efficiency 'pay-offs' (North, 1990). Women more than men are portrayed as 'natural' catalysts of the nutritional, educational, and health improvements of other household members, notably children (Mair et al., 2012).

In many developing countries, women are discriminated against in the market and are not paid a fair price for their labour or products. The question of mobility and capacity to manage finances also limits their ability to benefit from interactions with markets. Exclusion from asset ownership and the lack of entitlement to capital are also seen as significant drivers of female poverty. The economic and institutional mindset provides an auspicious terrain and an economic rationale for development agencies to support gender equality through market-based interventions such as microfinance delivery and asset transfers (World Bank, 2005). Women's 'empowerment' – defined broadly as an expansion in women's ability to make choices that have an impact on their lives and that they consider important – became the ambitious goal of development agencies.

Understanding inequalities through intersectionality

To understand the relationship between poverty and gender we need to consider the 'intersectionality' between gender and other social, economic, cultural, and political factors. The literature on race helps illustrate why this is important. The powerful critique of feminism by black feminists in the 1970s exposed omissions of other significant, and often interrelated or interdependent, class and race dynamics in the feminist struggle (White, 2006). The core proposition of black feminists was that the condition of women is comparable to that of other minorities whose agency is reduced by the economic and social systems that privilege the interests of dominant groups. The intersection between being a woman and wider factors means that inequalities converge and their impacts reinforce each other.

The notion of intersectionality can help us recognize the multiplicity of social differences, their diverse nature, and their interaction. In development, the notion has rarely been used as a framework for understanding power configurations (Kabeer, 2001). However, the value of an 'intersectional approach' is that it considers the multifaceted and diverse identities of women as a group, and explores the diversity of their experiences. It therefore calls for context-specific analyses that capture the nuances underpinning the creation and reproduction of inequalities.

Data and methods

Data collection and analysis

This chapter draws on original data from a qualitative and longitudinal dataset gathered through a programme working towards the Economic Empowerment of the Poorest called EEP/Shiree.[1] A life history methodology was used to collect information on poverty experiences and on poverty dynamics from 72 extreme poor households located in different regions of Bangladesh. In this chapter, I use simplified visual representations of household life trajectories to demonstrate the prevalence of hazards, events, and shocks and to examine the significance of their effect on household well-being. For each diagram, the vertical axis indicates five categories of well-being for households: namely, middle elite, low-earning non-poor, moderate poor, working extreme poor, and destitute poor. These have been constructed using diet, employment, and assets as indicators of well-being. The horizontal axis indicates time.

The data was analysed by systematically coding it according to themes that emerged from the research process itself. During the analysis, health shocks and the death of the primary income earner emerged as key drivers of female poverty. In looking for gender-specific processes, the significance of male guardianship through marriage emerged as a recurrent and important factor defining women's social identity and their relations with the labour market and capital.

Guardianship in Bangladesh

The focus on intersectionality argues for an understanding of the feminization of extreme poverty in Bangladesh in relation to wider social structures and processes. This section places the notion of guardianship as central to understanding women's experiences of poverty. As a concept, this combines the ideas of care and responsibility, but also control and power. It is a particularly relevant concept because the English term 'guardian' is also used literally in Bengali. It can relate to male–female relationships, but also to relationships between people of the same sex, implying a close dependency. A guardian may therefore refer to a husband, but it can also be used to refer to what in other terminology would be conceptualized as a 'patron' (Osmani, 2007; Goetz and Gupta, 1996).

Women in Bangladesh require a male guardian in order to engage on respectable terms with wider society. It is most often through the institution of family that women have a male guardian, be it a father or a husband; however, it is not confined to this context. These relationships are embedded within norms around expected and acceptable roles and obligations of both men and women. It is these relationships that determine the ways in which women then relate, for example, to the labour market, property, and productive assets. The argument here is that the dynamic processes that both result in and maintain extreme poverty are also embedded within the relationship of guardianship.

Marriage and mobility

Getting married equates to a search for a guardian who can bring security, well-being, and respectability to a young woman. In this sense, marriage can represent a significant opportunity. However, for the extreme poor, the high pressures for dowry payments result in significant hardship (Davis, 2008). This can force poorer households to send their girls to work or marry them into relations where the dowry expectations are lower, such as when a woman marries someone much older or someone with ill-health.

'Material' marital games

In Bangladesh, marriage has the potential to bring honour to families and to form binding relationships that can be instrumental to their socio-economic advancement. It can also turn girls born into poor families into 'liabilities for their family' (Kabeer, 2001). Aligned with the findings in Baulch and Davis (2008) and Davis and Baulch (2010), our data shows that marital relationships are heavily 'material' and create webs of guardianship as young brides are transferred at marriage from their parents to their new family-in-law. A common aspiration in Bangladesh is for girls to 'marry up': that is, to marry a man with higher socio-economic status. In practice, it is less common for men to try to 'marry up'. The capacity to 'marry up', however, is contingent upon a family's social status and the dowry price. Although the practice of dowry payments is legally banned, it constitutes one of the most common features of patrilineal inheritance systems on the Indian subcontinent (Goto et al., 2012). It is a transfer of resources through which parents expect to secure their daughter's long-term well-being. Once exchanged, the two families are connected through marital bonds. A number of considerations influence the setting of dowry prices, including the two families' perceived wealth, the reputation of the lineage, prospects for social mobility, and the bride-to-be's beauty and dutifulness (Crenshaw, 1989). South Asian beauty is commonly characterized by a fair complexion and a healthy-looking figure (van der Hoogte and Kingma, 2004). 'Dutifulness' generally refers to a woman's modesty embedded in *purdah* norms, according to which, interactions with men external to their family are considered a transgression and bring disrepute (*durnam*) to their family. In general, if the bride's family's wealth or perceived status is lower than those of the groom's, the dowry will be higher.

The life histories data shows that the pressure to pay a dowry strongly determines extreme poor families' livelihoods, savings, and expenditure behaviour. In trying to maximize potential dowry payments, however, families can in fact compromise their capacity to find an advantageous guardian, and as a consequence negatively affect their daughter's long-term well-being. Families are aware of the pressures with regard to dowry payments for their daughters, and when they can they will save early for them. In order to save, they often compromise on their children's education by sending them to work in order to increase household incomes. Daughters born into extreme poor households with high dependency ratios are considered less productive than their male counterparts because of their limited contribution to the household's income. Although female infanticide and selective abortion are very rare in Bangladesh, parents tend to justify favouring male children because they know they will receive as opposed to pay out a dowry, and because they know that sons tend to stay in the household while daughters leave on marriage. Many female respondents explained that, when young, they were asked to labour in order to save money towards their own dowry and to secure their own future. However, those forced to perform physical work in the sun are more likely to be 'dark-skinned', which adversely affects their marriage prospects. Life history data shows that, because of the reputational risks associated with pubescent daughters being 'exposed' to men outside their kin circle, extreme poor families tend to pick working locations that are distant from prospective grooms. Without parental guardianship, however, working girls are vulnerable to verbal or physical abuse.

The pressure to pay dowries poses a real dilemma for extreme poor households. On the one hand, they allow their daughters to work outside in order to increase the household income, thereby increasing the ability of the household to pay a dowry. On the other hand, daughters who work struggle to retain the socially constructed ideals of beauty and modesty, and in so doing they may have to pay higher dowries or enter into less favourable marriage arrangements.

The costs and benefits of time

Time is an important factor in arranging a marriage, and particularly in situations where households are trying to 'marry up'. Although the cost of the dowry and marriage expenditure (jewellery, clothes, and furniture) vary significantly, the trend is an upward one, with some claiming that expenses have more than doubled over the past 10 years and can amount to more than 200 times the daily wage (Baulch and Davis, 2008; Davis and Baulch, 2010). Risks and costs associated with delaying a daughter's marriage are greater than for a son, hence creating incentives for girls to marry early. This, we find, can be due to two main reasons. The first one is cultural.

Customary preference is for grooms to be older than brides at the time of marriage (Goto et al., 2012), so men can play their role as socio-economic guardians and brides can fulfil their reproductive function. The second one is economic. Although postponing a wedding would in theory allow parents to save more, age increases the dowry price and hence the burden for families. This 'imbalance' in the marriage market gives the groom's family a stronger position to negotiate terms (Rozario, 1992), an observation that is particularly true for extreme poor families and for those with more daughters than sons.

The heads of extreme poor households face a clear trade-off between needing additional income to pay for marriages, usually generated by daughters taking on paid work, and knowing that daughters who work can be more 'expensive' to marry off. To escape this dilemma, many poor and extreme poor families end up borrowing money to pay for dowries. The two life history examples presented below illustrate this. Fahmida was born in 1963 into a working extreme poor family and her parents faced a huge challenge to find husbands for their three daughters. Her father had sold his land in order to pay for dowries. Being the youngest, Fahmida dropped out of school at the age of eight to earn money and contribute to her own dowry. Her life trajectory (Figure 4.1) shows how, by the time of her marriage, she had already fallen into a state of destitution despite having worked from the age of eight. Marriage, however, gave her an opportunity to improve her well-being – reinforcing the point made earlier of the importance of finding appropriate male guardianship. Unfortunately, however, her male guardian suffered a serious accident that left him disabled. The lack of effective male guardianship signalled the start of a gradual return to destitution for Fahmida and her family.

Jalmai was born in 1981 into a low-earning non-poor family. Losing both parents when she was four meant that her brother became her guardian. Given the high dependency ratios in his household, Jalmai began to work to save for her dowry at the age of six. Despite finding a male guardian when she married at 13, her overall well-being did not improve. Her future in-laws requested a share in her brother's newly established tobacco business as part of her dowry, in addition to the monetary payment. Her husband, meanwhile, spent the dowry payment on luxury consumption items. Furthermore, after a few years of marriage, Jalmai's husband decided to marry for a second time in order to benefit from a further dowry. Jalmai's position in her in-laws' house was undermined with the arrival of a second wife, and she soon suffered discrimination and exclusion. When her husband became ill in the mid-1990s, she went into debt and started working as a day labourer in order to pay for his treatment. By this time, she had eroded most of her assets and credit sources and had become destitute. After her husband's death in 2000, she continued to repay her debts and slowly worked her way out of destitution.

High levels of poverty in relation to incomes and assets are exacerbated by wider forms of marginalization. Our data also shows the intersections between material poverty and belonging to a religious or ethnic minority, or suffering social stigma due to family history or the mental or physical disability of a household member. In an attempt to reduce dowry demands and secure a marriage, extreme poor households with backgrounds considered 'undesirable' tend to arrange early marriages. Although estimates show that in Bangladesh 29 per cent of girls are married by their fifteenth birthday and 65 per cent by their eighteenth, the available data does not account for the influence of social marginalization and stigma. Our data shows that marriage arrangements among the extreme poor that entail little or no dowry payment typically involve the marriage of a young bride to a physically or mentally disabled man, to an older man, or to a married man looking for a second wife. Such marriages can ensure a form of male guardianship, albeit one that probably entails high risks.

Women, labour, and capital

In the context of extreme poverty, women's access to paid work and property rights reflects patriarchal norms in ways that are neither linear nor predictable. Although women are often prevented or strongly disincentivized from wage labour and owning assets by their guardians and the wider community, social norms are evolving and guardians differ in their attitudes.

Paid work

The gender gap in wage employment in Bangladesh is wide, with 24 per cent of rural men and only 3 per cent of rural women working in wage employment (Chowdhury, 2010), and the share of women's labour in the paid non-agricultural sector as low as 18 per cent (White, 2013). The institution of *purdah* represents a normative framework that defines women's relationship with paid work outside the home. Women's paid labour is usually weighted against her primary responsibilities of care and other domestic duties for household members. Beyond financial considerations, there are significant socio-cultural factors that determine how *purdah* norms and values are interpreted and sanctioned. Expectations around women's application of *purdah* often transform and adapt during their lifecycle according to age, socio-economic condition, marital status, household composition, and the woman's relation to the household head. They constitute an ever-changing and complex set of explicit and implicit patterns that shape their spiritual, economic, political, and social behaviour. Extreme poor women interviewed for our data indicated that the social prejudice associated with women performing paid work is slowly eroding. They point to the rise of garment work opportunities in Dhaka, NGO and government-led rural development initiatives, and smaller household size as determining this change.

Our findings suggest that women who have to negotiate social norms in order to earn a livelihood find themselves engaging on largely unfavourable terms with an exploitative labour market. This means being systematically discriminated against in terms of earning a fair wage, being excluded from the labour market, and facing greater risks in terms of abuse and violence. Female participation in paid labour is concentrated in lower-level hazardous and precarious jobs where wages are about half those of male wage rates. Again, these challenges are made more complicated when issues of status, ethnicity or race, religion, or social marginalization are considered. Extreme poor male household members belonging to *adivasi* groups such as the Santal and the Mro, Marma and Chakma reported that they were reluctant to allow their wives and daughters to work outside their immediate and known community circle because of the risks associated with being extreme poor, being a woman, and belonging to a minority group. This reinforces the argument rehearsed above about intersectionality and how gender-based discrimination interacts with other factors to create exacerbated forms of inequality.

Property rights and assets

Inheritance systems, entitlements, and intra-household allocations of resources are significant in determining women's fortunes (Rozario, 1992). Assets matter because, aside from being a source of pride and status, they can be used to earn a livelihood or collect rents, and can be sold in times of distress.

Despite the significance of assets as a source of security, young extreme poor women reported feeling disincentivized from owning them. This seems to be particularly significant for some extreme poor young mothers with a living husband and unmarried daughters. They described feeling 'uneasy, embarrassed, or vulnerable' if they were to acquire a productive and valuable asset because they would fear being labelled a 'bad wife' by their community. A married woman creating her own wealth and status is considered a threat to the tenets of patriarchy, and a threat to the community. However, relationships with the community are crucial to extreme poor women's survival because the community is often a source of livelihood support, patronage, and charity. Furthermore, women reported that displaying wealth would inflate dowry demands for their daughters' marriages. Notwithstanding this, many extreme poor women do try to maintain a small business or build up their asset base. This has led to uncertain outcomes. In some cases, the business or asset base is accepted as an important part of the household's survival and livelihood; in other cases, having an independent financial base has become a source of tension and the cause of domestic violence.

While accumulating assets through their own means is contested, Muslim and Hindu inheritance practices also disadvantage women's capacity to own property, whether as mothers, wives, or widows (Rozario, 1992). Customarily, it is inappropriate for a daughter to claim her share of her parents' property unless they bequeath it willingly to her. Furthermore, some women waive any claim to their father's land in favour of their brothers in exchange for future assurance of support. In theory, young Hindu and Muslim brides retain

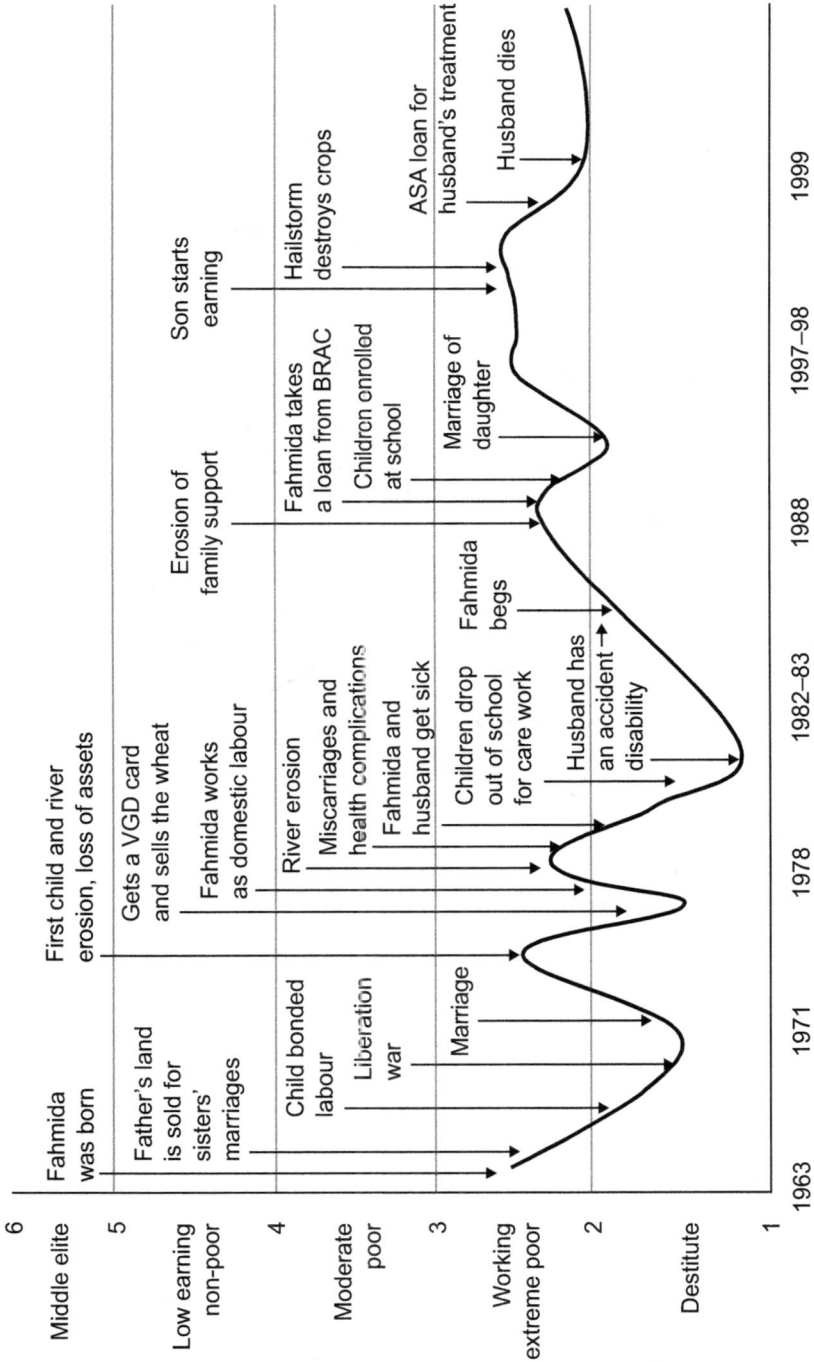

Figure 4.1 Fahmida's life trajectory

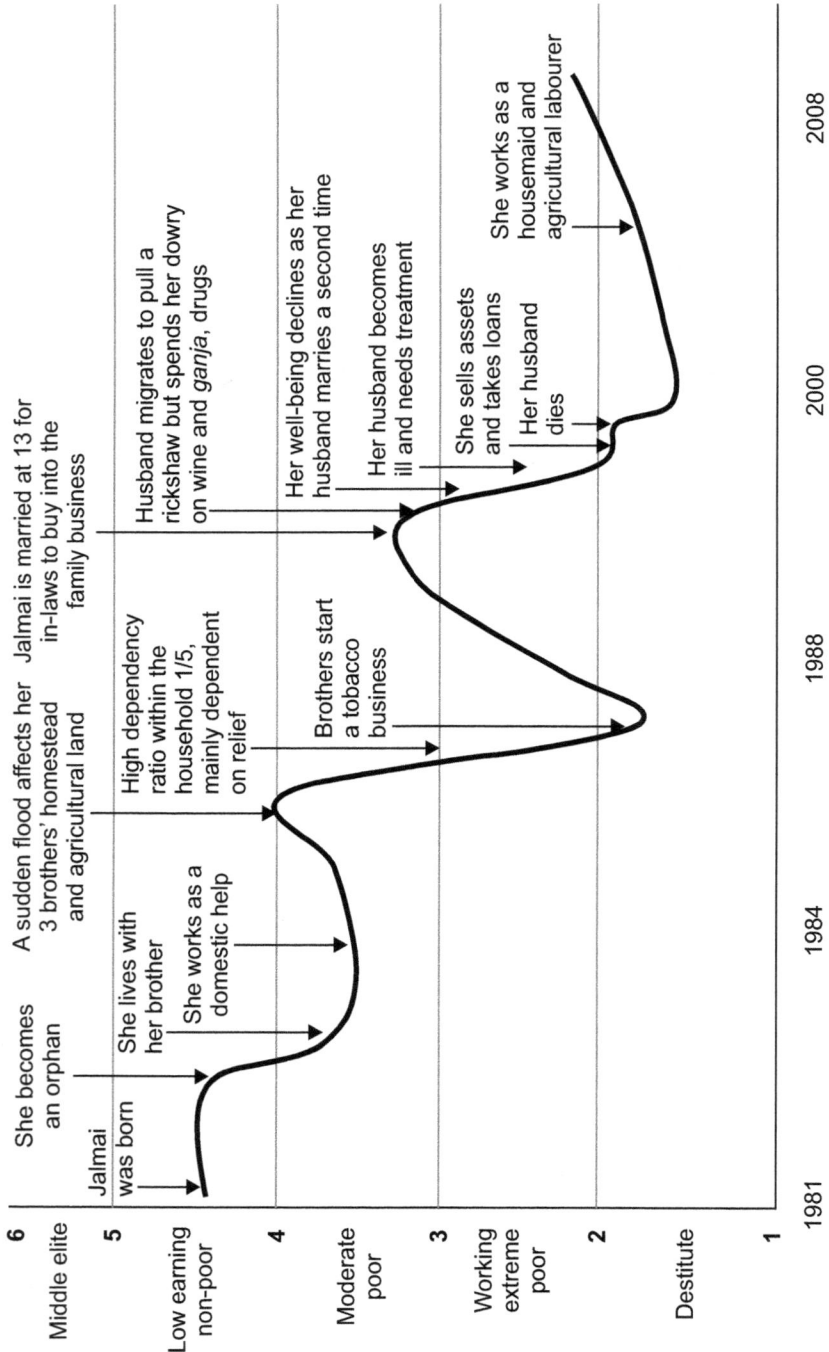

Figure 4.2 Jalmai's life trajectory

some entitlement to their fathers' household after marriage and have a dual membership that should allow them to pay regular visits to their natal homes and to access financial support in times of hardship. Although this support is prescribed by religious and cultural norms, it is more likely to be forthcoming when daughters have renounced their inheritance entitlement at the time of their marriage. Brides might be denied support from their natal home after marriage if the dowry exceeded the value of their inheritance. Given that, in extreme poor settings, dowries are mobilized primarily through the labour of the male members of the household, the men see dowries as advance compensation for their daughters' and sisters' inheritance.

Furthermore, a large number of women reported that as young brides they had very limited control over their dowry. In-laws and husbands generally decide how dowries should be spent. In most cases, part of the dowry is used for investing in the in-laws' business, purchasing assets for the joint household, or investing in dowries for the bride's new sisters-in-law.

Being alone

In Bangladesh, there is very limited national data on the status of female-headed households. In 2012, the Bangladesh Bureau of Statistics (BBS) published a report based on census data, indicating that the incidence of poverty in female-headed households is actually lower than in male-headed households (26.6 per cent and 32.1 per cent respectively). It notes, however, that female-headed households include cases where male members have migrated abroad, later stating that if male migrant cases were excluded from the estimate, 'the results would have been the opposite' (Philips, 2004).[2]

Previous sections have demonstrated how women have unequal and limited relationships to property and the labour market. Male guardianship is supposed to offer indirect access to resources and protection for women. This section analyses moments when male guardianship is removed or erodes, and explores the impact of this on women's well-being. The analysis focuses on two critical life events: widowhood and the abandonment of women.

Widowhood and separation: the guardianship deficit

Although widowhood is generally associated with old age, it is not uncommon to find young widows among the extreme poor. The occurrence of widowhood particularly affects women given that the number of female widows is around 10 times higher than that of male widowers (6.52 per cent of the population and 0.62 per cent respectively) (Davis, 2008). This could be due to age preferences at the time of marriage. The BBS report (2011) indicates that the mean age at marriage is 17.5 years for women and 24 years for men. A larger proportion of extremely poor women are widows compared with women from higher socio-economic groups. With men experiencing higher mortality risks (Amin and Bajracharya, 2011), the chances of women being widowed increases. This is reinforced by the high probability that extreme poor women marry men with poor health or who work in hazardous conditions.

Losing a husband considerably impacts upon the socio-economic condition and status of women. For most of our young widows, the process of becoming a widow triggered a rapid and steep descent into extreme poverty (Kabeer, 2007). The responsibility for guardianship of a widow is most commonly held by her in-laws. Widows, however, described being deprived by their in-laws of their husband's assets, home, and savings immediately after their deaths. This process of ostracism and estrangement can often be violent for women who have limited legal capacity to claim their marital share. Any attempt to claim ownership or rights runs the risk of terminating all relations with their in-laws and the wider community. These are relationships that they may need in the future for protection or support. The data indicates that young widows with young dependants are even more vulnerable if they have no sons or if the joint household includes other daughters-in-law. Young widows have few places to turn to for help. If they become widows relatively soon after marriage, they may try to seek help from their natal home. Our data suggests, however, that very few of such cases were actually offered support.

Separation or estrangement from the household epicentre can be immediate or gradual, symbolic or drastic, as members are slowly pushed away. When women and/or their husbands are considered unproductive dependants by the head of the household, they risk being excluded, especially if they do not have any working sons. The detachment can be formalized symbolically by a decision that forces the unproductive dependants to 'eat separately': that is, they are expected to purchase and prepare their own food. It can also be drastic when, for example, household members are forced to geographically relocate outside the homestead land. Deserted women highlight the significance of dowry in justifying their discrimination (World Bank, 2014). Dowry-related conflicts come to the fore particularly when the bride's natal family fails to satisfy the financial demands of the bridegroom's family. According to our data, such conflicts can lead to deprivations in food, refusal to pay medical expenses, and physical abuse. When these 'punishments' continue over time, they can have an impact not only on mothers but also on their children. In many cases, the 'punishment' is made public with the physical separation of the bride from the joint household.

The chance that a deserted bride will find support from parents and relatives also depends on dowry arrangements. If the bride's family was not able to satisfy the bridegroom's demands, it is probable that her natal family does not have the financial capacity to care for her. Particularly in extreme poor families, where dowries are gathered through a combination of labour, loans, savings, and asset sales, the young bride is likely to be rejected by her natal home. Although women's remarriage is generally discouraged by social norms and tradition, it is not uncommon – indeed, it is the normal response if a new groom can be found. However, those who do remarry generally cannot afford a dowry and therefore enter into a new marital relationship with someone who is either much older, disabled, ill, or already married. Some abandoned women said that they refused to remarry to avoid the risk of their children being rejected or abused by a new husband. In rare instances, some managed to secure guardianship without remarrying. Typically this means that a local elite or a distant relative might help the widow.

Coping alone

This section analyses the forms of coping women use in order to support themselves and sometimes their dependants (disabled husband, old parents, or children). The power and reach of patriarchy means that, in general, women are forced to consider fewer, riskier, and more precarious coping strategies.

When they need to find paid employment, women without male guardians reported experiencing abuse and exploitation. In terms of employment conditions, for example, they often found themselves having to take on advanced labour, bonded labour, or 'food for work'. As one of our respondents noted:

> I do not get paid instantly for my work. Many of them [employers] deliberately pay late. Despite this, I still work for the same employer because I do not have any option.

Being without male guardians can also expose women to physical abuse and exploitation. This is captured in the account of another of our respondents:

> A man once gave me an indecent proposal to have a forbidden relationship with him. In return he promised to feed my children and me as long as the relationship continued. He would not dare to make such a proposal if I had a husband or a son. Many other men also wanted to do the same but I always avoided them.

The gender ratio of children also determines women's livelihood options. Although girls can work as housemaids and perform their mother's domestic duties, they are perceived as less productive than boys. For a woman without a working husband, having a boy who can perform activities that are different from the ones she can perform is a significant advantage. For socio-cultural reasons, it is more acceptable for boys and men to scavenge food in public spaces, work in restaurants, be employed in transport-related businesses, and go to markets. Boys are generally perceived as requiring less guardianship and their actions or behaviour are less likely to have detrimental effects on their marriage prospects or those of their siblings.

Having a daughter, therefore, further limits extreme poor working mothers' labouring options:

> I didn't work outside in the *upazila* cash-for-work programme because I have a daughter. People would say: 'She works on the street, it's better not to get married to her daughter.'

> I left my restaurant job thinking about my daughter because it will affect her marriage, although this decision deteriorated my situation.

Working extreme poor mothers are caught at the intersection where gendered relationships and socio-economic rules and norms limit the choices they can make. This adversely impacts on their livelihood options and, by implication, on the well-being of their dependants.

Our data also suggests that community support and guardianship are limited. Destitute women report cases where they have become the object of gossip, rumours, and disdain. They feel that the community is indifferent to their plight and report of incidents when community neighbours will hide food from them or avoid eye contact because they are frightened they will be asked for food, money, or support. Female-headed households claim that they are excluded from community-based loans with virtually zero interest rates and yet cannot afford 'expensive' loans from moneylenders. Vulnerable extreme poor women will turn to the community for other forms of help. For example, in some cases community support is needed if mothers try to send their children to orphanages. Equally, there is some acceptance and some sense of community obligation towards older women and widows in particular if they beg or ask for religious donations. It is culturally acceptable for older women and widows to beg and benefit from religious donations.

Many of our respondents rely on food leftovers gathered from trees or fields, or food items neighbours or small shop-holders let them collect because they are considered imperfect or defective. They will also change their eating practices, for example by consuming the kernel or middle stem of banana plants, eating wild vegetables or the stems of water lilies, and drinking the thick water produced by boiling rice. Some mothers reported resorting to stealing food to stop their children crying from hunger.

Conclusion

This chapter has used the life histories of extreme poor households to analyse key experiences of being female and the process of 'descending' into extreme poverty. The life history approach has helped highlight the plurality of women's experiences at different life stages and underlined how these experiences are influenced by class, marital status, ethnicity and race, religion, and social marginalization. Although experiences are very diverse, there is an underlying common narrative about gendered inequalities and the multiple negative effects of their progressive convergence, articulated powerfully in the institution of marriage.

The empirical section of the chapter explored how marriage arrangements are central to the social and economic identity of a young bride and that of her family because they define her access to male guardianship. In Bangladesh, male guardianship defines identity and can bring benefits and open up opportunities. It can also, however, be violent and exploitative. Our data shows that the way in which male guardianship unfolds has a direct bearing on the movement of women in and out of extreme poverty. Marriage quite often brings short-term improvements in people's socio-economic status. However, dowry payments are a major cause of movement into extreme poverty and destitution. Women born into extreme poor households are therefore caught up in this process. In need of male guardianship, they rely on good marriage terms and arrangements. Our data suggests that the poorer the household, the more chance that the marriage terms and arrangements for women are unfavourable.

The significance of male guardianship is highlighted in cases where that guardianship is lost, removed, or reduced. When an extreme poor woman is widowed or abandoned, the risk is that she will quickly fall into irreversible destitution. In order to try to offset this, widows or abandoned women will attempt to find guardianship through their remaining family members, by remarrying, or by securing community support. These are critical life decisions with consequences for the women themselves as well as for their dependants. In dealing with these decisions, extreme poor women start from a position of vulnerability, disadvantage, and inequality. As our research indicates, in most cases extreme poor women also end up in positions of vulnerability, disadvantage, and inequality.

Notes

1. See <www.shiree.org>.
2. Around 10 per cent of Bangladesh's total male labour force is international migrants, and their remittances amount to more than 12 per cent of the country's GDP (Das et al., 2014).

References

Agarwal, B. (1994) 'Gender and command over property: a critical gap in economic analysis and policy in South Asia', *World Development* 22(10): 1455–78.

Agee, M.L. and Walker, R.W. (1990) 'Is there any truth to the buzz words "feminisation of poverty"?', *International Journal of Social Economics* 17(5): 18–30.

Amin, S. and Bajracharya, A. (2011) 'Costs of marriage–marriage transactions in the developing world', *Promoting Healthy, Safe, and Productive Transitions to Adulthood*, Brief no. 35, New York: Population Council.

Baulch, B. and Davis, P. (2008) 'Poverty dynamics and livelihood trajectories in rural Bangladesh', *International Journal of Multiple Research Approaches* 2(2): 176–90.

BBS (2011) *Report of the Household Income & Expenditure Survey 2010*, Dhaka: Bangladesh Bureau of Statistics (BBS), Government of Bangladesh.

Byrne, N. (1988) 'The feminisation of poverty', *Women's Studies International Forum* 11(4): 367–9.

Chant, S. (2004) 'Dangerous equations? How female-headed households became the poorest of the poor: causes, consequences and cautions', *IDS Bulletin* 35(4): 19–26.

Chowdhury, F.D. (2010) 'Dowry, women, and law in Bangladesh', *International Journal of Law, Policy and the Family* 24(2): 198–221.

CIDA (1999) *CIDA's Policy of Gender Equality*, Hull, Quebec: Canadian International Development Agency (CIDA).

Crenshaw, K. (1989) 'Demarginalizing the Intersection of Race and Sex: A Black Feminist Critique of Antidiscrimination Doctrine, Feminist Theory, and Antiracist Politics', *University of Chicago Legal Forum* 1989 (1), Article 8: 139–67.

Das, N., de Janvry, A., Mahmood, S. and Sadoulet, E. (2014) 'Migration as a risky enterprise: a diagnostic for Bangladesh', CUDARE Working Papers, Berkeley: University of California at Berkeley, <http://escholarship.org/uc/item/6574658k>.

Davis, P. (2008) 'Marriage dowry as major cause of poverty in Bangladesh', *Science Daily*, <www.sciencedaily.com/releases/2008/10/081030075654.htm> (posted 31 October 2008) [accessed 8 January 2016].

Davis, P. and Baulch, B. (2010) 'Casting the net wide and deep: lessons learned in a mixed-methods study of poverty dynamics in rural Bangladesh', Working Paper 155, Manchester: Chronic Poverty Research Centre, University of Manchester.

Goto, R., da Corta, L., Mascie-Taylor, N. and Devine, J. (2012) *Quantitative & Qualitative Analysis of the Changes in Extreme Poor Households (March 2010 – March 2011)*, <www.shiree.org/wp-content/uploads/2012/02/Q2-report-2010-2011.pdf> (posted 31 October 2012) [accessed 8 January 2016].

Fuchs, V. (1986) 'The feminization of poverty?', Working Paper 1934, pp. 1–22, Cambridge, MA: National Bureau of Economic Research.

Gallagher Robbins, K. and Morrison, A. (2014) 'National snapshot: poverty among women & families, 2013', Poverty & Family Supports, Washington, DC: National Women's Law Center.

Gimenez, L., Jolliffe, D. and Sharif, I. (2014) 'Bangladesh, a middle income country by 2021: what will it take in terms of poverty reduction?', *Bangladesh Development Studies* 37(1&2): 1–20.

Goetz, A.-M. and Gupta, R.S. (1996) 'Who takes the credit? Gender, power, and control over loan use in rural credit programs in Bangladesh', *World Development* 24(1): 45–63.

Grichting, W.L. (1986) 'The impact of education on the will to redress the feminisation of poverty in Australia', *Journal of Sociology* 22: 427–45.

Kabeer, N. (ed.) (2001) 'Reflections on the measurement of women's empowerment', in *Discussing Women's Empowerment: Theory and Practice*, Sida Studies Vol. 3, Stockholm: Swedish International Development Cooperation Agency (Sida).

Kabeer, N. (2007) 'Marriage, motherhood and masculinity in the global economy: reconfigurations of personal and economic life', Working Paper 290, Brighton: Institute of Development Studies.

Kodras, J.E. and Jones, J.P. (1991) 'A contextual examination of the feminization of poverty', *Geoforum* 22(2): 159–71.

Mair, J., Martí, I. and Ventresca, M.J. (2012) 'Building inclusive markets in rural Bangladesh: how intermediaries work institutional voids', *Academy of Management Journal* 55(4): 819–50, doi: 10.5465/amj.2010.0627.

Mallick, D. and Rafi, M. (2010) 'Are female-headed households more food insecure? Evidence from Bangladesh', *World Development* 38(4): 593–605.

Medeiros, M. and Costa, J. (2008) 'Is there a feminization of poverty in Latin America?', *World Development* 36(1): 115–27.

Mies, M., Bennholdt-Thomsen, V. and von Werlhof, C. (eds) (1988) *Women: The Last Colony*, London: Zed Books.

Moser, C. (2005) 'Has gender mainstreaming failed?', *International Feminist Journal of Politics* 7(4): 576–90.

North, D. (ed.) (1990) *Institutions, Institutional Change and Economic Performance*, Cambridge: Cambridge University Press.

Osmani, L.K. (2007) 'A breakthrough in women's bargaining power: the impact of microcredit', *Journal of International Development* 19(5): 695–716, doi: 10.1002/jid.1356.

Pearce, D. (1978) 'The feminization of poverty: women, work, and welfare', *Urban and Social Change Review* 11(1&2): 28–37.

Peterson, J. (1987) 'The feminization of poverty', *Journal of Economic Issues* 21(1): 329–37.

Philips, A. (2004) 'Gendering colour: identity, femininity and marriage in Kerala', *Anthropologica* 46(2): 253–72.

Quisumbing, A.R. and Maluccio, J.A. (2003) 'Resources at marriage and intra-household allocation: evidence from Bangladesh, Ethiopia, Indonesia, and South Africa', *Oxford Bulletin of Economics and Statistics* 65(3): 283–327.

Rahman, R.I. and Islam, R. (2013) *Female Labour Force Participation in Bangladesh: Trends, Drivers and Barriers*, Asia-Pacific Working Paper Series, New Delhi: International Labour Organization (ILO).

Rozario, S. (ed.) (1992) *Purity and Communal Boundaries: Women and Social Change in a Bangladeshi Village*, North Sydney, Australia: Allen & Unwin.

van der Hoogte, L. and Kingma, K. (2004) 'Promoting cultural diversity and the rights of women: the dilemmas of "intersectionality" for development organisations', *Gender and Development* 12(1): 47–55.

White, S.C. (2006) 'The "gender lens": a racial blinder?', *Progress in Development Studies* 6(1): 55–67.

White, S.C. (2013) 'Patriarch investments: marriage, dowry and economic change in rural Bangladesh', Working Paper 19, Bath: Centre for Development Studies, University of Bath.

World Bank (2005) *Enhancing Women's Participation in Economic Development*, Washington, DC: World Bank.

World Bank (2013) 'Poverty assessment: assessing a decade of progress in reducing poverty, 2000–2010', Bangladesh Development Series, Paper No. 31, Dhaka, Bangladesh: World Bank.

World Bank (2014) *Gender Equality Data and Statistics*, Washington, DC: World Bank.

Wright, R.E. (1992) 'A feminisation of poverty in Great Britain?', *Review of Income and Wealth* 38(1): 17–25.

About the author

Dr Mathilde Maîtrot is a Research Associate at the University of Bath. Her research focuses on the dynamics of microfinance, civil society, extreme poverty, and social protection in Bangladesh. She has worked closely on the EEP/Shiree programme and recently led a research project on knowledge creation. Dr Maîtrot received her PhD from the University of Manchester in 2014, exploring the complex relationships between microfinance institutions and clients in rural Bangladesh.

CHAPTER 5

Financial exclusion and extreme poverty in Bangladesh

Mustafa K. Mujeri

Bangladesh's development strategies treat financial inclusion as a powerful accelerator of economic growth and development and an effective means for achieving the goals of reducing extreme poverty and building shared prosperity. Various indicators of financial inclusion show that extreme poor households have the least access to financial services. Their exclusion is involuntary and created by price and non-price barriers. Four promising avenues are identified as effective vehicles for financial inclusion of the extreme poor: 1) linking microcredit with formal financial services; 2) building financial inclusion components into safety net systems; 3) promoting effective and targeted insurance programmes; and 4) expanding the mobile banking network. The policy priority is to create an efficient, transparent, and integrated financial system, along with improved financial literacy for all segments of the population. Key aspects of the policy response include working towards achieving a 'cashless society' through investments in the electronic infrastructure of financial services and other supportive measures, and the development of an efficient national payments system.

Keywords: extreme poverty, financial inclusion, formal financial services, microfinance

Introduction

Over the last two decades, Bangladesh has achieved rapid reductions in poverty due to a number of factors such as high economic growth and favourable demographic transitions, including declines in fertility and the shift to lower dependency ratios. In addition, rural transformations, including the growth of non-farm employment and incomes, supported by large inflows of remittances, have played a key role in reducing rural poverty. Despite this impressive track record, addressing poverty, especially extreme poverty, remains a major challenge for Bangladesh. Extreme poverty levels remain high, with around 13 per cent of the population subsisting in distressed living conditions.

It is widely recognized that finance is a powerful tool of economic growth especially in a resource-poor developing country such as Bangladesh.

http://dx.doi.org/10.3362/9781780443463.005

Access to finance for the poor is essential for promoting inclusive economic growth and eradicating poverty.[1] There exists growing evidence of the beneficial impacts of access to financial services on different social and economic outcomes at household and business levels (Levine, 2005; Demirgüç-Kunt et al., 2008). Bangladesh's current development strategies recognize that national development will be undermined if expanded financial services are not made available to the population. This concerns the extreme poor in a specific way since they are the most deprived and are most in need of access to these services. In an inclusive financial system, no segment of the population should remain excluded from accessing financial services.[2]

This chapter aims to identify opportunities for the poor in Bangladesh, especially the extreme poor, to access financial services through banks and financial institutions. It explores how these can help the extreme poor invest in livelihoods, and develop their skills to make informed financial decisions.[3] The chapter has two main objectives: first, to assess the present level of access of the extreme poor to financial services; and second, to recommend a set of policies and measures that will enable the regulatory agencies and financial institutions to provide access to financial services to the excluded groups.

Access to financial services in Bangladesh: an overview

In Bangladesh, financial markets consist of three broad segments: financial services offered by the formal markets (financial institutions and banks); quasi-formal markets (microfinance institutions and cooperatives); and informal markets (moneylenders, traders, friends, and relatives). Various indicators are used to measure the level of access to financial services in an economy (Mehrotra et al., 2009). Broadly speaking, these indicators refer to two aspects of financial access: 1) the outreach dimension; and 2) the actual usage dimension. In terms of the outreach dimension, there are two types of indicators: geographical penetration and demographic penetration.

In Bangladesh, indicators of both outreach and actual usage dimensions show that overall access to financial services has increased rapidly, especially in recent years (see Table 5.1). Access as a share of the total population increased from 44 per cent in 2005 to more than 65 per cent in 2013. As a share of the total adult population, it increased from 71 per cent to 101 per cent over the same period (BBS, 2013). This figure, however, includes multiple account-holders and multiple memberships in microfinance institutions (MFIs) and cooperatives. Available evidence shows that the incidence of such multiple memberships is quite high among those with access to financial services.

Despite the rapidly expanding network of both formal and quasi-formal institutions in Bangladesh, informal markets continue to be widely used. This is because they offer flexibility, proximity, and ease of operation. While poor households have managed to deal with their lack of access to formal institutions by turning to quasi-formal providers such as MFIs, the extreme poor

Table 5.1 Overall state of financial inclusion in Bangladesh (2014)

Financial access indicator	Value (%, age 15+ years)
Account at a formal financial institution, all adults	31.0
Account at a formal financial institution, females	26.5
Account at a formal financial institution, poorest 40%	23.1
Account used to receive wages	1.6
Account used to receive government payments	0.4
Account used to receive remittances, % recipients	8.6
Saved at a financial institution in the past year	7.4
Saved using a savings club in the past year	5.2
Loan from a financial institution in the past year	9.9
Loan from family or friends in the past year	25.2
Used a debit card to make payments	1.0
Used a credit card to make payments	0.2

Source: World Bank financial inclusion data, accessed online 24 November 2015.

have far fewer options. Many extreme poor have limited access even to MFIs because they are perceived as vulnerable and therefore risky.

Recent technological innovations in the information and communication technology (ICT) sector have played a significant role in providing financial services more efficiently, at lower costs and more quickly, especially in remote areas. In Bangladesh, financial institutions, particularly banks, have rapidly adopted new technologies such as the installation of ATMs and points of sale (PoS), the introduction of credit and debit cards, the use of mobile phones, internet banking, online banking, and tele-banking. In recent years, mobile banking has emerged as a powerful instrument for increasing the outreach of financial services, aided by the already high mobile phone penetration rates in rural areas (Mehrota et al., 2009).[4]

Access to finance for the extreme poor in Bangladesh: key issues

For policy purposes, it is important to identify those households who have access to financial services and those who do not have such access. Table 5.2 provides an overview of the characteristics of households accessing different kinds of financial services.

The results suggest a correlation between household access to particular kinds of financial services and wider household characteristics. In general, households with less education, low income, and lower-end occupations are more likely not to have access to financial services. For example, almost 34 per cent of the daily labour-headed households do not have access to any financial services. Furthermore there seems to exist an inverse relationship

Table 5.2 Characteristics of households with access to financial services (2009–10)

Characteristics	Access to any financial services (%)	Access to formal services (%)	Access to quasi-formal services (%)	Access to informal services (%)	No access to financial services (%)
Occupation					
Service-holder	76.7	54.8	22.9	19.4	23.3
Self-employed	77.0	31.7	48.0	29.8	23.0
Daily labour	66.3	13.6	51.9	24.5	33.8
Education					
Illiterate	68.7	17.8	50.0	25.8	31.3
Up to grade 5	73.1	25.1	48.8	28.0	26.9
Up to grade 9	74.5	36.5	38.9	30.0	25.6
SSC	78.1	51.7	32.7	26.8	21.9
HSC	82.4	66.5	22.2	18.4	17.6
Above HSC	90.1	85.7	12.0	15.6	9.7
Income quintile					
Lowest	64.6	18.5	43.3	24.7	35.4
Second	67.8	14.9	51.9	24.7	32.2
Third	73.0	25.2	49.3	27.1	27.0
Fourth	76.0	35.9	40.9	26.2	24.0
Highest	86.0	63.2	30.5	28.6	14.0

Source: Khalily and Khaleque (2013a).
Note: SSC is secondary school certificate and HSC is higher secondary certificate.

between the level of education of the household head and the degree of access to quasi-formal and informal financial services. In particular, household heads with less education are more likely to be excluded from accessing any financial services. Similarly, households belonging to lower-income quintiles are less likely to have access to financial services.

Access to credit for extreme poor households

Access to credit is critical to improving the livelihoods of extreme poor households in Bangladesh because it can ease capital constraints, help minimize production vulnerability, and increase labour and capital productivity by enabling access to better inputs and the adoption of higher-yielding technologies (Eswaran and Kotwal, 1990; Zeller et al., 1997). However, in the context of Bangladesh, the extreme poor have only limited access to these productivity gains even when supported by credit, as they are either landless or have limited or no access to cultivable land. Nevertheless, credit can increase the risk-bearing ability and change the risk-coping strategies of extreme poor households. It can also improve their consumption-smoothing ability. Although extreme poor households have some access to quasi-formal credit through the targeted programmes of government agencies and MFIs, they remain excluded from the formal markets and have limited access to the informal credit market due to their low and uncertain incomes and extremely limited asset ownership.

Key constraints to improving financial access

For policy purposes, it is important to identify the key barriers that prevent extreme poor households from accessing financial services. In view of the large number of financially excluded people, one of the major barriers is the low geographical or physical access to banks. The banking infrastructure is inadequate, particularly in remote areas of Bangladesh. Where services are available, low financial literacy and awareness, as well as the complex requirements relating to the documentation needed to open an account, act as barriers for the extreme poor to access the banking system. Furthermore, banks and other financial institutions mostly focus on large-scale loans as part of a competitive and cost-effective business strategy. Consequently, small-sized loans that would be suitable for extreme poor households are a low priority for mainstream banking institutions.

The literature confirms that most MFIs reach 'upper poor' groups and that they are less successful in reaching extreme poor groups. While households in upper-income quintiles may access financial services in locations in which the extreme poor live, the extreme poor are often unable to secure the same access due to a number of constraints operating on both the demand and supply sides. Many of the MFI products offered, for example, are inappropriate because they lack flexible options for loan terms and repayment schedules. They are also expensive products, and the practice of charging higher interest rates for smaller loans relative to the larger ones reflects the fact that the per unit administration cost is higher for smaller loans. The failure of MFIs to reach the extreme poor encouraged a number of institutions to design programmes aimed specifically at this group, such as BRAC's 'Challenging the Frontiers of Poverty Reduction–Targeting the Ultra-poor' (CFPR-TUP) and the Shiree programme supported by the Department for International Development (DFID). Shiree's targeting criteria explicitly focused on households who did not have access to credit.[5]

Transaction costs of borrowing

The transaction cost of borrowing is one of the key determinants of access to credit and is determined by both demand- and supply-side considerations. The transaction cost involves both interest and non-interest costs. In the case of lending, the interest rate is usually lower in the formal credit market and is highest in the informal credit market. The quasi-formal credit market also offers loans at high interest rates because of high operating costs; however, in most cases, it is lower than the lending rate of the informal credit market. A higher lending interest rate increases the expected average borrowing cost.

Table 5.3 Transaction costs of borrowing from different markets (2009–10)

	Borrowing cost (in BDT) per BDT100 Credit market		
	Formal credit market	Quasi-formal credit market	Informal credit market
Conveyance cost	0.61	0.62	1.57
Cost of loan fees	0.52	0.69	–
Cost of informal payments (bribes)	1.20	0.03	–
Total non-interest transaction cost	*2.33*	*1.34*	*1.57*
Interest cost	12.14	13.07	22.94
Total borrowing cost (interest + non-interest cost)	**14.47**	**14.41**	**24.51**
Non-interest cost as % of total transaction cost	16.1	9.2	6.4

Source: Khalily and Khaleque (2013b).

Together, the transaction cost of borrowing (interest plus non-interest costs) is likely to be higher in the informal credit market than in the other two markets. The normal expectation is that, with homogeneous products, borrowers are more likely to access credit from the quasi-formal markets since these are relatively easy to access and have features that are more in line with their expectations of formal credit. In reality, the products across markets are not homogeneous: they vary in terms of loan conditions and size, among other factors. Given the variety of products on offer, firms and individuals will behave in ways that optimize the transaction costs of borrowing.

Khalily and Khaleque (2013b) examine several characteristics of the transaction costs of borrowing from different markets (Table 5.3). They find that the non-interest cost is higher in the formal credit market but the average nominal interest rate is lower. The quasi-formal market is characterized by low transaction costs but high interest rates compared with the formal market. On the other hand, the average lending rate is higher in the informal credit market but explicit non-interest costs fall between those of the formal and the quasi-formal credit markets. Although these results indicate that the interest cost of borrowing is lowest in the formal credit market and highest in the informal credit market, the total transaction cost of borrowing is similar for formal and quasi-formal credit markets. The transaction cost of borrowing is highest in the informal credit market, indicating that the extreme poor face the highest costs of borrowing.[6]

Recent policies for improving access to financial services

In recent years, the government, especially the Bangladesh Bank (the central bank), has taken several initiatives to enhance the coverage of financial services in the formal financial system, especially by expanding coverage to poor and disadvantaged sections of society.

One of the significant efforts of the Bangladesh Bank is to expand the availability of banking services to small and marginal farmers. In order to bring these farmers within the networks of commercial banks, banks now offer new bank accounts with less stringent conditions. For example, with these new accounts, applicants need to make an initial deposit of only 10 Bangladeshi Taka (BDT) and to show their national identity card or birth registration certificate and the Agriculture Inputs Assistance card issued by the Agriculture Extension Department. Banks are no longer required to fill in the 'Know Your Customer' (KYC) form, and there are no conditions around maintaining a minimum balance. Importantly, these accounts are free from additional charges or fees. As of 2014, a total of 9.6 million such accounts had been opened by farmers. These accounts are used to disburse government input subsidies to farmers; to facilitate small savings, the disbursement of revolving loans, and receipt of remittances; and to allow access to other financial services. In addition, 3.5 million accounts have been opened by beneficiaries of different social safety net programmes and by young school students under separate targeted programmes.

Another innovative step taken by the Bangladesh Bank is the provision of agricultural credit to sharecroppers, considered to be among the poorest groups in the rural areas. The Bangladesh Bank has also encouraged creative partnerships between banks or MFIs and mobile phone and smart card technology platforms to provide cost-effective financial service packages especially for poorer clients. In 2010, the Bangladesh Bank introduced no-frills accounts (NFAs) for farmers; in 2011, it started mobile financial services (MFS) to facilitate the provision of financial services to unserved and underserved areas; and then, in 2013, it began agent banking services to provide banking services in the most remote areas. Furthermore, the Bangladesh Bank has encouraged banks and financial institutions to embrace a specific commitment to financial inclusion as a corporate social responsibility (CSR) obligation.

The existing banking initiatives are, however, still inadequate to resolve the issues that prevent the extreme poor from accessing financial services from the formal and quasi-formal markets. There are a number of barriers, including poor banking infrastructure, cumbersome documentation requirements, inadequate financial literacy or education, inadequate technological infrastructure, low incomes, the limited availability of a suitable product structure, relatively high product costs, and the absence of a credit bureau and insurance for borrowers.

The policy framework: challenges and opportunities

Bangladesh's development strategies treat financial inclusion as a powerful accelerator of economic growth and development and as an effective means of achieving the goals of reducing extreme poverty and building shared prosperity. The approach involves three mutually reinforcing objectives:

1. reduce the amount of time and money that poor people spend to conduct financial transactions;

2.   increase the capacity of poor people to manage financial shocks and make use of income-generating opportunities;
3.   generate macro-level efficiency by digitally connecting poor people, financial institutions, government service providers, businesses, the private sector, and other stakeholders.

The government's efforts have increasingly focused on expanding innovative ways to improve the extreme poor's access to financial services and to encourage financial institutions to offer these services. Since these interventions often involve technologies that need to be adapted to the targeted clients, product design experiments are needed to develop appropriate and user-friendly services and packages.

The challenges

Increasing access to financial services for the extreme poor is critical to enable new and more productive income-earning opportunities, to manage personal financial crises and unforeseen risks, and to increase the chances of moving out of poverty. In this respect, the present challenge is to capitalize on rapid advances in mobile communications and digital payment systems to connect these households to affordable and reliable financial services. This involves making available effective tools for savings, payments, credit, and insurance, especially at critical moments, to help extreme poor households exploit opportunities to move out of poverty or manage a crisis or emergency.

The opportunities

Over the past few years, financial inclusion policies, coupled with the explosion of mobile penetration and the launch of MFS, have created an environment for reaching unbanked populations in all locations. However, these developments have not benefited all groups in a similar manner, and extreme poor households have benefited the least.

Available evidence shows that digital means are the most effective way to significantly expand poor people's access to formal financial services. In addition to cost savings, digital financial services have many other advantages, such as: 1) they connect the poor to the formal financial sector and with the wider economy; 2) financial flows can be accurately tracked through digital means, enabling safer and speedier transactions that are less susceptible to corruption and theft; 3) the deposit of loans and other transfers directly to the banks helps recipients save more and also gives women more financial authority within the household and is thus seen as empowering; 4) financial institutions can use the financial histories of poorer clients to develop products that are better suited to their needs, cash flows, and risk profiles; and 5) information sharing – such as sending reminders and providing default options and other choices – is convenient and saves time if performed through mobile phone and/or other digital means (see Kendall and Voorhies, 2014; World Bank, 2014).

Digitizing financial transactions can be seen as a first step in introducing low-income populations to banking and other financial services and can have a transformative effect on the overall financial landscape of the country. When transactions that previously circulated outside the formal economy are channelled within it, new relationships and opportunities among users, providers, and commercial entities are created. However, it must also be recognized that extreme poor families require products that meet their day-to-day needs, with small payment sizes and safe ways to save money for purposes such as education and important life events. By going digital, it is possible to lessen the financial divide that currently exists, especially in rural areas and between different income groups. It is estimated that transaction costs can be reduced by as much as 90 per cent (World Bank, 2014). There also exists the advantage of reach. Operating a traditional bank branch may be impractical in many rural and remote areas where the majority of the poor live; however, 94 per cent of the poor in Bangladesh are covered by a mobile signal. This implies that digital means can take banking to the people and to places that have been underserved or completely excluded so far.

However, availability does not always mean adoption. For successful adoption, it is necessary to establish an environment in which digital payments are also accepted. Digital money has to become a more convenient and commonly supported way of buying goods, paying school fees, sending money to family members, and performing other transactions central to the lives of extreme poor people.

One of the major challenges of serving extreme poor households is the lack of adequate information on the kinds of financial services they need. While progress has been made on understanding the needs of different poor groups, relatively little is known about the financial service needs of the extreme poor and of harder-to-reach segments of the population. A detailed understanding of their financial service needs requires a comprehensive analysis of the lives of different extreme poor groups and their specific characteristics. It is important to understand how the extreme poor manage their cash flows, their preferences, attitudes, and behaviours, and the nature and significance of different barriers that these groups face in determining the scope for diversifying their income sources as an effective path out of poverty. It is also important to analyse what policy and other incentives need to be adopted so that financial service providers feel encouraged to take an active interest in serving these marginalized populations, understanding how they access information, and adapting existing technologies to make that information available.

Digital financial services

Since digital payment systems have already taken hold in rural communities in Bangladesh, there is an opportunity to work with banks and other financial service providers to increase the range of financial services that the extreme poor can access digitally. As a reasonable degree of connectivity in rural areas is already established, efforts should be made to extend the reach of digital payment systems into rural communities and to encourage the extreme poor to adopt these systems. Public–private cooperation represents one way in which cost, distance, and regulatory complexities can be managed.

It is important to note that the financial sector and digital operators have already started a process in Bangladesh that involves simple yet powerful innovations in the use of mobile phones. This includes the introduction of the digital wallet; this is an electronic prepaid card with mobile banking facilities that utilizes ATMs, mobile phones, and other forms of e-banking. It is expected that these innovations will help reach a greater number of the poor and drive down transaction costs to levels that could pave the way for the more effective use of financial products and applications that were previously considered unprofitable. This may also lead to the creation of savings products that are more accessible to the extreme poor, better suit their cash flow challenges, and help address future spending needs.

Providing efficient financial services and relevant products

To ensure the productive use of financial services, deeper and more comprehensive knowledge is required about the products that exist for extreme poor households, the institutions that provide these products, and the success factors behind effective and innovative models. This will involve both development and piloting of more tailored products and services for extreme poor households. The government should encourage relevant organizations to explore ways to work with mobile network operators (MNOs) and other private sector actors to identify not only how technology can help drive down costs so that poorer clients can benefit, but also how different types of providers can collectively reach these clients in an effective manner.

The fact remains that the specific characteristics of different groups of extreme poor households and their demand for financial services are still not well understood and the risk of extending credit to these groups is perceived to be high. The small size of their transactions also makes it difficult to capture savings, channel remittances, build money transfer systems, and offer individual micro-insurance products. On the other hand, significant opportunities to improve access to financial services do exist, as shown by positive experiences across a wide range of delivery channels, products, and financial service providers.

It also needs to be recognized that the challenges of providing financial services that offer effective support to the multiple goals of extreme poor households are complex. In view of such complexities, it may be useful to characterize, as precisely as possible, their demand for financial services within a segmented framework. Developing a broader range of high-quality, transparent, and affordable financial services, based on the informed needs of different extreme poor groups, is an imperative for financial inclusion in Bangladesh. Ensuring the availability of a broader range of services and products will benefit both the recipients and the financial service providers. Through effectively responding to the needs of the extreme poor with the right range of products, financial providers will also be able to deepen their relationships with service recipients, broaden their market share, expand their business in a socially responsible manner, and reduce their own risks.

In the above context, the relevant strategies should highlight three core requirements for unleashing innovations in product development:

- *Incentives*: encourage the relevant authorities to invest in research and development for innovation and risk appetite.
- *Organizational capacity*: provide the necessary support for integrating systematic ways to interact and learn from extreme poor groups about their product development needs and management buy-in.
- *Regulatory environment*: bring about required changes, as necessary, in the regulatory environment so that it allows for, and encourages, the development of new products and approaches to financial inclusion and for product innovation to flourish.

Partnership between formal and quasi-formal institutions

In the present situation, formal banks and financial institutions have significant limitations in extending financial services to extreme poor households due to the technologies through which they operate, their service provision mechanisms, their work environment, and other characteristics. In this respect, the quasi-formal financial institutions may have some comparative advantage and they have made progress in establishing closer contacts with extreme poor groups. Thus, while the formal financial institutions have more resources, the quasi-formal institutions have higher levels of capability, efficiency, and experience in reaching the extreme poor in Bangladesh. This suggests scope for developing mutually beneficial partnerships between formal and quasi-formal financial institutions based on their relative comparative advantages: for example, the formal institutions may adopt detailed programmes based on agreed guidelines to capitalize quasi-formal institutions for on-lending to extreme poor households. This will provide an effective mechanism to reach out to larger numbers of extreme poor households, covering unserved regions, households, and enterprises in a sustainable manner.

Learning from MFIs and informal markets

There exist instances in Bangladesh which show that MFIs and informal markets have successfully rendered credit services to extreme poor households without any collateral or third-party guarantees. A major reason for their success is that the loans are provided under intensive monitoring mechanisms along with appropriate incentive structures. The formal financial sector also has experience of diversifying loan products to meet the needs of specific client groups. The formal financial institutions (especially the banks) could learn lessons from these experiences to adapt their activities accordingly. The risk on the part of the lending institutions can be significantly reduced by strengthening the Credit Information Bureau and decentralizing its operation in order to facilitate the quick generation and dissemination of relevant information on targeted financial programmes and specific client groups.

Transaction costs are one of the major determinants of access to finance. The transaction costs of borrowing matter for access to finance and for determining the loan size. For the formal financial institutions, transaction costs may be reduced by adopting a number of supply-side approaches such as increasing bank branch density and improving the efficiency of their operation through innovation in loan production technology: for example, minimizing waiting periods for loan approvals and focusing on better governance so that efficiency is increased and illegal transaction costs are reduced for the borrowers.

Promoting a competitive financial system

Bangladesh Bank is in a position to develop an enabling environment for creating a competitive financial system with appropriate incentives and governance systems so that banks can provide financial services that ensure a high degree of efficiency. Despite the trend towards convergence in performance between public and private sector banks, the non-interest cost of borrowing is higher for the public sector banks compared with the private sector ones (Sufian and Kamarudin, 2014; Mohan and Ray, 2004). In addition, the moral hazard problem (non-repayment and delinquency, for instance) is a dominant issue within public sector financial institutions. The government and the Bangladesh Bank should take prudent action to address these issues and to create a congenial environment so that borrowers are able to receive services at low cost and depositors can get a fair return.

Specific targeting issues for the extreme poor

In the absence of insurance or safety net mechanisms, the extreme poor cannot protect their assets and incomes against hazards and shocks such as illness or natural or man-made disasters. Access to finance helps extreme poor households minimize the risks of and vulnerability to economic crises, and can also act as a 'circuit breaker' for vicious intergenerational cycles of poverty and hunger. However, both drivers are related in that they steer the ability of extreme poor households to generate income and cash flows, and increase resilience. Moreover, inclusive finance can enable the extreme poor to build new livelihoods, obtain jobs, and pursue entrepreneurship opportunities.

While in the past efforts to achieve financial inclusion in Bangladesh focused on extending credit, these have now widened to cover other financial services such as savings and insurance. The 'credit alone' approach will not deliver financial inclusion, especially for the extreme poor (Wood and Sharif, 1997). A broader approach to accessing financial services has particular relevance for the poorest as it enables them to smooth erratic income streams in order to ensure regular access to food and invest in children's education, acquire better capacity to respond to various shocks, and invest in income-earning opportunities. In this context, four promising avenues may be used as effective vehicles for financial inclusion for the extreme poor. These are: 1) linking microcredit with formal financial services; 2) building financial inclusion components into safety net systems; 3) promoting appropriate insurance programmes; and 4) expanding the mobile banking network.

Microcredit programmes are widespread in Bangladesh, but significantly less so among the extreme poor groups. Where they are present, they are rarely linked with formal financial services. Linking microcredit groups with formal financial services could help formal financial organizations reach extreme poor people and remove some of the limitations faced by microcredit borrowers. The key issue for the extreme poor is to be able to deposit frequently in small amounts and near home. Solutions must therefore be low cost and geographically accessible. If the microcredit system and formal financial institutions are linked effectively, banks will gain new customers and will profit in the long run. Some pilot experiments in Bangladesh suggest that the results can be very promising in terms of improving socio-economic conditions, and especially in improving consumption and nutrition and the economic empowerment of women (Faruqee and Badruddoza, 2011).

Adding components to safety net programmes such as the digital payment of benefits, the formation of savings groups, financial literacy education, transfers conditional on saving and taking out insurance could become an important channel towards financial inclusion. As the country's safety net programmes are targeted to the extreme poor, this is arguably the quickest way to enhance their financial inclusion.[7] While making safety net payments conditional on saving or insurance could be a positive step, the difficulties that the poorest households have in ensuring adequate day-to-day consumption indicate that savings and similar steps may have to be introduced in phases at appropriate times.

Micro and other variants of the insurance programmes have significant potential to help extreme poor households manage the risks of flood and other disasters – the main environmental hazards to which they are exposed regularly. There are several examples of pilot programmes from which lessons can be drawn for scaling up. While, in most cases, the government and the projects have subsidized the insurance premiums as a way of expanding coverage, longer-term expansion can best be achieved by addressing the underlying obstacles: for example, through customer education, by creating effective delivery channels, by reducing the risk that payments do not reflect actual losses through better data or product design, and by bundling with other services. Other stakeholders aiming to support low-income populations may also take out such insurance to protect their activities; relevant covariance problems may be explored to design appropriate programmes for this.

The relevant authorities, such as the Bangladesh Bank, are in a position to develop comprehensive financial inclusion programmes for the extreme poor in which each financial institution would be assigned specific under-banked districts or areas to promote financial inclusion. To improve access to financial services in remote and disadvantaged locations – including *char* and *haor* areas where there exists a greater concentration of the extreme poor – a number of policy initiatives are needed, such as exploring more viable solutions, enhancing the capacity of formal financial institutions to serve these areas in a flexible and cost-effective manner, creating partnerships between formal and quasi-formal institutions, and developing customized financial products to meet the specific needs of *char-* or *haor*-dwellers based on the experience of the MFIs.

Conclusion

Financial exclusion implies the existence of both price and non-price barriers to the use of required financial services. For policy purposes, exclusion can be voluntary (that is, the households can access financial services but are not using those services by choice); alternatively, exclusion can be involuntary, where price and/or non-price barriers prevent access to these services. For extreme poor households, exclusion is involuntary since they have multiple and compelling reasons to smooth their income over short-term fluctuations and meet income-earning and other needs by accessing credit.

Overall, a wide variety of policy initiatives is needed for scaling up the delivery of formal and quasi-formal financial services to extreme poor households. This will help improve the access of extreme poor families to financial services and help prevent serious problems such as falling into debt or losing their productive assets. In this respect, the private sector has an important role to play in better serving extreme poor households.

The public sector has the capacity to increase savings and ensure greater use of formal financial services among extreme poor households. By working closely with the private sector, it could encourage and incentivize financial institutions to serve extreme poor populations. The government and the Bangladesh Bank can also play an important regulatory role, which includes overseeing financial providers to ensure that they provide a range of poor-friendly financial services and implement better protection for the extreme poor receiving financial services. The public sector can also encourage saving by low-income families by implementing different incentive mechanisms and matched savings plans.

Over the years, the challenge of financial exclusion has received increased policy attention in Bangladesh. In order to provide access to financial services for extreme poor households, Bangladesh needs to create an efficient, transparent, and integrated financial system along with financial literacy across all segments of the population. In this respect, several key aspects of the policy response concern links between microfinance and the formal financial system. These relate to moving towards a 'cashless society' through investments in electronic infrastructure for financial services, complementary reforms and supportive measures, and the development of an efficient national payments system.

Notes

1. The term 'access to financial services' can refer to households with or without access to financial services currently or in the future.
2. Financial inclusion can be defined as the 'delivery of banking services and credit at an affordable cost to the vast sections of disadvantaged and low income groups. The various financial services include savings, loans, insurance, payments, remittance facilities and financial advisory services by the formal financial system' (RBI, 2008).
3. Limited access to finance prevents the extreme poor from making improvements to the quality of their lives. For example, in Bangladesh there have been recent attempts to develop high-quality solar-powered solutions that can satisfy the energy needs of the poor. These are being brought to poorer households in off-grid areas using new distribution models. However, for most of the extreme poor living off-grid, the lack of access to financing options prevents them from adopting modern solar solutions. There are many similar innovations in key services such as health and education where access is not possible because of a lack of appropriate financing options.
4. The first mobile-based financial service was launched in Bangladesh in 2011. By the end of 2013, the technology was being used by 22 per cent of the country's adult population, and to date Bangladesh Bank has approved more than 20 licences to offer mobile financial services in the country.
5. Some MFIs, such as BRAC, include technical training in their programmes with the rationale that extreme poor people do not have the entrepreneurial skills or assets to use business loans productively. On the other hand, other programmes take the view that minimalist programmes can be sustainable and can help the extreme poor stabilize their income and build a buffer against possible future crises. Experience shows that it is important to understand why extreme poor people value particular aspects of microfinance programmes and in what contexts, and how these may be incorporated into the programmes as a tool for accessing financial services.
6. The information costs are not made explicit in the study mentioned above. One aspect about information costs relating to informal moneylenders is that they are usually known locally. Moreover, normally one would expect interest rates in the informal credit markets to be much higher than those cited in the study, reflecting local monopolies and the

high risks of lending. It is possible that interest rates have decreased in recent years due to competition from the quasi-formal markets. If so, MFIs have made a positive contribution to the financial inclusion agenda.

7. The Safety Net Systems for the Poorest project, launched in 2013, also focuses on expanding the provision of cash-based transfers through the banking system or other financial channels as well as strengthening access to information and grievance redress mechanisms to enhance transparency in programme implementation.

References

BBS (2013) *Statistical Yearbook of Bangladesh 2012*, Dhaka: Bangladesh Bureau of Statistics (BBS), Statistics and Informatics Division, Ministry of Planning, Government of Bangladesh.

Demirgüç-Kunt, A., Beck, T. and Honahan, P. (2008) *Finance for All: Policies and Pitfalls in Expanding Access*, World Bank Policy Report, Washington, DC: World Bank.

Eswaran, M. and Kotwal, A. (1990) 'Implications of credit constraints for risk behaviour in less developed economies', *Oxford Economic Papers* 42: 473–82.

Faruqee, R. and Badruddoza, S. (2011) *Microfinance in Bangladesh: Past, Present and Future*, Occasional Paper, Dhaka: Institute of Microfinance.

Kendall, J. and Voorhies, R. (2014) 'The mobile-finance revolution: how cell phones can spur development', *Foreign Affairs*, March/April. Available at <https://www.foreignaffairs.com/articles/africa/2014-02-12/mobile-finance-revolution>.

Khalily, M.A.B. and Khaleque, M.A. (2013a) 'Access to financial services in Bangladesh', paper presented at the National Conference on Microfinance and Development, PKSF Auditorium, Institute of Microfinance, Dhaka, 24–25 August.

Khalily, M.A.B. and Khaleque, M.A. (2013b) *Access to Credit and Productivity of Enterprises in Bangladesh: Is There Causality?* Working Paper 20, Dhaka: Institute of Microfinance.

Levine, R. (2005) 'Finance and growth', in P. Aghion and S.N. Durlauf (eds), *Handbook of Economic Growth*, vol. 1A, pp. 865–934, North Holland: Elsevier BV.

Mehrotra, N., Puhashendhi, V., Nair, G. and Sahoo, B.B. (2009) *Financial Inclusion: An Overview*, Occasional Paper 48, Mumbai: Department of Economic Analysis and Research, National Bank for Agriculture and Rural Development.

Mohan, T.T.R. and Ray, S.C. (2004) 'Comparing performance of public and private sector banks: a revenue maximisation efficiency approach', *Economic and Political Weekly* 39(12): 1271–6.

RBI (2008) *Report of the Committee on Financial Inclusion*, Mumbai: Reserve Bank of India (RBI).

Sufian, F. and Kamarudin, F. (2014) 'Efficiency and returns to scale in the Bangladesh banking sector: empirical evidence from the slack-based DEA method', *Engineering Economics* 25(5): 549–57.

Wood, G.D. and Sharif, I. (eds) (1997) *Who Needs Credit? Poverty and Finance in Bangladesh*, London and New York: Zed Books.

World Bank (2014) *The Opportunities of Digitizing Payments*, Washington, DC: World Bank Development Research Group, Better Than Cash Alliance, and Bill & Melinda Gates Foundation to the G20 Global Partnership for Financial Inclusion.

Zeller, M., Schrieder, G., von Braun, J. and Heidhues, F. (1997) *Rural Finance for Food Security for the Poor: Implications for Research and Policy*, Food Policy Review No. 4, Washington, DC: International Food Policy Research Institute.

About the author

Dr Mustafa K. Mujeri is the Executive Director of the Institute for Inclusive Finance and Development (InM). Dr Mujeri has published extensively on development. His expertise lies in poverty and macro policy analysis, and the application of quantitative techniques in development issues. He has previously served as the Director General of the Bangladesh Institute of Development Studies (BIDS), Chief Economist of Bangladesh Bank, and Adviser to the United Nations Development Programme in Cambodia.

CHAPTER 6

Dynamics of regional poverty and real wages: policy implications for development interventions

Shamsul Alam and Kazi Iqbal

In Bangladesh, the question of regional poverty dynamics and their drivers has received very little attention in the literature. This chapter is the first attempt to study poverty dynamics at the sub-district level in Bangladesh and then link them to changes in real wages. Drawing on primary data, we argue that aggregate poverty data disguises important local realities. Thus, while poverty rates have decreased significantly at the national level as well as at divisional levels, our analysis shows that there is a large number of sub-districts that have seen an increase in poverty levels. One of the reasons for these spatial variations in poverty is the disparate distribution of real wages. The chapter argues that knowledge of local-level poverty conditions and their covariates is an important tool for effective policy interventions.

Keywords: regional poverty dynamics, real wage, local planning

Introduction

National-level planning, such as the Five Year Plan instrument, primarily stresses the overall macro-economic situation, growth projections, sectoral performances, and priority policy areas. Even policies on social protection, which by definition require local planning, are usually crafted at the national level and focus on efficient targeting and delivery mechanisms. Regional and local-level planning, therefore, has on the whole been overlooked in development discourse and planning in Bangladesh, despite the widespread recognition of regional variations in growth, human development progress, employment opportunities, and income disparities. As argued by Sen and Ali, geographical exclusion, ecological vulnerability, and policy bias all contribute to the persistence of 'poverty pockets' in Bangladesh (Sen and Ali, 2015). We would argue that the three causes identified by Sen and Ali also manifest themselves in regional variations in real wages. As such, we advocate for a more informed understanding of the regional distribution of income and poverty, as well as of their drivers. Furthermore, we argue that poverty dynamics at the

http://dx.doi.org/10.3362/9781780449463.006

aggregate or national level not only mask important regional facts, but are also a misleading foundation upon which to base national policy.

This study is the first attempt in Bangladesh to identify key characteristics of regional poverty dynamics and relate them to changes in agricultural real wages. The chapter does not investigate all the potential causes of the variations in sub-district poverty levels, but focuses instead on the nexus between poverty and real wages introducing, where appropriate, some key stylised but relevant facts.

In Bangladesh, there already exists an extensive literature analysing poverty at the aggregate level, covering a wide range of issues including poverty trends and drivers; linkages with growth and inequality; as well as non-income dimensions of well-being including health, education, nutrition, and access to safe water. Although recent literature using panel data has helped enrich our understanding and knowledge of poverty dynamics (Osmani and Sen, 2010; Quisumbing and Baulch, 2009; Hossain and Bayes, 2009), most studies of poverty in Bangladesh present a rather static picture of selected poverty indicators. The World Bank's report on Bangladesh's poverty assessment (World Bank, 2013) redresses this situation to some extent with an examination of the dynamics of poverty at a national level over the period 2000–10.

One of the weaknesses of the current literature on poverty is that it examines only aggregate or national trends, which tend to disguise regional disparities. The few studies we have into regional disparities focus on the east–west divide in Bangladesh or on very specific geographical areas such as the coastal regions, the *haor* or *char* areas (Shilpi, 2008; Zohir, 2011). Inevitably, these same studies call for more robust disaggregated data that can help understand local-level dynamics of income and poverty. We support these calls because we believe in the policy value of more localized understandings of poverty conditions. For example, we already know that the rate of poverty has been declining in all of the country's divisions since 2000 (GED, 2013). However sub-district-level analyses of 2005 and 2010 data also show that a large number of sub-districts have in fact experienced an increase in poverty, both extreme and moderate, despite the fact that poverty levels have decreased in their respective divisions (GED, 2013). In fact, levels of moderate and extreme poverty were found to have increased in 158 sub-districts in 2005 and in 144 sub-districts in 2010.

In policy terms, analysis at the sub-district level is important for a number of reasons. First, national-level top-down planning tends to pay far less attention to regional differences and, as a consequence, risks recommending interventions that may be completely inappropriate. Second, in-depth understanding of local-level realities can also help authorities at the sub-district and union levels plan poverty reduction interventions more effectively, and allocate resources more efficiently.

Bangladesh has sub-district-level poverty estimates for 2005 and 2010 but this data has not been used extensively. In this chapter, we offer a first attempt at a more comprehensive analysis of poverty dynamics at the sub-district level, and in so doing identify several key characteristics of poverty dynamics as they manifest themselves at district and sub-district levels. To begin our analysis, we map out changes in the rate of poverty from 2005 to 2010 and identify the 20 most poverty-stricken sub-districts in the two years.[1] Our aim then is to identify some stylized facts about changes in sub-district-level poverty and to examine the possible links to changes in real wages.

Our analysis reveals some striking observations that are worth highlighting briefly here. First, we find that poverty rates have decreased in almost all sub-districts in the north-west of the country, which is traditionally known to be a 'lagging region'. This suggests a certain convergence of regions whereby previous 'lagging' areas are 'catching up' with more prosperous ones. Second, we also find that a substantial number of sub-districts experienced an increase in the levels of both moderate and extreme poverty, and that the increase in poverty is more pronounced in the eastern part of the country than in the western part. Third, regional poverty maps also indicate the existence of 'poverty pockets' throughout the country. For example, although Sylhet is known as a rich district, most of the poor and extreme poor are to be found in the greater Sylhet region. Finally, the hill tract region in the south-east, again known traditionally as an extreme poor region, is no longer on the list of the 20 most poverty-stricken sub-districts.

Furthermore, we argue, in line with the World Bank (2013), that real wage increase is the single most important factor responsible for the sharp decline in poverty observed nationwide. We reached this conclusion by first studying the aggregate trends of real wages, defined in terms of the amount of rice (in kilograms) an agricultural wage labourer can purchase with his nominal daily wage. Data shows that, nationally, trends in real wages have seen a steep rise in the last few years. For example, an agricultural labourer can now buy about 10 kg of coarse rice with his daily wage, while as recently as 2009–10 this was below 6 kg. This indicates that the rural labour market has reached a 'Lewis's tipping point' (Lewis, 1954), beyond which the wage rate increases very sharply.

We then link regional poverty data with the spatial distribution of real wages. We first map the regional distribution of real wages at the sub-district level and identify 20 sub-districts with the highest and lowest real wages. The data shows that there is a huge variation in real wages across regions, ranging from 4.3 kg to 22.5 kg of coarse rice. In general, the regions with the lowest real wages tend to be in the northern part of Bangladesh while those with some of the highest real wages are found in Chittagong and Natore. However, across the country, there are discrete pockets with very high and very low real wages.

In order to understand the relationship between the rate of poverty and the real wage rate, we graph these two variables, and the results show a clear negative relationship. We then regress poverty rates on real wages to study whether regional variations in real wages explain the regional income disparity at the sub-district level. Community-level Household Income and Expenditure Survey (HIES) data from 2010 shows that if an increase in nominal wages in a sub-district buys one more kilogram of coarse rice, it will help reduce poverty by about 1 or 2 percentage points. The association between rates of poverty reduction and real wage increases is stronger when we consider sub-district variations of panel data. In this case, an increase of one kilogram of coarse rice in the real wage is associated with about a 4 percentage point decrease in poverty rates.

The rest of the chapter is organized as follows. The next section provides an overview of the data used in our analysis. We then focus on two main issues: the significance of real wages in reducing poverty, and the reasons for increasing real wages. The following section dwells on regional poverty dynamics at the sub-district level and highlights some insightful stylized facts. This is followed by an examination of regional variations in real wages using available national data. The next section then builds on the previous one to explore the relationship between regional poverty rates and real wages. The final section offers a conclusion that focuses on policy implications and recommendations.

Data on poverty and wages

We use two sets of data for our analysis. First, the sub-district poverty data was collected from the poverty maps produced jointly by the Bangladesh Bureau of Statistics and the World Food Programme (BBS-WFP). Second, the wage data was collected from three BBS sources. From these sources, we construct three sets of real wage data: one at the national level and two at the sub-district level. National-level wage data was compiled from various issues of the BBS's *Monthly Statistical Bulletins*, while sub-district-level wage data was collected from district statistics (BBS, 2011) as well as the HIES. Note that daily wage data is the annual average of without-food wages for males alone.[2]

We use rice prices to deflate nominal wages. Data on rice prices was collected from various issues of the BBS's *Statistical Pocketbook*. Note that the rice price is the annual average retail price from all divisional headquarters. In order to create a panel of real wage data, we use community modules of HIES 2005 and HIES 2010. Despite a large number of sub-districts being missing from the community dataset of HIES 2005 and 2010, this is the only data through which changes in real wages can be observed at the sub-district level. The panel regressions are based on this HIES data. To map real wages at a regional level, we use recently published district statistics (BBS, 2011). This data has also been used in cross-sectional regression analysis.

Increase in rural real wages: the most important driver of poverty reduction

The steep increase in real wages in agriculture can be identified as the most important driver of poverty reduction in rural areas. Figure 6.1 shows that real wages began to increase quickly from 2000, with a dip during the period of international food price hikes in 2007–8. After this shock, the real wage doubled in the span of five years or so. At the time of writing, an agricultural labourer can buy about 10 kg of coarse rice with his daily wage, which is significantly more than the 6 kg of rice that could be purchased just about five years ago. Even with the very sharp increase from 2010, the upward trend of real wage increases evident throughout the 2000–10 period explains why the rate of poverty reduction was faster in the 2000s than in the previous decades.

Recent literature suggests that the rural economy may have reached 'Lewis's tipping point' (Lewis, 1954), beyond which agricultural wages increase very quickly (Zhang et al., 2013). One interesting feature of the transitional dynamics of Lewis's model is that the steep increase in rural wages precedes the increase in urban wages. Zhang et al. (2013) also found evidence in support of this finding, indicating that the economy would – and indeed may have begun to – experience a sharp increase in urban real wages. Further comparative analysis of the dynamics of real wages in rural and urban areas is required to verify this. We identify three major factors behind this sharp increase in real wages in recent years.

The first is that the rural labour market has tightened because the demand for agricultural wage labour is growing faster than its supply. The surplus wage labour in the agricultural sector has arguably been exhausted and this has exerted tremendous upward pressure on the wage rate. The shrinking share of households in which the main occupation is agricultural wage labour indicates strongly that labour surplus is waning (Hossain and Bayes, 2009). Underlying this trend, two major structural shifts can be observed in the rural labour market.

- The vibrant non-farm sector in rural areas, as well as the burgeoning labour-intensive service sector in urban and semi-urban areas, is argued to have absorbed a large share of surplus labour. There are a number of important references that can be made to support this statement. For example, we know that the manufacturing sector has maintained steady growth over the last decade, employing a huge pool of unskilled and semi-skilled labour. We also know that demand for non-farm activities such as agricultural services, which employ mostly contract as opposed to wage labour, has also increased. The increased demand for contract labour also reflects an increase in the number of absentee landholders in rural areas. The overall shift from wage to contract labour has created upward pressure on the wages of the former.
- Data on land ownership also shows that the share of land being used by the landowners themselves has increased. This has led to an increased share of tenancy arrangements, especially around fixed-rent contracts (Hossain and Bayes, 2009). Migration to urban areas, international migration, and intergenerational occupational mobility towards more productive non-farm jobs have freed a large amount of cultivable land for the tenancy market. This has created opportunities for landless farmers and marginal farmers to gain access to land, allowing wage labourers the option to become tenant farmers. The overall impact of this is to tighten the agricultural labour market and put pressure on the wage rate of farm labour.

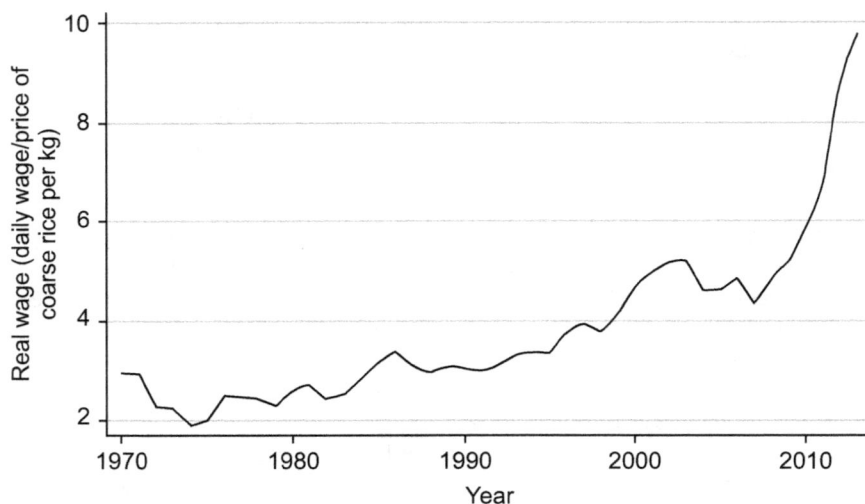

Figure 6.1 Trends in real wages in agriculture
Source: Data on rice prices is from *Statistical Pocketbook* (BBS) and wage data from *Monthly Statistical Bulletin* (BBS).

Evidence suggests that the second factor behind wage increases comes from an increase in the productivity of agricultural labour due to the mechanization of agriculture and the adoption of HYV (high yield variety) or hybrid crops and modern irrigation systems (Rahman and Salim, 2013). Osmani (2015) argues that recent increases in real wages may represent a 'catching up' stage whereby real wages are catching up with the higher productivity of labour. The reduction in the gap between real wages and the productivity of labour has direct implications for poverty, as it reduces income inequality.

The third factor behind the recent sharp increase in real wages is that nominal wages have been increasing much faster than food inflation (see Figure 6.2). Locally strong harvests and declining international food prices have contributed to the relative stabilization of food prices in Bangladesh.

Poverty dynamics at the sub-district level

This section further examines the dynamics of poverty at the sub-district level, offering stylized facts that emerge from our data. We are aware that some of the trends we identify will need to be tested and analysed using separate and extensive studies. Here we reflect on the trends by making use of secondary data analysis. Figures 6.3 and 6.4 offer an overview of the changes in poverty levels over the 2005–10 period using both the upper and lower poverty lines. Positive changes (i.e. from 0 to 60) signify an increase in poverty while negative changes (from 0 to –60) illustrate a reduction in poverty levels.

Both maps indicate that the regional distribution of the change in poverty rates is more or less the same for both the upper poverty line (UPL) and the lower poverty line (LPL). This can be seen even in the north-west and in the southern coastal belt of the country, where higher levels of poverty have historically been documented. This suggests two important findings. First, at the sub-district level, both moderate and extreme poverty change in tandem. Second, patterns of poverty reduction at the sub-district level broadly follow patterns observed at the national level. These are important findings because they cast doubt on a fairly well established argument that the extreme poor in Bangladesh are somehow caught up in a 'poverty trap' and that the benefits of economic growth and human development investment are not sufficient to help them. Our analysis suggests otherwise. The maps show that, in broad terms, the rate of reduction in extreme poverty is as fast as that of moderate poverty, and that both seem to be in line with national trends. Using aggregate data, Sen and Ali (2015) have made a similar argument, suggesting that there is little indication of non-linearity in poverty reduction in Bangladesh.

While the country experienced a substantial decrease in overall poverty between 2005 and 2010, the decline in poverty rates has been sharper in the west compared with the east. The River Jamuna acts as a natural barrier splitting the country into west and east. However, the eastern part contains two major growth poles: Dhaka, the capital city, and the coastal seaport city of Chittagong, the country's second largest city. Previous poverty maps based on headcount ratios highlighted the differences in terms of poverty levels between the west and east, with the former noticeably much more impoverished than the latter. Our data suggests that the rate of poverty reduction is

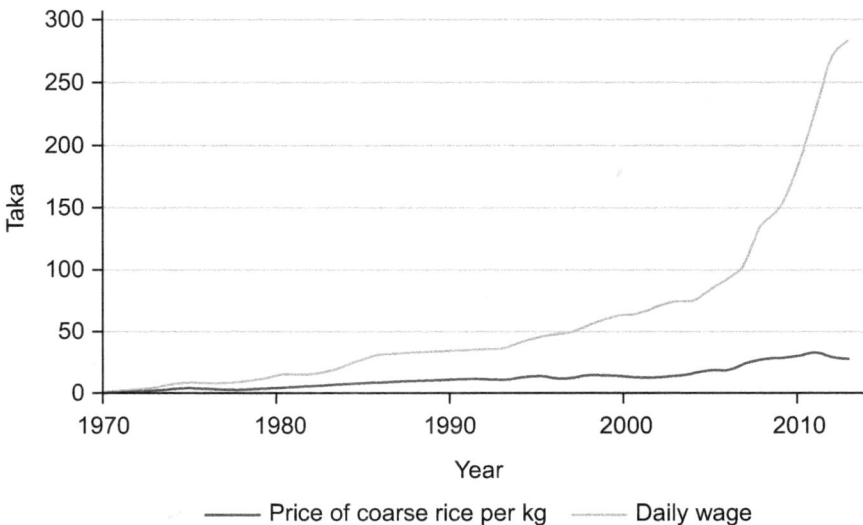

Figure 6.2 Trends in nominal wages and rice prices

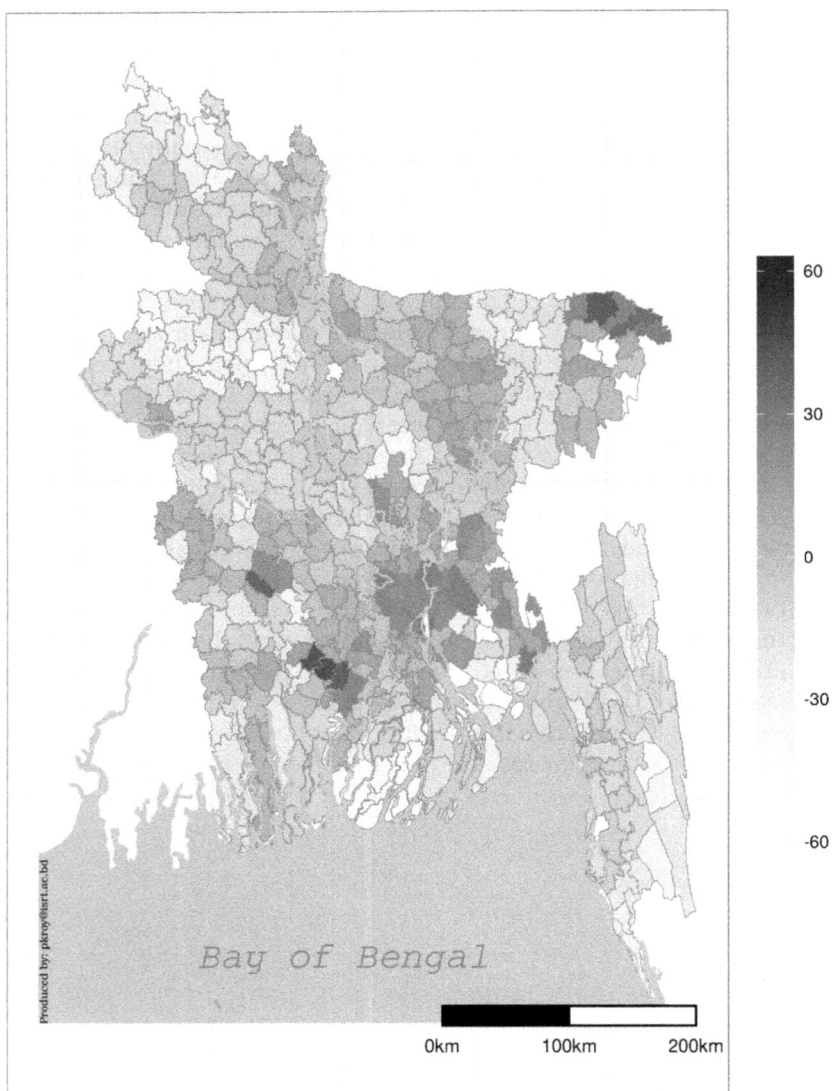

Figure 6.3 Change in poverty rates by sub-district (UPL)

highest in the southern regions of Barguna and Patuakhali and also in some parts of Nilphamari, in the north-west of the country. Parts of Khulna (a major city in the south), Rajshahi, and Rangpur (both in the north-west) have also seen significant poverty reductions. At the same time, poverty has increased dramatically in parts of Sylhet (north-east), Comilla (east), and other areas of the south, and has also increased – albeit more moderately – in some parts of greater Mymensingh districts in the north. Both the UPL and LPL maps indicate that southern parts of Chittagong division in the south-east

(Cox's Bazar and Bandarban) experienced faster poverty reduction than northern regions (Khagrachari and Rangamati).

These findings therefore challenge the traditional 'east–west' divide that has dominated poverty studies in Bangladesh. If we look closer at regional poverty reduction patterns, the picture that emerges is much more fluid. This finding supports Khondker and Mahzab's (2015) work, which examined income and wider socio-economic indicators and demonstrated the presence of underdeveloped districts in the east and developed districts in the west. Not only do our findings challenge the 'east–west' divide, they also highlight the emergence of regional pockets of poverty. Recent studies have suggested that the location of these pockets has moved from the north to the south (PKSF, 2012). Our findings offer some confirmation of this, with certain areas in the coastal belt showing significant increases in extreme poverty. The extreme poor therefore also reside in the most ecologically disadvantaged areas of the country.

Furthermore, it is interesting to observe that almost all sub-districts in the north-west region – again considered historically as an impoverished area – have experienced significant decreases in their respective poverty levels. To a great extent, these improvements are a consequence of the construction of the Bangabandhu Bridge,[3] which has substantially enhanced connectivity between the north-western part of the country and growth centres such as Dhaka. However, although the rate of poverty has declined in the north-west, this remains the most poverty-stricken region in the country. In 2010, Kurigram (situated in the north-west) was the poorest district in the country, with 63.7 per cent of the population classified as moderate poor and 44.3 per cent as extreme poor. Meanwhile, the districts of Gaibandha and Rangpur (both again in the north-west) were in the list of the 10 most poverty-stricken districts in Bangladesh. Perhaps not surprisingly, nine sub-districts of Kurigram and two from Rangpur and Gaibandha made the list of the 20 most poverty-stricken sub-districts in the country. In short, poverty levels in the north-western part of Bangladesh traditionally have been so high that even with recent substantial poverty reductions the region still has a high proportion of moderate and extreme poor citizens. Again, it is important to note that – like some areas in the coastal south – the north-west region is both ecologically vulnerable and economically depressed. It is therefore a region where we find regular cases of river erosion and extensive flooding; where crop yields and wages are low; where infrastructural developments lag behind; and where off-farm employment opportunities are weak (Mahmud, 2011).

Let us now turn our attention to the eastern part of the country, which has traditionally been considered the most prosperous part of Bangladesh. Our analysis provides two interesting findings for the Chittagong and Sylhet regions. In 2005, Alikadam in Bandarban (located in Chittagong region) was the poorest (upper line) sub-district in the whole country. Four other sub-districts of Bandarban – Thanchi, Ruma, Rowangachhari, and Naikhongachhari – were also on the list of the 20 most poverty-stricken sub-districts. By 2010, however, none of these sub-districts appeared on this list. Indeed, they were the sub-districts

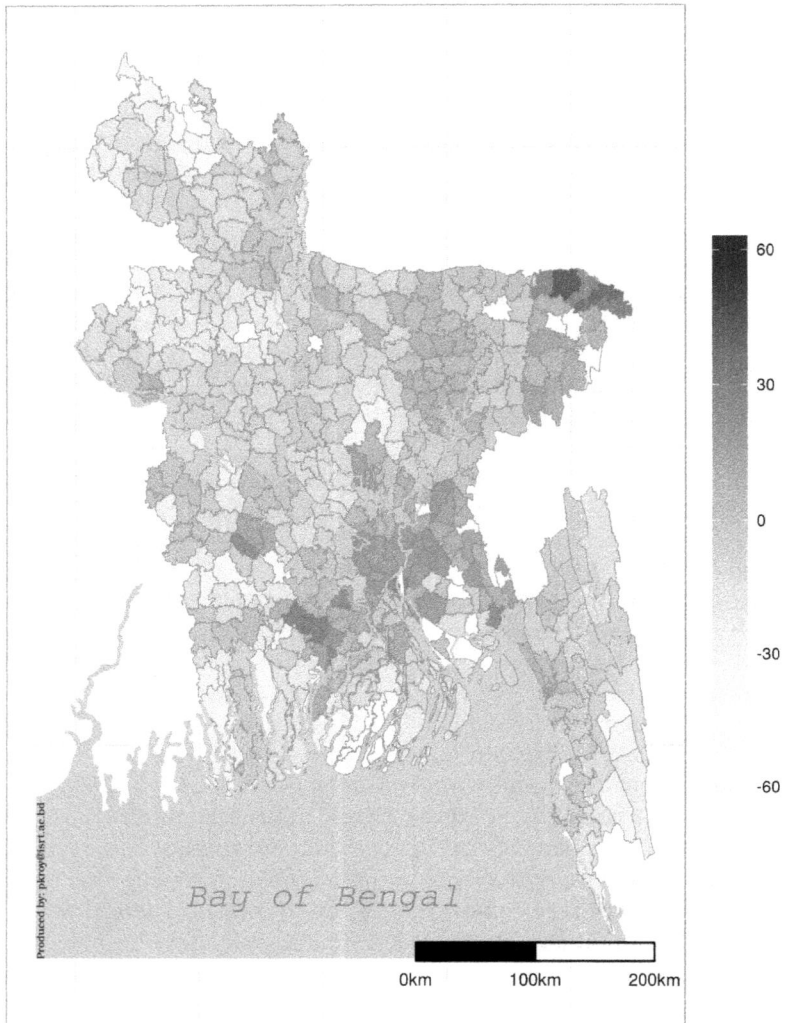

Figure 6.4 Change in poverty rates (LPL)

with the highest levels of poverty reduction in the 2005–10 period. Furthermore, no sub-district in the hill tracts region[4] has experienced an increase in poverty during this period (see Figure 6.4). It is difficult to speculate on the reasons for such a change within a short period of time. It could simply reflect the in-migration of Bengali people into the hill tract region or it may be the result of the impactful work and attention of government and NGOs responding to the fact that the region was so poor.

In contrast, the greater Sylhet region, located in the north-east of the country, is home to high levels of extreme poverty. However, there is an unusual phenomenon in this region because most of the poor are extreme poor. Indeed, if we look at the 2010 list of the 20 most poverty-stricken sub-districts, we see that those with the highest levels of extreme poor as a proportion of the total poor are all from the greater Sylhet region. According to the 2010 HIES, more than 85 per cent of the poor are extreme poor in Gowainghat and Kanaighat sub-districts of Sylhet district and in Jury sub-district of Moulvibazar district. This is quite a dramatic change. In 2005, it was in the sub-districts of the southern part of the country, such as Barisal, Patuakhali, Sathkhira, Pirojpur, Bagerhat, Khulna, Jessore, and Narail, that we found the greatest concentrations of extreme poverty.

Regional variations in real wages

This section examines regional variations in real wages, using HIES and district statistics. A comparison of 2005 and 2010 indicates that the distribution of real wages has shifted slightly upwards in 2010. However, given the paucity of data for 2010, we also investigated the distribution of real wages using district statistics from 2011. This clearly confirms the upward shift suggested by the 2005 and 2010 comparison, with the mean real wage hovering around 7–8 kg of coarse rice. District statistics for 2011 show that the average real wage for the country in 2010–11 was 8.54 kg of coarse rice, with a standard deviation of 3.36. Data from the 2011 district statistics has also been used to map regional variations in real wages (illustrated in Figure 6.5).

Our analysis suggests that there is a wide variation in real wages across the different regions of the country. The highest real wage (22.5 kg of rice) is found in the Gurudaspur sub-district of Natore district, and the lowest (4.29 kg) in the sub-district of Durgapur in Netrokona district. At a district level, evidence suggests that Natore has the highest real wages (20.78 kg) and Gaibandha has the lowest (5.71 kg) in terms of the coarse rice equivalent to the wage rate per day.

It is worth noting at this point, given the discussions above about poverty reduction rates, that 12 sub-districts of Chittagong district (where we have observed significant progress in poverty reduction) are among the list of 20 sub-districts with the highest real wages. The real wages of Lohagara and Banshkhali sub-districts, for example, were more than 20 kg of coarse rice. Conversely, and as expected, real wages in the northern sub-districts (where extreme poverty is more concentrated) were among the lowest in the country, particularly in Gaibandha, Kurigram, Naogaon, and Sirajgonj districts. Again, it is worth highlighting that these same sub-districts were also among the poorest in terms of headcount poverty measures. All of this suggests a strong association between increased real wages and the rate of poverty reduction.

There are also distinct pockets of high and low real wages. Figure 6.5 identifies a number of locations where real wages are extremely high (>20 on the scale) and low (<5 on the scale). Some pockets in Rangpur, Kishoreganj, and Laxmipur districts have very low real wage rates while some sub-districts of Chittagong and Natore have very high real wages. As far as we can tell, neither researchers

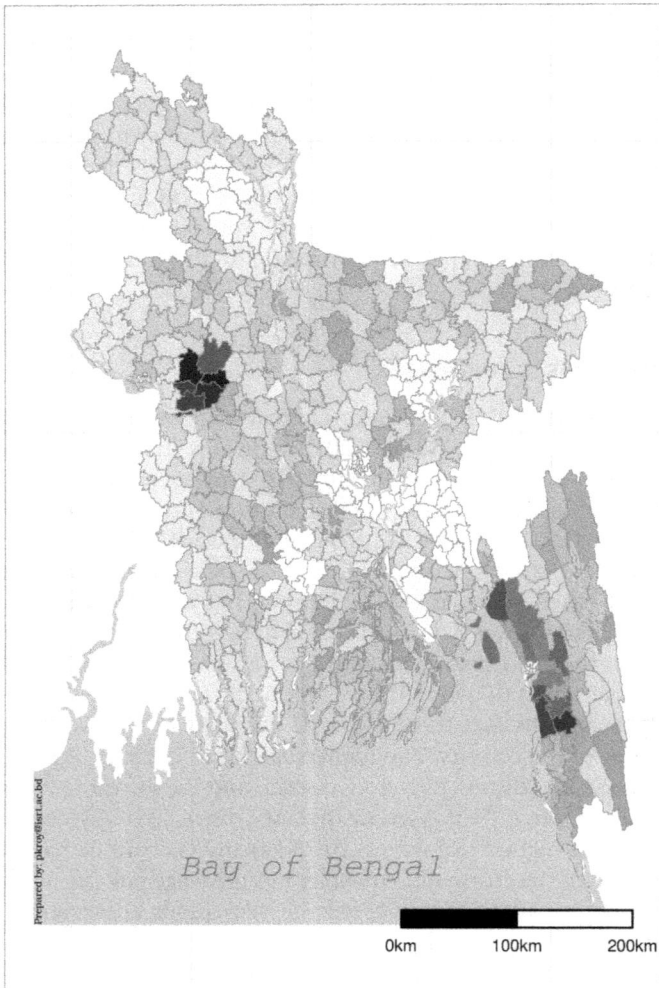

Figure 6.5 Real wages by region
Source: District statistics (2011).

nor policymakers have insights to help explain these regional anomalies. This observation raises two key questions: why do such large regional variations in real wages exist? Why do rural agricultural wage labourers not migrate, temporarily or permanently, to take advantage of better opportunities? Finally, we have always assumed that the development of rural communications, especially rural roads, as well as the huge penetration of mobile phones in rural areas would bring real wages across the regions together or at least closer. This has not happened. Why? Clearly our analysis has identified key areas for further research and investigation.

Association between poverty and real wages

The analysis so far has touched on the question of whether or not there is a relationship between poverty and real wages. Here, we attempt to examine this question. Figures 6.6 to 6.9 plot poverty rates against real wages for both 2005 and 2010. The figures show a clear negative relationship in both years and in the case of both the UPL and LPL.

In order to investigate the relationship further, we introduce a regression model with both cross-sectional and panel data:

$$Poverty\ rate_i = \beta_0 + \beta_1 \cdot Real\ wage_i + u_i$$

where i signifies sub-district.

This regression model states that the poverty level of a sub-district depends on real wages and on other observed and unobserved factors (u) relating to the sub-district. In other words, poverty rates across sub-districts may vary because of observed or unobserved differences in the sub-districts. As above, we use three sets of data (HIES 2005, HIES 2010 and district statistics for 2011) to capture the regional variations of poverty and real wages.

In order to deal with variations (panel), we apply:

$$Poverty\ rate_{i,t} = \beta_0 + \beta_1 \cdot Real\ wage_{i,t} + \alpha_i + u_{i,t}$$

where i signifies sub-district, t = 2005 and 2010, and α_i represents sub-district-level observed and unobserved characteristics, which are fixed over time. Observed characteristics include agricultural productivity, distance from the growth poles, non-farm opportunities, and so forth. Unobserved characteristics include norms, culture, and other social institutions, which have a bearing on people's well-being. It is realistic to assume that these factors are fairly fixed in the short run and can be captured by sub-district fixed effects. One advantage of using panel data in our analysis is that it allows us to exploit variations over time of each sub-district, free from unobserved heterogeneity that may confound the results. We use HIES 2005 and HIES 2010 to construct the panel.

It is important to note that the purpose of the regressions is not to establish causality, but to show some association between poverty and real wages in a robust way.[5] Table 6.1 records the regression results for both cross-sectional and panel data. Columns 2 and 3 present the ordinary least squares (OLS) results for 2005 for both the UPL and the LPL. The regional variations in 2005 show that an increase of 1 kg of rice in real wages is associated with a reduction in poverty of about 2 percentage points for both moderate and extreme poverty. This confirms our earlier observation about the way in which both forms of poverty seem to move in tandem with each other. In other words, if an increase in real wages is a direct outcome of economic growth, our findings suggest that growth is not only pro-poor but also pro-extreme poor.

However, in 2010, we observe that the extent of the association diminishes, with an increase of 1 kg of rice in real wages being associated with about

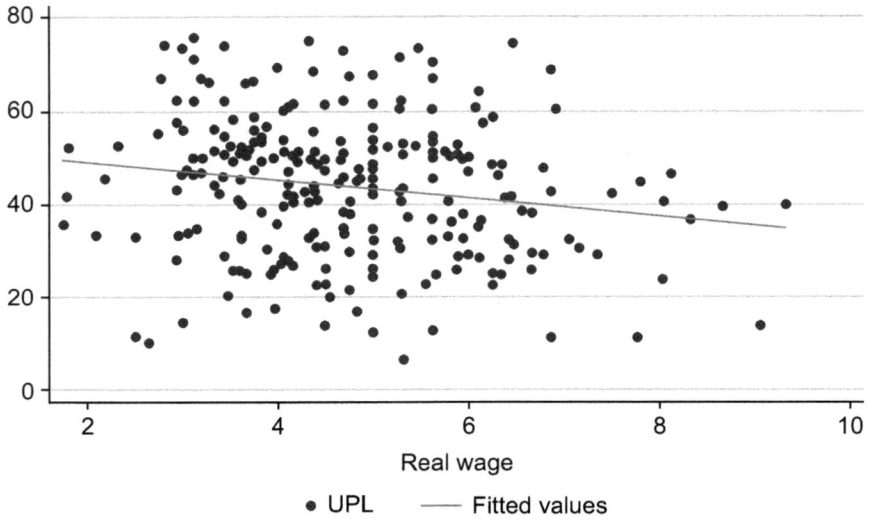

Figure 6.6 Relationship between poverty (UPL) and real wages
Source: HIES (2005).

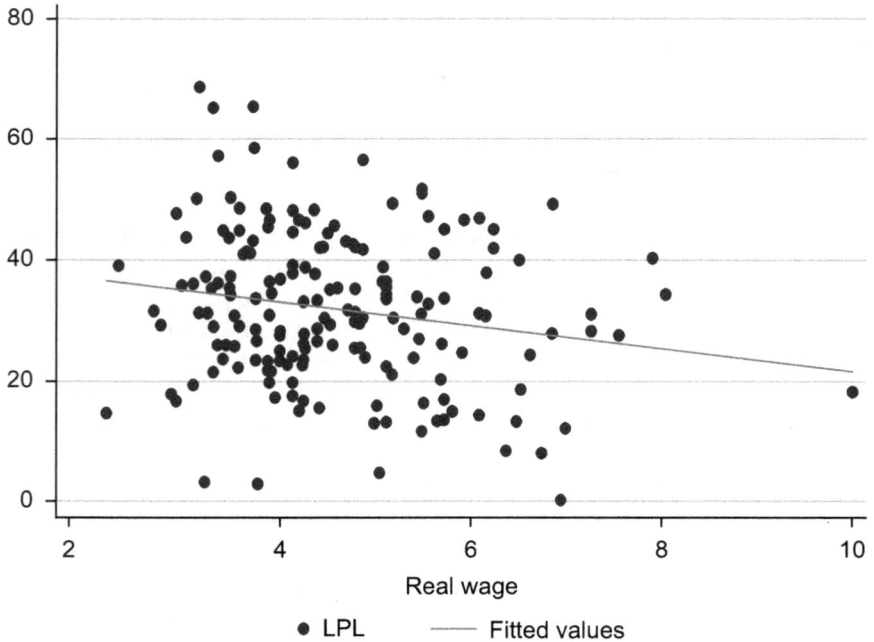

Figure 6.7 Relationship between poverty (LPL) and real wages
Source: HIES (2005).

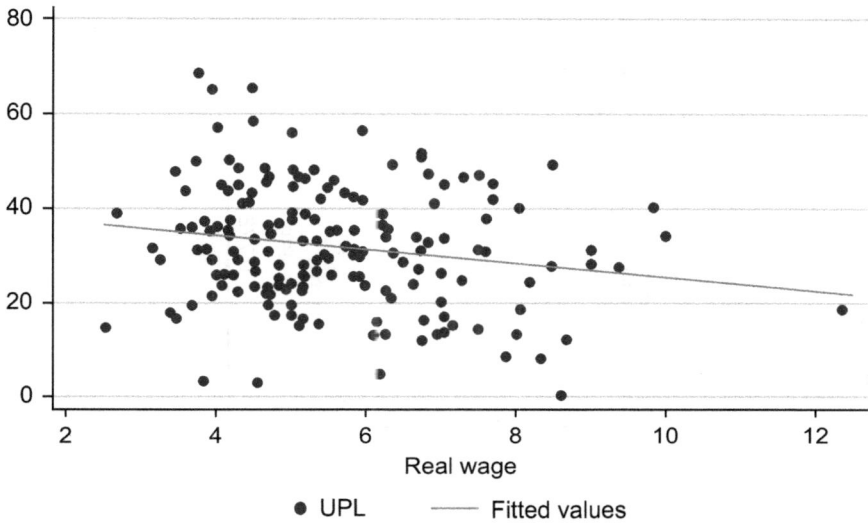

Figure 6.8 Relationship between poverty (UPL) and real wages
Source: HIES (2010).

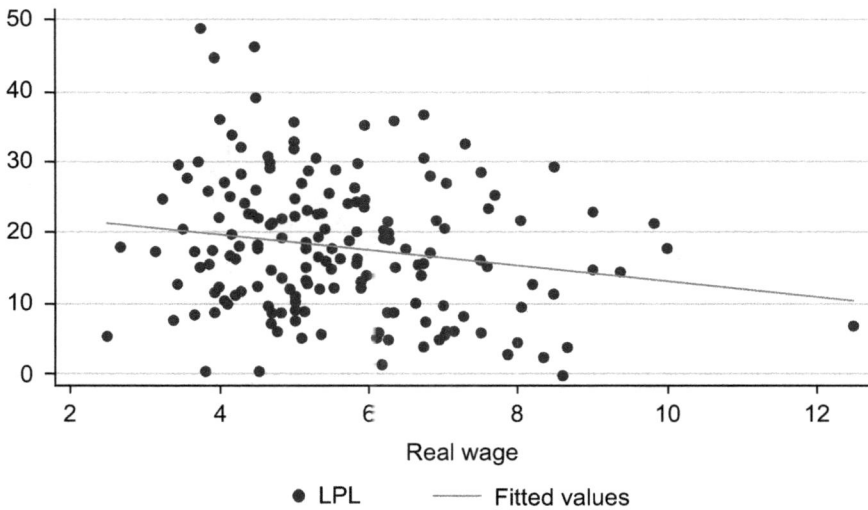

Figure 6.9 Relationship between poverty (LPL) and real wages
Source: HIES (2010).

Table 6.1 Association between poverty and real wages

Variables	HIES 2005		HIES 2010		District statistics, 2011		Panel (sub-district, 2005, 2010)	
	Moderate poverty	Extreme poverty	Moderate poverty	Extreme poverty	Moderate poverty	Extreme poverty	Moderate poverty	Extreme poverty
1	2	3	4	5	6	7	8	9
Real wage	−1.941***	−1.959***	−1.460**	−1.109**	−0.826***	−0.611***	−3.926***	−3.706***
	(0.663)	(0.593)	(0.599)	(0.450)	(0.243)	(0.189)	(1.020)	(0.903)
Constant	53.135***	38.430***	39.981***	24.206***	39.96***	24.352***	64.099***	49.138***
	(3.256)	(2.910)	(3.480)	(2.612)	(2.300)	(1.791)	(10.848)	(9.599)
Sub-district dummy	No	No	No	No	No	No	Yes	Yes
Observations	262	262	177	177	425	425	439	439
R-squared	0.032	0.040	0.033	0.034	0.027	0.240	0.778	0.767

Note: Standard errors in parentheses: *** $p<0.01$, ** $p<0.05$, * $p<0.1$

a 1.5 percentage point reduction in moderate poverty (columns 4 and 5). Interestingly, the regression results show that the effect on extreme poverty in 2010 is smaller than it is on moderate poverty, with extreme poverty reduced by only 1.1 percentage points. It is unclear why this should be the case but perhaps it indicates that the global food price increases of 2007–8 may have had a greater impact on the extreme poor.

We also use real wage data from 2011 district statistics in our regression analysis (columns 6 and 7); the results show that the degree of association is lower than what we found with the HIES data. The district statistics data indicates that poverty rates are reduced by 0.6 to 0.8 percentage points if an increase in nominal wages can buy one extra kilogram of coarse rice. When we use panel data controlling for regional heterogeneity (columns 8 and 9), we find that the association between the rate of poverty reduction and the increase in real wages is higher than the cross-sectional results reported in columns 1 to 6. In this case, an increase in real wage terms of 1 kg of coarse rice is coupled with around a 4 percentage point decrease in poverty levels.

Figure 6.1 above shows that real wages in Bangladesh started to rise very sharply from 2009–10. Our study period ends in 2010 and so we are waiting to see the full impact of the rise in real wages of 2009–10. Our analysis to date suggests that the 2009–10 increase will have an impact upon future poverty reductions. Using growth elasticity of poverty, the government's seventh Five Year Plan projected that the level of moderate poverty would be 24.8 per cent in 2015. Our regression results suggest that the rate of poverty reduction will be much faster.

Conclusion and policy implications

The research underpinning this chapter underscores the importance of understanding local-level poverty dynamics and their covariates for effective development interventions. For the purpose of our study, we concentrated our analysis on the income dimension of poverty even if we recognize that there might not be a linear relationship between income and non-income dimensions of poverty. Our research makes a number of key arguments. First, it confirms that aggregate poverty data disguises local realities, which are important for crafting effective policies and designing public investment programmes. Second, through descriptive statistical and regression analyses, we found that variations in real wages actually help explain the variations in poverty rates at the sub-district level. We draw some specific suggestions from these core findings that we believe are important for future policy interventions.

The most obvious recommendation builds on the observation that our understanding of regional poverty is weak. We actually know very little about why some sub-districts have experienced a substantial increase in poverty while others have experienced the opposite. This calls for a need to conduct rapid appraisals in the sub-districts that have experienced substantial changes in poverty rates. The Government of Bangladesh, especially the General Economics Division (GED) of the Planning Commission, should take the lead in conducting such appraisals. Our attempt to rank the 20 most poverty-stricken sub-districts is a promising start that can help organize these appraisals. Equipped with a clearer picture of regional variations in poverty, policymakers can devise more effective intervention strategies. In arguing for a better understanding of regional variations of poverty levels, we are arguing not only for better 'snapshots' of poverty levels but also for a more nuanced understanding of the ever changing dynamics of poverty. Our analysis already suggests that some regions may have relatively lower poverty levels but are also moving in an upward direction. The analysis of poverty dynamics at the local level can therefore be part of an early warning system that captures impacts from such developments as the country's rapidly changing economy or its increasingly fragile ecology.

Our second broad recommendation is that, in addition to the incidence of poverty, it is essential to understand relevant observed covariates such as real wages. Again, we would recommend that the GED of the Planning Commission take the lead in preparing a database on regional wage rates and costs of living (food prices, for example) at the sub-district level and in preparing a map for effective use in local policymaking. In principle, this could be matched by regional maps on other pro-poor policies and interventions such as the Annual Development Programme (ADP) or safety net programmes. In this way, we could, for example, have a sub-district-level database with information on total budget outlays spent on social protection and ADP, which can then be represented in the form of maps similar to the poverty maps.

Notes

1. Note that sub-district poverty estimates are based on small area estimations in which out-of-sample information is used to compensate for the small number of observations. Since the use of the actual number of observations in testing mean differences would underestimate the level of significance, we prefer not to use it. Therefore, the change in poverty rates is calculated using the mean difference without statistical significance.
2. BBS reports both without-food wages and with-food wages, the former generally being 30 to 40 Bangladeshi Taka (BDT) more than the latter.
3. Bangabandhu Bridge was constructed in 1998 over the River Jamuna, connecting the eastern part of the country to the western part. The 5.6 km bridge was the eleventh longest bridge in the world at the time of its construction.
4. The Chittagong Hill Tracts combine three hilly districts in the southeastern part of the country. They are home to 11 indigenous groups and are one of the most diverse regions of the country in terms of geography, ethnicity, culture, and traditions.

5. Establishing causality with clean identification strategies is beyond the scope of this study. For an insightful identification strategy, see Emran and Shilpi (2014).

References

BBS (2011), *District Statistics 2011*, Dhaka: Bangladesh Bureau of Statistics, Ministry of Planning.

Emran, S. and Shilpi, F. (2014) 'Agricultural productivity, hired labor, wages and poverty evidence from Bangladesh', Policy Research Working Paper 7056, Washington, DC: World Bank.

GED (2013) *Millennium Development Goals: Bangladesh Progress Report 2013*, Dhaka: Planning Commission, Government of Bangladesh.

Hossain, M. and Bayes, A. (2009) *Rural Economy and Livelihoods: Insights from Bangladesh*, Dhaka: AH Development Publishing House.

Khondker, B.H. and Mahzab, M.M. (2015) *Lagging District Development*, Background Paper, Seventh Five Year Plan, Dhaka: Planning Commission, Government of Bangladesh.

Lewis, W.A. (1954) 'Economic development with unlimited supplies of labor', *The Manchester School* 22(2): 139–91.

Mahmud, W. (2011) *Mitigating Seasonal Hunger: Evidence from North-West Bangladesh*, Occasional Paper, Dhaka: Institute of Microfinance.

Osmani, S.R. (2015) *Linking Equity and Growth in Bangladesh*, Background Paper, Seventh Five Year Plan, Dhaka: Planning Commission, Government of Bangladesh.

Osmani, S.R. and Sen, B. (2010) *Dynamics of Poverty in Rural Bangladesh: A Research Framework*, Working Paper 9, Dhaka: Institute of Microfinance.

PKSF (2012) *Annual Progress Report, 2011–12*, Dhaka: Palli Karma-Sahayak Foundation (PKSF).

Quisumbing, A. and Baulch, E. (2009) *Assets and Poverty Traps in Rural Bangladesh*, CPRC Working Paper 143, Manchester: Chronic Poverty Research Centre (CPRC), Institute for Development Policy and Management (IDPM), University of Manchester.

Rahman, S. and Salim, R. (2013) 'Six decades of total factor productivity change and sources of growth in Bangladesh agriculture (1948–2008)', *Journal of Agricultural Economics* 64(2): 275–94.

Sen, B. and Ali, Z. (2015) *Ending Extreme Poverty in Bangladesh during the Seventh Five Year Plan: Trends, Drivers and Policies*, Background Paper, Seventh Five Year Plan, Dhaka: Planning Commission, Government of Bangladesh.

Shilpi, F. (2008) *Migration, Sorting and Regional Inequality: Evidence from Bangladesh*, Policy Research Working Paper, Washington, DC: World Bank.

World Bank (2013) *Bangladesh Poverty Assessment: Assessing a Decade of Progress in Reducing Poverty 2000–2010*, Washington, DC: World Bank.

Zhang, X., Rashid, S., Ahmad, K., Mueller, V., Lee, H., Lemma, S., Belal, S. and Ahmed, A. (2013) 'Rising wages in Bangladesh', IFPRI Discussion Paper 01249, Washington, DC: International Food Policy Research Institute (IFPRI).

Zohir, S. (2011) *Regional Differences in Poverty Levels and Trends in Bangladesh: Are We Asking the Right Questions*, Dhaka: Economic Research Group.

About the authors

Professor Shamsul Alam is a Member (Senior Secretary) of the General Economics Division, Bangladesh Planning Commission. He has held this position since July 2009. He had a distinguished career as Professor of Agricultural Economics at the Bangladesh Agricultural University, Mymensingh, before joining the Planning Commission. Under his leadership, a number of national policy documents, including the First Perspective Plan of Bangladesh, and the sixth and seventh Five Year Plans, have been prepared.

Dr Kazi Iqbal is an Economist and Research Fellow at the Bangladesh Institute of Development Studies (BIDS). He has conducted a wide range of research, including on macro-economics, microfinance, migration, health, taxation, climate change, and agricultural productivity. On completion of his PhD in 2006 at the University of Washington, USA, he spent three years working at the Poverty Reduction and Economic Management Division of the World Bank Institute in Washington, DC.

CHAPTER 7

Agricultural commercialization and employment generation: implications for the extreme poor

K.A.S. Murshid

This chapter explores the significance that commercialization in the agricultural sector has for the extreme poor in Bangladesh. In particular, it examines the non-farm opportunities emerging from this transition, taking the case of the potato value chain. It finds that the consequences of commercialization for the extreme poor are mixed. On the one hand, the extreme poor appear to benefit from improved agricultural labour opportunities and wages, as well as increased non-farm labour opportunities elsewhere in the value chain. At the same time, they remain excluded from entering higher-value forms of employment and trade, continue to attract temporary and casual work, and their wages increase at a lower rate than those for higher forms of labour.

Keywords: value chains, employment, commercialization, agriculture

Introduction

The Bangladesh economy is experiencing rapid structural change with a declining contribution of agriculture to gross domestic product (GDP) and a corresponding rise in the contribution of manufacturing and, especially, of services. Moreover, substantial transformation has also been taking place within both the crop and non-crop sub-sectors. Thus, livestock and fisheries have performed very well while non-rice crops, fruits, and vegetable production have begun to respond strongly to growing demand in the face of rising incomes, especially in urban areas (Faruqee, 2012; World Bank, 2008).

Despite the dwindling share of agriculture in GDP, the rural economy of Bangladesh appears to have contributed enormously to both growth and poverty reduction. The broad development narrative associated with this process relates historically to the spectacular success of the Green Revolution, securing food security in relation to rice production, rising rural wages, a growing number of women in the rural as well as urban labour markets, and a rapidly expanding off-farm and non-farm sector. In addition, important complementary and supportive changes have taken place across

http://dx.doi.org/10.3362/9781780449463.007

a wide front, involving road infrastructure; communications, including mobile telephony; rural commodity and financial markets; remittance flows; microcredit; the rise of rural institutions such as non-governmental organizations (NGOs) and community-based organizations (CBOs); and improved health, education, and safety nets (Murshid, 2015).

This chapter seeks to examine the nature of rural transformation and its underlying processes, focusing particularly on the role of the non-farm sector, especially in relation to the reduction in extreme rural poverty. A case study approach is adopted using the evolving potato value chain sector to explore how increasing commercialization impacts upon employment generation and the livelihoods of the poorest workers.

Agricultural value chain development can be a powerful tool for the eradication of extreme rural poverty in a land-constrained economy such as Bangladesh. Bangladesh's agriculture has performed well, especially in the last decade, with the success of the Green Revolution, rising productivity and growth rates, and an excellent record of extreme poverty reduction (Osmani, 2015). This has happened mainly by reaping productivity gains from technological change and innovations, especially through the continued varietal development of seeds, subsidized access to fertilizers and diesel fuel, and access to finance. Developments in infrastructure, markets, remittance inflows, and rural telephony have also contributed immensely to capital accumulation and investment in rural areas, including in milling, processing, storage, trade, and transport.

Evidence of significant investment in agricultural value chains has been presented recently by Reardon et al. (2012) as well as by Minten et al. (2013) in the context of the rice sector. These reviews have shown, for example, that the milling sector has expanded in Bangladesh at an exponential rate, resulting in a decisive shift from more traditional milling techniques to completely automated modern systems. These changes have had important ramifications for labour employment, and have brought positive changes across the value chain (Murshid, 2015; Reardon et al., 2012).

A typical value chain in agriculture (such as for rice or potatoes) involves a number of actors, stages, and roles, as indicated in Figure 7.1. Possible entry points for the extreme poor (men and women) can be found at 'traditional entry points' (TEPs) or 'new or emerging entry points' (NEPs). TEPs will continue to remain important as long as farm-level productivity grows. NEPs, however, are more related to investment and technological change further down the value chain, and seem to be especially important in processing, milling, cold storage, and modern retailing, where demand for female labour is especially strong. In addition, there is expanding demand for transport and handling services at NEPs, which are dominated by male labour. At the level of modern retailing, there is considerable potential for new types of employment opportunities, both directly as well as indirectly through demand for a range of processed, packaged, and branded products. The modern retail sector in Bangladesh is still in its infancy but appears to be growing quickly.

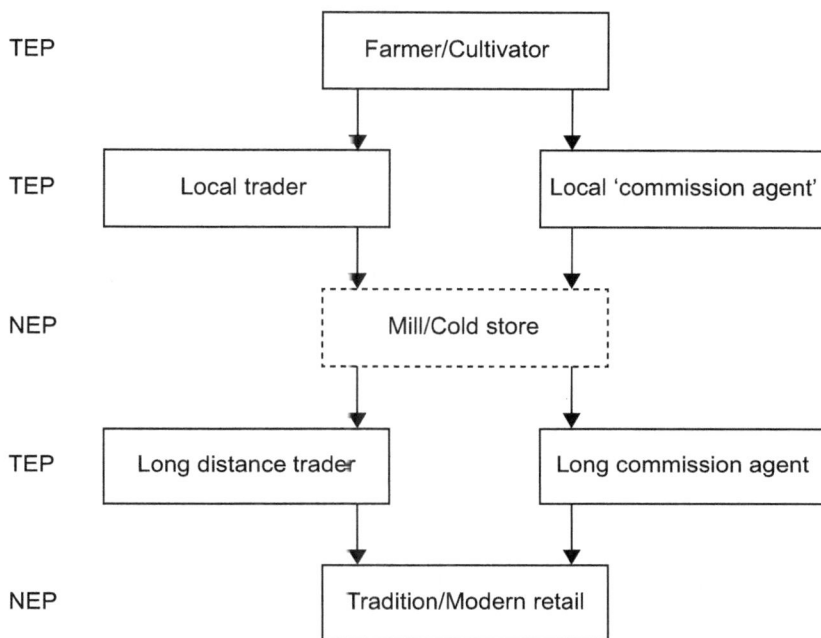

Figure 7.1 Typical value chain for agriculture in Bangladesh

In what follows in this chapter, I focus on the potato value chain case study to explore the role of value chain development in reducing extreme poverty. Given dwindling crop productivity and acute land constraints, these value chains could potentially be of great importance in the fight against extreme poverty.

Methodological approach

This chapter draws on primary data generated using an agricultural value chain approach, starting from the farm to the retail point. It asks whether agricultural transformation – through, for example, higher value addition in agriculture or crop diversification – leads to faster poverty reduction; and if it does so directly through the production process or indirectly through processing and trading. A general observation underpinning the key question is that, with increased diversification away from traditional cereals, which involves the adoption of new products such as *IRRI-boro* or new employment opportunities such as horti-culture, there is a proliferation of agricultural service roles that offer more entry points to the extreme poor and poor. These new service roles are crucial to the rural labour force because there are increasingly fewer land-based employment options available. The value chain data is explored through a combination of cross-section and (pseudo)[1] panel data analysis. Additional relevant data was also generated through a community survey that attempted to capture broad trends over time (2006–7 to 2013–14) for basic socio-economic and infrastructural indicators.

The top four potato-growing regions or districts of Bangladesh – Rangpur, Munshiganj, Bogra, and Rajshahi – were chosen as the core study areas. Surveys on potato-growing households, retailers, traders, *aratdars* (commission agents), and cold storage owners were conducted in each of these districts. From each district, two *upazilas*[2] (sub-districts) were sampled, and from each *upazila* two villages were chosen. The criteria for choosing the *upazilas* and villages were that one would be from the 'more developed' region of the district while the other would be from the 'less developed' or more remote part. This selection process allowed us to capture different socio-economic as well as infrastructural conditions. In total, 252 households were selected from 16 villages along with different traders and cold stores. The fieldwork was carried out in 2014 and a six-year recall period was used to generate the 'pseudo' panel.

The changing village context, 2007–13

Over the past decade, the rural landscape of Bangladesh has changed dramatically. This is confirmed in our community-level data generated from our 16 selected villages.

Human resources

The labour force participation rate over the 2007–13 period was significantly higher than the population growth rate (34.6 per cent compared with 24.5 per cent). This was primarily due to increasing female participation in the labour market, with more and more female workers travelling outside the village to work. This has been accompanied by significant improvements in education, with the 2007–13 period witnessing a dramatic rise in the number of adults reporting more than 12 years of schooling (now standing at 53.6 per cent of the adult population).

There has also been a sharp increase in the number of college students in our selected villages, increasing by around 57 per cent in the reference period. At the same time, the number of local associations ('*samiti*') has also risen substantially, from 20 in 2007 to 41 in 2013–14. These are both formal and informal associations, mostly of poor and extreme poor women who are organized to facilitate savings or credit. The increase in the number of associations is an indication of growing social capital in the area, which allows individuals to borrow small amounts of money at relatively short notice and receive support in other ways from friends, family, and neighbours. Our research suggests that these associations have played an important role in promoting cooperation and collective action among villagers, leading to improved networking, access to information, and productive outcomes.

Social and physical infrastructure

Important changes have taken place in the sample villages in terms of access to schools, clinics, and utilities. The total number of schools increased by 12.5 per cent, from 32 to 36; while the number of clinics rose sharply by 133 per cent from three to seven. In terms of utilities, access to tap water rose by 72 per cent while electricity connections increased by around 45 per cent. The rise in the number of households with mobile phones was dramatic: in 2007, 3,950 households owned a mobile phone; by 2013–14, the number had risen to 10,882.

Access to irrigation is an important determinant of productivity in an agrarian economy. Irrigation usage by farmers increased by 26.5 per cent over the reference period while both ownership rates and the renting of equipment rose in parallel by around 30 per cent. At the same time, there was almost a 10 percentage-point rise in the area covered by irrigation, going up from 82 per cent in 2007 to 91 per cent in 2013–14. A slight decline in cultivated area is also noted over this period.

There is no surface water available in the selected villages, and people depend almost entirely on groundwater for drinking and irrigation. However, the level of groundwater is reported to be receding, on average dropping by more than 5 feet over the reference period. This reflects a sharp worsening trend in groundwater availability due to excessive mining. Distance to a water source point has declined a little, mainly due to the large number of tube-well installations. Access to brick or cement roads has improved significantly, even if this has not necessarily or always translated into improved connectivity or time saving. The reason for this is not entirely clear. In some cases, it may reflect the fact that transport systems have not changed to keep pace with better roads, or that transport is dominated by traditional non-mechanized vehicles or locally adapted motorized vehicles. In such scenarios, improved access to roads will not necessarily reduce travel time.

Land and cropping patterns

Although landlessness (defined here as owning less than 5 decimals[3] of land) increased a little (around 10 per cent over the reported six-year period), we actually observed that landlessness as a proportion of total households declined slightly. This suggests that the total number of households in the area is rising at around the same rate or at a slightly higher rate than the number of landless households. Although this is difficult to explain with certainty, we know that households are fragmenting and subdividing into smaller units. We know far less about how households subdivide and whether this occurs more or less frequently among poorer groups. Our data confirms that the average household land ownership declined from 0.79 acres to 0.62 acres, and for arable land it declined from 0.61 acres to 0.49 acres. This is quite a significant drop over a relatively short period of time and highlights the problem of generating land-based employment for the rural poor and extreme poor.

The main crops grown in the selected villages are rice (*aus*, *aman*, and *boro*), jute, wheat, and potatoes. The area under potato and *aman* rice accounts for over 75 per cent of the gross cropped area, with potato alone accounting for around 28 per cent. The contribution of *aus* rice is also significant; however, the jute and wheat area is insignificant, pointing to the challenge of crop diversification into higher-value activity.

This period has seen significant change in the non-farm economy, which has expanded by around 20 per cent in terms of the number of businesses (shops, rice mills, and so forth). What is much more significant than the sheer number of businesses is their nature. In our selected villages, service businesses renting out machinery and equipment to farmers account for more than a quarter of all establishments. This kind of business was barely known before 2002. Not only is it a growth sector for employment, but it is generally regarded as making agricultural production more efficient. The emergence of these new work opportunities is reminiscent of earlier studies that looked at the role of irrigation service provision by landless workers as an innovation in employment that was particularly suitable for the landless poor and helped them improve their well-being (Wood and Palmer-Jones, 1991).

Wages

Over the 2007–13 period, the wage rate for women grew more than that of men during the busy agricultural season. However, during the slack season, the reverse was observed. Thus, the female-to-male wage ratio in the busy season improved from 0.54 to 0.6 while it fell from 0.64 to 0.6 in the 'off' season. The general pattern of rising real wages and increasing participation of women in the rural labour market is borne out by national-level data (see, for example, the Labour Force Survey[4]), especially for the period after 2000. This has been accompanied by a sharp reduction in poverty, including extreme poverty (Bangladesh Planning Commission, 2015).

Disposition of sales

Potato farmers have the option to either sell at harvest or rent cold storage space and wait for higher prices before selling. Given the wide price fluctuations in the potato market, cold storage options have become increasingly popular. However, the decision to store is not straightforward, as storage does not necessarily protect farmers from price shocks. For example, there have been situations in the past when farmers chose not to release their products from storage because the market price was not profitable. The decision by farmers not to sell their products then meant that cold storage owners were left holding a large volume of unwanted stock. In a sense, both cold storage owners and their farmer clients share the risk of storing products. In some cases, the risk leads to losses, but in general both groups benefit from the storage arrangements.

Cold storage capacity in the areas under study almost trebled over the reported period, rising from over 66,000 tonnes to 190,000 tonnes. More and more farmers appear to be using cold storage options before deciding to sell their products. In 2007, around half the farmers reported using cold storage but by 2013–14 this figure had risen to 65 per cent. We also observed small changes in sales to traders and wholesalers, with a slight increase in sales to traders and a slight decline in sales to wholesalers. However, these did not appear to be significant changes.

In three villages, we found evidence of the beginnings of contract farming and sales to processors. This could be of great significance and may be an early indicator of a major shift in farming in the years ahead, especially as modern agro-processors such as supermarkets expand their operations. In other words, further transformation of the farming system may well be driven not so much by newer crops but by better and more efficient marketing and services such as contract farming or better input delivery systems. Indeed, the Government of Bangladesh's seventh Five Year Plan (Bangladesh Planning Commission, 2015) suggests that this trend has already gained some momentum. If this holds, it is likely that new employment opportunities will be created for the poor and extreme poor.

Access to credit

Our village-level data shows that the number of microfinance institutions (MFIs) located in the villages has remained at 15. The demand for credit from MFIs, however, has increased, judging by the increase in minimum and maximum loans provided in 2007 and 2013–14. The minimum loan amount increased by over 5 per cent while the maximum amount rose by over 62 per cent. By contrast, there has been little expansion or access to loans from informal sources, commercial sources, or specialized banks. MFIs therefore may not be expanding in numbers but their operations continue to grow and demand for their services remains very high.

Performance of farm households

Crop production

Table 7.1 captures the change in crop production over the 2007 to 2013–14 reference period. It confirms that seed production increased modestly by around 9 per cent but the quantity retained rose even more by over 14 per cent, while the purchased quantities remained similar in absolute terms, showing rising demand. The relative shares, however, reveal a small increase in retained share of approximately 2 percentage points and a small decline in purchase shares of 3 percentage points. In other words, over the 2007 to 2103–14 period, there has been no dramatic change in seed production, retention, or purchase.

Table 7.1 Potato production (2013–14 and 2007) by land size group (*maunds*/household)

Land size	Seed potato production in total plots (2013–14)	Seed potato production in total plots (2007)	Commodity potato production total plots (2013–14)	Commodity potato production in total plots (2007)
Marginal	12.3	10.0	88.3	97.0
No.	4	5	15	15
Small	78.8	88.1	168.5	164.0
No.	15	14	29	28
Medium 1	70.6	70.3	346.8	352.4
No.	62	58	99	99
Medium 2	83.9	80.9	758.7	750.4
No.	33	32	62	62
Large	126.3	107.6	1,713.7	1,246.4
No.	11	10	19	19
Total	82.1	75.8	536.4	498.4
No.	125	119	224	223

Notes: One *maund* equals 40 kg. Data for Table 7.1 was collected in February and March.

For commodity potato production, the growth rate was also modest at below 8 per cent. However, looking at the disaggregated picture by land ownership, we observed that the 'large' farmers have in fact registered significant increases in seed and commodity production while other groups show a more stagnant return. Thus, large farms reported an increase of over 17 per cent in seed production and around 37.5 per cent in commodity potato production over our reference period. This suggests that there may be important financial or resource constraints that have served to keep overall potato yields repressed or stagnant.

The implication for the extreme poor is that labour demand from the larger farms will continue to rise even though the direct impacts may be small due to the limited crop productivity response from marginal and small farms. This aspect is dealt with in greater detail below when we analyse labour costs.

Storage

Most households in the sample reported renting modern storage facilities equipped with temperature control systems. Thus, 71 per cent of households reported utilizing the services of private cold storage companies, mostly on the basis of a fixed rate per unit of weight by season or for the whole year.

Small and marginal farms were found to store higher amounts per household (average of storing households) than other farmers. However, it is important to note that only 22 per cent of marginal households actually used

Table 7.2 Storage of table and seed potatoes by land size group (*maunds*)

Land size group (N)	Table potatoes (2013–14)	Table potatoes (2007–8)	% change	Seed potatoes (2013–14)	Seed potatoes (2007–8)	% change
Marginal (18)	0.56	5.11	–89.03	0.56	1.61	–65.23
Small (39)	70.54	48.50	45.40	85.79	56.82	50.11
Medium 1 (110)	121.11	69.35	74.50	96.66	62.34	54.31
Medium 2 (64)	358.30	137.27	161.02	351.56	110.78	217.33
Large (21)	713.57	144.09	395.02	455.71	112.86	303.80
Total (252)	214.28	85.01	152.00	182.77	73.66	148.00

rented storage space while the figure for larger sized groups reaches 70 per cent. This suggests that a large proportion of marginal farmers are constrained in their ability to use cold storage facilities, and thereby unable to benefit from the advantages these offer.

The storage of table potatoes and seed potatoes registered a sharp increase over time across all land size groups except marginal farmers (see Table 7.2). On average, storage of both table and seed potatoes went up by around 150 per cent, with the largest group showing increases in the order of three to four times. This suggests a rapid rise in demand for storage space, especially in modern facilities. Our research suggests that this is being supported through credit being extended to farmers by cold store owners. If true, this implies that those standing to gain most from investments in storage are those likely to be in a position to access credit. In other words, this is an investment context where there is little room for the extreme poor.

Access to agriculture inputs and labour costs

Farmers reported purchasing inputs up to a maximum of four times per year, although the modal value is three times. The most popular months for input purchases are November (100 per cent of households), July (47.2 per cent), and April (24.6 per cent). Input costs per farming household for 2013–14 and 2007 are shown Table 7.3. Two points are worth noting. First, there has been a substantial decline in both absolute and relative terms in outlays for chemical fertilizers, and a sharp rise in seed costs. Second, the total input costs have declined by 33 per cent, and this is likely to be the result of a more careful use of chemical fertilizers.[5]

From 2007 to 2013–14, we observe a 29.7 per cent increase in labour costs, which rose from 16,234 Bangladeshi Taka (BDT) to BDT21,062 per farmer. At the same time, labour costs due to mechanized activities rose by 37.7 per cent, from BDT8,011 to BDT10,952 per farmer. For labour operations, costs related to land preparation, fertilizer and pesticide application, and irrigation increased faster compared with total manual operation costs. Costs relating to seed potato cutting, seeding, weeding, and harvesting also increased but

Table 7.3 Agricultural input costs (BDT/household)

Inputs	2013–14		2007	
	BDT	%	BDT	%
Organic	2,462	3.5	2,118	3.4
Chemical F	33,232	47.1	48,259	76.9
Pesticide	9,941	14.1	13,058	12.4
Irrigation	8,154	11.6	29,679	28.2
Seed	16,433	23.3	12,188	11.6
Other	350	–	–	–
Total	70,572	100	105,302	100

at a lower rate. In terms of the mechanization costs associated with manual operations, costs for irrigation, seed potato cutting, and land preparation increased most significantly.

Across all our selected sites, it is clear that the use of machinery in farming has expanded significantly, as has the ownership of machinery. The most common piece of equipment owned by farmers is the spraying machine used to apply pesticides. We found that 243 farmers out of 252 owned such a machine. After this, 26 per cent of farming households (65 in total) owned a tractor or tiller. The greater need for and use of machinery are not only evidenced in ownership but also in hire and rental services. There has been an explosion of providers offering different machines for hire. This can be a lucrative business. Our data suggests that the average income for those renting out machines has increased from BDT28,700 in 2009 to BDT44,893 in 2013–14. In the vast majority of cases, those who rent out machines bought them with their own money without resorting to borrowing or loans.

From this analysis, it is worth highlighting two points that are particularly relevant for the extreme poor. First, the sharp rise in labour costs suggests higher agricultural wages and opportunities for rural labourers. This is without doubt a positive development for all those working in the sector. Second, the growing importance of mechanization in agriculture points to the strong labour-employment impact of agriculture even in the face of modest growth. On the one hand, mechanization replaces jobs and makes agricultural production more efficient. This may not bode well for the extreme poor. On the other, the mechanization of value chains opens up new employment opportunities that could prove to be useful entry or merging points for the extreme poor and poor.

Traders: producing areas and Dhaka

More than 76 per cent of sample traders in our selected sites own a wholesale stall in the local market, and, of these, around 12 per cent reported investing in a cold store and 9 per cent in some form of retail outlet. This suggests that people put considerable investments into fixed assets. The average initial investment per trader was just over BDT184,000 in 2013–14 prices. This is not an insignificant amount of money, and indeed even the smaller traders needed to invest around BDT90,000 on average.

Over 93 per cent of traders reported investing in a stall; this includes those who have made an initial deposit to secure a pledge of purchase, but do not yet own one. Around 26 per cent invested in activities related to potato processing, and 7 per cent reported making investments in transport equipment. We also came across a few cases of traders investing in cold storage and warehouses. Much of the financing for the initial investment (over 91 per cent) came from the traders' own resources with only 12 per cent reporting that they had to borrow in order to invest. It is clear from the structure and level of interest rates on money borrowed that traders are able to borrow from formal sources. Most traders (over 70 per cent) reported making additional investments after the business was in operation. Some 50 per cent of this additional finance was obtained from their own resources.

Cold storage owners or operators are a crucial source of credit, with 41 per cent of traders reporting taking loans from cold storage owners; commercial banks are not far behind at 37 per cent. However, when we asked about the number of loans (as opposed to the size or amount of the loan), we found that NGOs were in fact the most popular source of lending, followed by cold stores at 29 per cent, and commercial banks at 14.4 per cent. On average, each trader took out 1.18 loans; small traders took out 1.04 loans, medium traders 2.71, *aratdars* 0.47, and wholesalers 0.6 each. As indicated above, it is worth remembering that traders enjoy much better access to the formal credit sector than producers. Almost 75 per cent of traders rent storage space; this is almost entirely from cold stores located in nearby wholesale markets. The amount of space rented depends on the amount of produce that needs to be stored. Among our sample, traders looked to store as little as 100 tonnes per annum to as much as 900 tonnes per annum.

A total of 19 traders, representing 9.7 per cent of the total, borrowed money in order to cover the cost of cold storage (mostly from cold store owners but also from wholesalers and MFIs), with each borrowing over BDT40,000 at an interest rate of under 18 per cent. However, 140 traders rented storage space from cold stores, spending over BDT20,000 per season each on average. This ranges from around BDT7,500 for small traders or BDT10,827 for *aratdars* to BDT39,000 for wholesalers and BDT35,400 for medium traders. The improved availability of credit has meant that the poorer cultivators and traders are able to participate in the value chain. However, most of these participants cannot be categorized as extreme poor. If there are benefits for the extreme poor, these are likely to be found in the world of employment.

We can distinguish four types of labour used by traders: family labour, employed salaried or white-collar workers, permanent labourers, and temporary workers. Family workers are almost never paid a wage and overall there seems to be little change over time in the use of family labour by traders. The number of salaried or white-collar employees, however, has increased significantly (82 per cent) over the reporting period. Wages for these employees have also risen significantly, from BDT3,500 in 2007 to BDT6,600 in 2013–14, representing an 88.6 per cent increase. These salaried workers tend to have some level of education and come from relatively well-off backgrounds. The number of permanent workers rose by about 40 per cent, with their wages increasing by around 36 per cent. It is, however, among the temporary workforce where we see some of the most dramatic changes. Here, traders reported an increase of almost 120 per cent in the number of people employed as temporary workers. The significance of this lies in the fact that this category of employee is most likely to include poor and extreme poor labourers. This suggests that even modest agricultural growth leading to greater demand from traders can have important downstream impacts on employment opportunities for the poor and extreme poor. However, it is important to note that the nature of this work is casual or temporary, indicating a significant degree of insecurity. It is also worth noting that wages for temporary labourers grew by around 6 per cent, representing a fraction of the increases seen by permanent and salaried labourers. Despite this, evidence from other studies (Faruqee, 2012) indicates that rural wages have been rising quickly, especially since 2005. It is possible that the increase in temporary employment opportunities will result in longer-term improvements in wages.

The role of cold stores

Over the period studied, cold storage firms become one of the most important downstream developments for the potato value chain. Arguably, these firms have had a significant impact on poverty and extreme poverty reduction. These impacts can be both direct and indirect; employment generated for both males and females is an example of the former and employment generated through financing both trade and production is an example of the latter. In this section, we want to examine the expansion of cold storage firms, drawing on our data as well as on other studies, especially that of Reardon et al. (2012). The research of Reardon et al. focused on 20 cold storage firms in the district of Bogra, which were also included in our sample. These two sources therefore complement each other well.

The capacity of the cold storage firms (measured in terms of the number of potato bags they can store) has increased substantially according to farmers and traders. The average start-up year for the cold storage firms in our sample was 1999, with the majority starting in the 1990s (43 per cent) and the 2000s (31 per cent). The cold storage firms with smaller capacity at their start-up points were generally established in the 1990s while the larger ones were established in the 2000s. In 2013–14, the average size of the cold storage firms in the study sample was 17,155 tonnes and their average capacity at their start-up point was 11,740 tonnes. The utilized capacity in 2014 was 12,910 tonnes per cold store, with the capacity utilization rate around 75 per cent. The cold storage firms' self-reported worth in 2014 was about US$4 m on average. Compared with the findings of Reardon et al.'s earlier study, the average size of the cold storage firms in our sample is larger, and they self-report higher levels of value and worth.

As indicated above, cold storage firms are now more involved in providing credit to the users of their facilities. Loans are used for a variety of purposes, including repayment of debts to input suppliers and consumption. A high proportion of the cold stores (57 per cent) provide credit to farmers in the form of advances before storage It is clear that this type of arrangement is increasing: in Reardon et al.'s study only 15 per cent of cold storage firms provided loans for this purpose Furthermore, in our study 74 per cent of cold storage firms provided advance payments after starting the cold store; this share was only 55 per cent just four years earlier in 2009, according to Reardon et al.'s study. In our study, 43 per cent of the farmers using cold storage firms took advances before storage while 41 per cent of them took loans using the stored potato as collateral. On average, the cold storage firms charged a 15 per cent interest rate annually on these loans, with the typical storage period being about six to seven months. However, the cold storage firms also reported that about 30 per cent of the clients who used their credit services ended up defaulting on their loans.

The cold storage firms also offer or support other important services such as intermediating transactions, arranging transportation services, and providing grading and sorting services. The most common service falls under the umbrella of intermediary transactions, with more than 95 per cent of the interviewed cold storage firms reporting that they had responded to requests from farmers and traders to arrange transactions by putting clients in contact with potential buyers. Those that provided this service did so for 28 per cent of their clients on average. This is consistent with the findings in Reardon et al.'s study, where roughly a third of all the cold storage clients received intermediation services from the firms.

When we compare Reardon et al.'s study with our own, we see some important differences in the cold storage firms' annual operating costs. For example, the total operating cost per cold storage firm in 2013–14 was reported to be $291,800, which is about $40,000 lower than the costs reported by Reardon et al. (2012). Energy costs now make up about 51 per cent of the total cost outlay compared with 63 per cent previously. Payments for labour now take up a larger portion of the total costs, their share having more than doubled (29.6 per cent as opposed to 13.5 per cent previously). This is an interesting finding because, although cold storage firms are relatively more capital intensive, labour payments have increased at a higher rate than any other item of cost. Labour payments are made up of two components: payment for permanent workers and payment for those on temporary contracts or arrangements. In 2013–14, the average cold storage firm employed 47 permanent and 445 temporary workers. The former were paid about $53 per month on average while the latter earned $127 yearly. In addition to this income, temporary workers also earned an average of $219 annually from unloading and loading potato bags to and from client transport.

Calculating the profits of cold storage firms is not an easy task. We have attempted to do this by subtracting the total operating costs from the revenues of the cold storage firms. In calculating revenues, we focused on the storage charges levied on users and we left out any earnings accrued from interest on advances paid to those using the stores. To calculate the profit rate, the profits of the cold storage firms were taken as the share of their total investment expenses including the cost of expansion. The rates were then averaged across the firms. The profit rate we calculated for our sample was just over 20 per cent. Given that this excludes interest earnings, it makes the cold storage sector a strong and profitable one. This helps explain why there has been so much investment in the cold storage market in recent years.

Conclusion

Transformative changes are taking place in rural Bangladesh and these have resulted in tightening labour markets, rising real wages, and increasing participation of women in the labour market, along with significant capital investments both in agriculture and in value chains and non-farm activities. The case study of the potato value chain has tried to highlight the role of value chain investments, especially in modern storage, and how this has stimulated labour demand, particularly among casual and temporary workers who are predominantly drawn from the ranks of the extreme poor. A similar – perhaps stronger – case can be made for the rice value chain, especially in modern milling and potentially also in modern storage. The processes described here, therefore have wide relevance for understanding the nature of agricultural changes in Bangladesh, and for understanding how the rural labour market can positively impact on attempts to reduce poverty and extreme poverty.

Another area that has led to increased demands for rural labour is closer to the upstream crop sector and derives from greater input use efficiency; capital investments in production as well as in input delivery systems; better linkages with markets; the emergence of a rental market for machinery and other agricultural equipment; and the beginnings of contract farming associated with better technology. These dynamics have been supported by both formal and informal financial intermediation, particularly for the trading and storage sectors.

In a situation in which there is an acute scarcity of cultivable land, all available land-augmenting or labour-generating activities that help address extreme poverty reduction need to be explored. Investments in value chain developments appear to present significant potential for extreme poverty reduction because of their direct and indirect effects on the labour market. While there are clear benefits to the opportunities presented by these transformations in both the agricultural and non-farm sectors, there are underlying questions relating to the insecure, temporary nature of these opportunities and the lower rate of increase in wages. In terms of future developments that might have an impact on extreme poverty reduction, a blended strategy is necessary. This needs to ensure that as many employment opportunities as possible are available for the extreme poor, address the underlying questions that emerge from new opportunities, and actively promote the development of new opportunities.

Notes

1. A pseudo panel was established through recall for the period 2006–7 to 2013–14.
2. *Upazilas* are the level of administration that lies below that of the districts.
3. One acre of land is equal to approximately 100 decimals of land.
4. The Labour Force Survey is conducted by the Bangladesh Bureau of Statistics periodically. The last survey was conducted in 2013 but the results are not yet available. The latest data currently available is from 2010.
5. Farmers in Bangladesh tend to use excessive amounts of chemical fertilizers, especially urea, partly because of available subsidies. The government has been trying to raise awareness about the dangers of excessive use and our results may reflect a degree of increased awareness.

References

Bangladesh Planning Commission (2015) *The Seventh Five Year Plan of Bangladesh, 2015–16 to 2019–20*, Dhaka: Planning Commission, Ministry of Planning, Government of Bangladesh.

Faruqee, R. (2012) *Stock-taking of Major Studies and Reports on Agriculture and Rural Development in Bangladesh*, mimeo, Washington, DC: World Bank.

Minten, B., Murshid, K.A.S. and Reardon, T. (2013) 'Food quality changes and implications: evidence from the rice value chain of Bangladesh', *World Development* 42(1): 100–13.

Murshid, K.A.S. (2015) 'Exploring transition and change in a complex traditional market: the case of the rice market in Bangladesh', *Journal of Agrarian Change* 15(4): 480–98.

Osmani, S.R. (2015) *Poverty and Vulnerability in Bangladesh*, Dhaka: Institute of Microfinance.

Reardon, T., Chen, K., Minten, B. and Adriano, L. (2012) *The Quiet Revolution in Staple Food Value Chains*, Mandaluyong, Philippines: Asian Development Bank and International Food Policy Research Institute.

Wood, G.D. and Palmer-Jones, R. (1991) *The Water Sellers: A Cooperative Venture by the Rural Poor*, London: IT Publications.

World Bank (2008) *High Value Agriculture in Bangladesh: An Assessment of Agro-business Opportunities and Constraints*, Bangladesh Development Series Paper 21, Washington, DC: World Bank.

About the author

K.A.S. Murshid is the Director General of the Bangladesh Institute of Development Studies (BIDS). Dr Murshid completed his PhD in 1985 at the Faculty of Politics and Economics, University of Cambridge. He has since published extensively on topics including food policy, infrastructure and irrigation, agricultural markets and value chains, and rural credit markets. He has extensive experience of operationalizing research to inform public policy and practice.

CHAPTER 8
Urbanization and extreme poverty

Nazrul Islam

Bangladesh has experienced rapid urbanization since its liberation in 1971, caused primarily by rural-to-urban migration. Urbanization in Bangladesh is characterized by a balanced distribution of urban centres but a highly uneven spatial pattern in the level of urbanization, with a persisting dominance of the capital city of Dhaka, which is already one of the largest megacities in the world. Nationally, poverty and extreme poverty have reduced steadily over time due to economic growth and targeted poverty reduction programmes. However, this chapter will argue that the urban extreme poor still suffer from inadequate access to key social services such as housing, education, and health. Addressing the needs of the urban extreme poor is vital if Bangladesh is to make progress on its national extreme poverty strategy.

Keywords: urbanization, extreme poverty, spatial patterns

Introduction

In the second decade of the twenty-first century, Bangladesh remains a predominantly rural and agrarian country which, however, is rapidly becoming more urbanized. While this observation is true of many countries in the world, both the nature and pattern of urbanization in Bangladesh are quite unique. An extraordinary mix of urban and rural characteristics can be found equally in both metropolitan cities and rural towns. These in turn reflect rapid developments in physical infrastructure and communication; significant advances in rural development; and investments in social sectors in both rural and urban locations. With a limited land base and a growing population, it is entirely reasonable to predict that in the next few decades, Bangladesh will be an entirely urban society. For this reason, it is important in any discussion about extreme poverty and inequality to focus on the pace and direction of the urban transition in the country. This chapter intends to shed light on the relation between extreme poverty and urban growth. It will first discuss the nature of urbanization in Bangladesh, highlighting recent trends and characteristics of urban growth, the significance of rural-to-urban migration, and the influence of economic development. The second part of the chapter focuses on urban extreme poverty and highlights the key challenges faced by the urban extreme poor in Bangladesh.

http://dx.doi.org/10.3362/9781780449463.008

Urbanization in Bangladesh: recent trends

When Bangladesh became independent in 1971, it had a small and predominantly rural population. It has since undergone a remarkable transformation towards urbanization. The continued move to urbanization has intensified over the past 16 years, leading some to claim that it represents a real turning point in Bangladesh's demographic transition (Mathur et al., 2013). The following observations help capture some of this remarkable transformation.

In 1974 (the year in which Bangladesh carried out its first census following independence in 1971), the urban population was just over 6 million. By 2011, this had risen to 39 million. The pace of growth of the urban population is significantly greater than that seen in the rural population, which moved from 65 million in 1974 to 107 million in 2011. As of 2011, 27.66 per cent of the entire population lived in urban areas compared with just 8.78 per cent in 1974 (BBS, 2014). Over the same 1974–2011 period, the exponential growth rate of the urban population was 5.18 per cent, while the same figure for the rural population was only 1.36 per cent. Indeed the long term trend of growth of the entire population was only 2.18 per cent.

Since 2000, the rate and growth of urbanization have increased and have become even more visible. Over the 2001–11 period, for example, the urban population has increased by 14.1 million while, over the same period, the rural population has increased by 12.5 million (Mathur et al., 2013). This is the first time we see comparatively more growth in urban areas in independent Bangladesh, a fact that gives weight to Mathur et al.'s claim about a turning point in the country's demographic transition.

The annual exponential growth rate of 4.01 per cent registered among the urban population during the 2001–11 period reversed the declining trend observed during the 1991–2001 period (see Figure 8.1). However, as Figure 8.1 clearly shows, the annual exponential growth rate of the urban population has consistently outpaced the growth rate of the rural population in every census conducted in the 1974–2011 period.

Figure 8.1 provides further insights into the pace and direction of urban growth. It shows, for example, that the annual rural and total population rates have also grown over the 2001–11 period. However, with the exception of 1974 (which captures growth from 1961 to 1974), the rural annual exponential growth rate has always remained below the 2 per cent level, and indeed fell as low as 0.68 per cent over the 1991–2001 decade. Rural population growth rates therefore have been monotonically decreasing in the 20-year period from 1981 to 2001.

The growth of the urban population is expected to continue in the future. By 2047, it is predicted that 50 per cent of Bangladesh's entire population of 240 million will live in urban areas, and from that point onwards the number of urban residents will outweigh the number of rural residents (Figure 8.2). The prospect of having around 120 million inhabitants living in urban areas in a matter of 30 years is a major and critical policy challenge, and will have a huge bearing on the country's ability to deliver prosperity and ensure the well-being of its citizens.

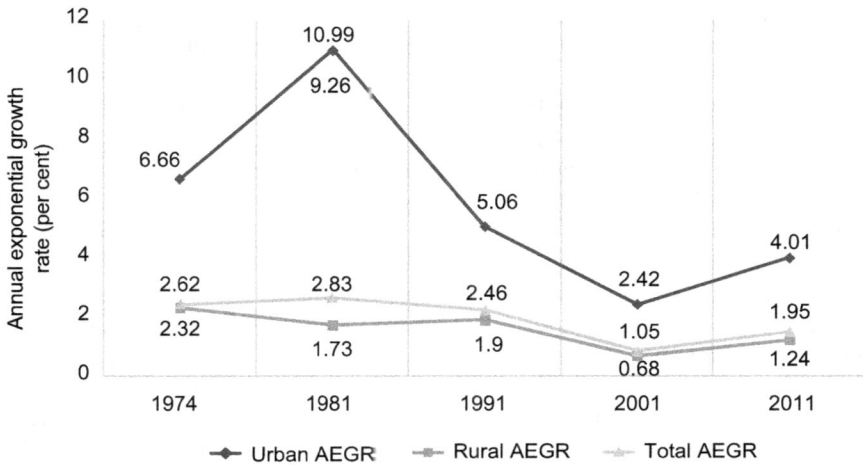

Figure 8.1 Annual growth rates of population (1974–2011)
Source: Mathur et al. (2013).

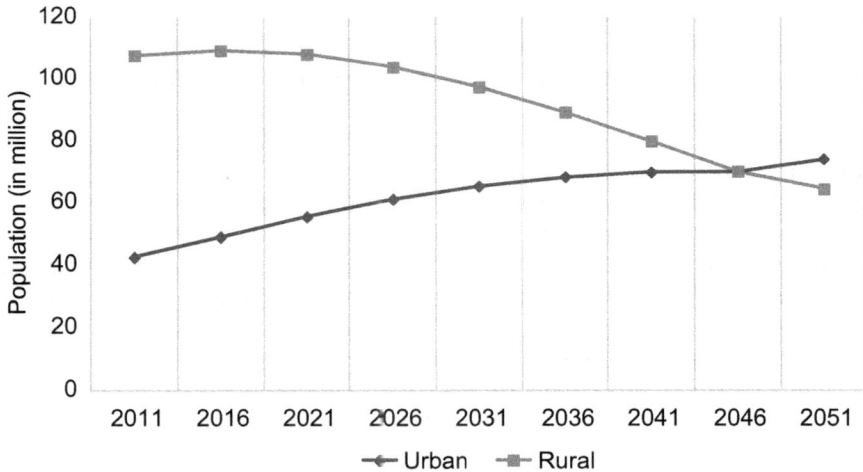

Figure 8.2 Projected rural and urban population in Bangladesh (2011–51)
Source: Mathur et al. (2013).

Urbanization and migration

Having outlined the broad trend towards further urbanization, it is important to identify the main factors behind the rapid urban growth. We would like to highlight four key factors. First, Bangladesh continues to experience persistently high population growth rates, and this is likely to continue for some time to come. Second, over the years, we have observed a gradual territorial extension of existing urban areas and the conversion of many rural centres into urban areas. Third, there has been a redefinition of what actually constitutes an 'urban' area. The most noticeable change to date took place in 1981, when the *thana*, later named *upazila* or sub-district headquarters, and other peripheral areas were reclassified as 'urban' areas. This change helps explain the significant increase in the annual growth rates of the urban population over the 1974–81 period, when the urban population grew by 10.99 per cent (see Figure 8.1). The fourth factor is arguably the most influential one and refers to the persistent levels of rural-to-urban migration observed throughout the country. Internal migration, we would argue, has had the greatest impact on the rate and pace of urban growth in Bangladesh. For large cities such as Dhaka, the capital city, migration may account for as much as 60 per cent of population growth.

Migration is a complex and multifaceted phenomenon. Although superficial and problematic in both analytical and empirical terms, there is some value in thinking about the push and pull factors underpinning migration in order to delineate its broad contours and characteristics. Migrants responding to pull factors at the point of destination can therefore be understood as making positive choices (these, however, can be problematic and 'coerced' choices) while migrants responding to push factors at the point of origin can be understood as being motivated by negative reasons (Islam and Saleheen, 2006).

There are a number of relevant push factors in Bangladesh. At one level, people often migrate because of population pressure or adverse people–land ratios in rural areas. In such instances, we also find conditions of poverty and large-scale unemployment. Migrants also move because they are forced to. For example, there are many cases of migration resulting from natural disasters such as riverbank erosion, floods, and cyclones. In many rural areas, the lack of core services, especially in education and health, force people to look for opportunities elsewhere. Finally, in some circumstances, people move because they feel threatened by a poor law and order situation. For example, some minority groups in Bangladesh migrate in order to avoid social, cultural, economic, or political oppression in their 'home' areas.

Pull factors are associated with the urban destination, and, in the case of Bangladesh, they often mirror the push factors. Thus urban centres are seen to provide more and better job opportunities as well as higher wages. Some of the urban centres such as Dhaka have real pockets of wealth and a relatively vibrant economy, which can provide diverse employment opportunities for both poor and not-so-poor migrants. Besides economic factors, social opportunities, particularly better education and health facilities, also act as strong pull factors. These again attract poor and non-poor households alike. Finally, the size of the urban population can offer some protection, even in the form of greater anonymity, for migrants who decide to move because of social discrimination or political oppression.

Rural-to-urban migration takes place in almost all districts of Bangladesh, but some districts or areas are more prone to out-migration. For example, there are a number of districts in Bangladesh that are traditionally known as 'home' to migrants moving to the country's two largest cities: Dhaka and Chittagong.[1] In line with our discussion on push factors, many of these districts are economically depressed areas and are vulnerable to natural disasters. However, the fact that some districts seem to have more migrants than others underlines the importance of what we call 'intervening factors': that is, factors that are not captured in the push–pull construct. Examples of 'intervening factors' include the distance between origin and destination, the cost and risk of travel, and so forth. These are factors that determine the pattern and shape of migration in the country. Districts close to large metropolitan areas such as Dhaka and Chittagong or districts with relatively better physical communication are therefore the main source areas of migrants.

Current and future urban profiles of Bangladesh

There is significant variation in the level of urbanization by district or other geographic or administrative region, such as divisions and *upazilas* or sub-districts.[2] In fact, by district, the level of urbanization varies from as low as 8.85 per cent in Gaibandha district in the far north-west of the country to more than 93 per cent in Dhaka district in the central region (BBS, 2014). Forty-four of the country's 64 districts have low levels of urbanization, with only 11 to 20 per cent of the population living in urban areas. There are three districts where the urban population is lower than 10 per cent: Panchagarh (9.86 per cent), Manikganj (9.28 per cent), and Gaibandha (8.85 per cent). While most of the less urbanized districts are located far from Dhaka, Manikganj, which has one of the lowest levels of urbanization, is in fact adjacent to Dhaka. While further analysis is needed to explain the phenomenon of Manikganj, it is worth recalling that there is intense communication between Dhaka and Manikganj; indeed, some see the distance between the two as 'commutable'.

Bangladesh has some 570 urban centres, of which one (Dhaka) is a megacity with a population of 14.70 million, and a further four (Chittagong, Khulna, Rajshahi, and Sylhet) are metropolitan areas. A further 25 urban centres are cities with populations over 100,000, and the rest are smaller towns. There are 11 city corporations and over 322 *pourashavas* (municipalities) administered under local governments. All the other towns have the union *parishad* type of local government, which tends to be associated with rural areas. The megacity of Dhaka spreads over Dhaka district and parts of four other districts, covering an area of over 1,400 square kilometres. Most commentators believe that Bangladesh has a fairly well balanced urban system (see Figure 8.3) in the sense that there is an urban centre in every region under the central government administrative authority. Furthermore, almost all divisional cities are metropolitan cities, all 64 districts have a town or a city of reasonable size (with populations varying from 30,000 to 400,000), and each of the old 450 *upazilas* have at least one small town.

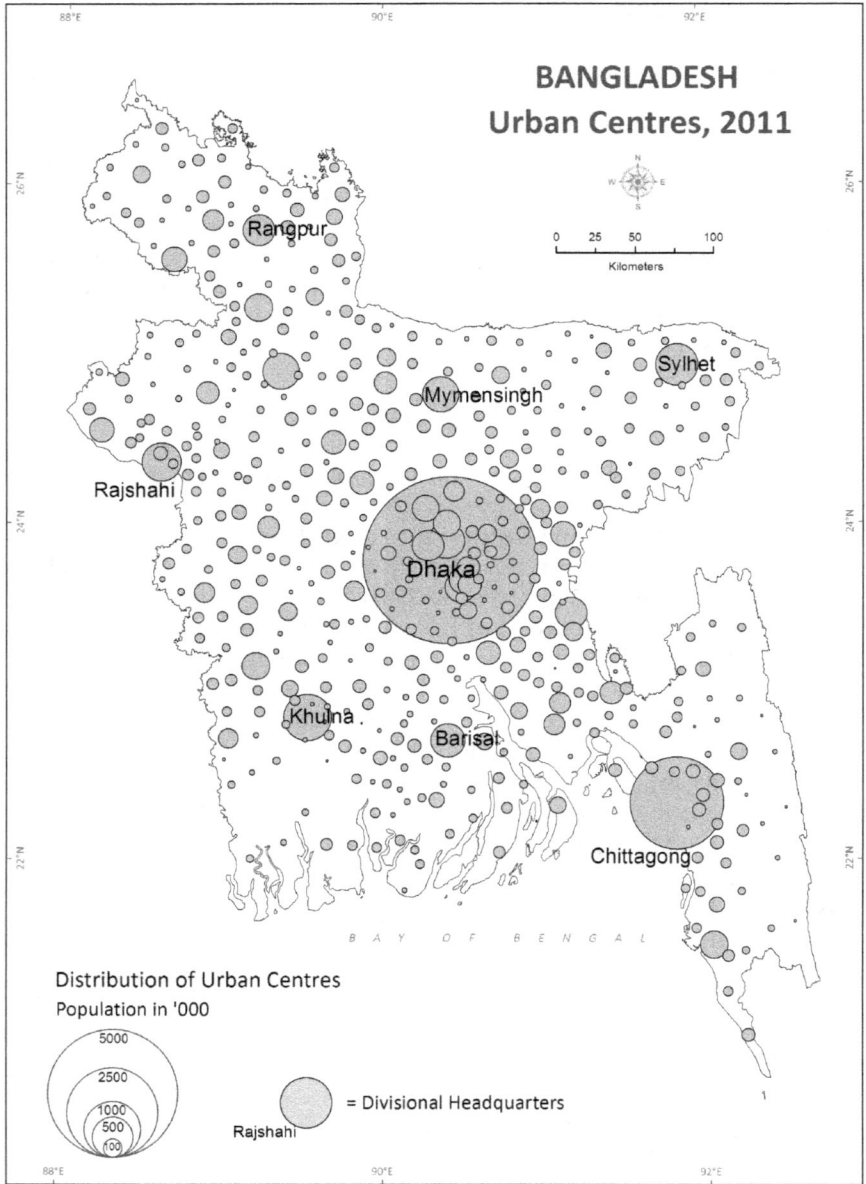

Figure 8.3 The distribution and size of urban centres in Bangladesh
Source: BBS et al. (2010).

The distribution of large and medium-sized cities and towns throughout the country offers some access to urban services to most of the country's inhabitants, including those in remote rural settlements.

Of all the urban centres, Dhaka stands out in terms of size and significance. In 2011, it comprised 44.26 per cent of the total urban population and 12.56 per cent of the national population. When compared with the country's second-largest city, Chittagong, Dhaka's population was 2.47 times higher in 1981 and 3.58 times higher in 2011. Even when compared with the sum of the other three largest cities in the country (Chittagong, Khulna, and Rajshahi), Dhaka's population was 1.50 times higher in 1981 and this rose to 2.26 times higher in 2011. The primacy of Dhaka rests not only on its population size, but just as much on the fact that it is the political, economic, and, some might argue, social epicentre of the country. As the capital city, Dhaka is home to parliament and all the bureaucratic, administrative, military, and law-enforcement authorities. In terms of economic dominance, it is estimated that Dhaka contributes over a third of the national gross domestic product (GDP). And finally, as an indicator of social dominance, of the country's 120 universities, 50 are located in the Dhaka metropolitan area (UGC, 2015).

Metropolitan cities with populations of more than 1 million also play important economic and socio-political roles in Bangladesh. In 1981, Bangladesh had only one metropolitan city (Dhaka), but by 2011 the number had increased to four, with Chittagong, Khulna, and Rajshahi joining the ranks. These four metropolitan cities accounted for 63.87 per cent of the total urban population in 2011, up from 35.69 per cent in 1981 (BBS, 2014). The prevalence of business services, particularly finance and real-estate services, is considerably higher in the four major cities relative to the rest of the country (GoB, 2011).

Rather than stagnating, all four metropolitan cities experienced higher rates of population growth in the most recent census decade (2001–11) than in the previous one (1991–2001). Moreover, the growth rates of the metropolitan cities exceeded the rate of the urban population as a whole, underlining the fact that the scope of urbanization in Bangladesh is not yet exhausted. As such, we can expect continuing rapid urban growth in Bangladesh in the coming decades, mainly fuelled by the growth in the metropolitan centres. This process is expected to be led by Dhaka, which, despite its current size, is still the fastest-growing metropolitan area in Bangladesh. The growth of Dhaka will most likely occur via the planned expansion of new satellite cities and the spontaneous growth of existing urban centres in the greater metropolitan region of Dhaka. Chittagong many also expand significantly in the future.

If, as predicted, the pace of urbanization continues or accelerates in Bangladesh, what are the likely impacts on the economic performance of the country? To answer this question it is perhaps worth recalling that urbanization worldwide has been found to be an effective engine of economic growth and a significant contributor to national economies. In Bangladesh, the urban sector contributes more than 65 per cent of GDP (ADB, 2010), up from 25 per cent in 1972–3 and 45 per cent in 1995–6. Within the country, there is also evidence of a clear correlation between regional economic development and levels of urbanization. Thus, those districts with higher levels of urbanization are also those with more developed and thriving economies. This is confirmed by the latest (i.e. 2001) district-level GDP per capita data, which shows a highly positive relationship (r^2 being 0.8295) between urbanization and economic development. Furthermore, we see a similarly positive relationship when we look at key social development indicators. Thus, where we see greater urbanization we also see higher literacy rates, improved quality of education, and better health indicators. Although it is difficult to be precise, urban centres in Bangladesh also tend to offer more cultural opportunities such as centres for fine arts, and political opportunities such as politically orientated associations or groups. As such, it could be claimed that urbanization brings important cultural and political benefits.

All of the above suggests that, on the whole, urbanization brings many important benefits to Bangladesh. However, it is important to be aware of the many challenges urbanization also brings, especially when the pace of change is rapid – and future projections point to even more intensity and concentration. There are many current and future challenges for Bangladesh, including the provision of efficient and affordable housing and transportation systems; the delivery of key urban social services including health, education, and sanitation; the maintenance of law and order; the protection of the natural environment; and the defence of residential areas from the worst impacts of natural disasters, including those caused by climate change. In addition to these, urban growth in Bangladesh poses a very unique challenge in terms of eliminating extreme poverty. Urban extreme poverty is not the same as rural extreme poverty, and, given the prognosis outlined above about the projected further urbanization of Bangladesh, it is safe to assume that in the future the country's extreme poverty challenge will be decidedly urban. We turn to this challenge in the sections that follow.

Urban growth and extreme poverty

As argued above, increased migration is without doubt the most significant factor behind the rapid growth of urban populations in Bangladesh. While not all migrants are poor, most are. This has made the task of poverty reduction in urban areas difficult. The levels of urban poverty have been positively affected by a combination of a sustained period of impressive national economic growth and the introduction of urban development programmes carried out by governmental as well as non-governmental agencies. As a result, the incidence of poverty has declined significantly in urban areas since the 1970s; indeed, urban areas have shown more dramatic rates of reduced poverty and extreme poverty than rural areas (see Sen and Ali, 2017). Thus, according to the 2010 Household Income and Expenditure Survey (HIES), the proportion of the rural population living in extreme poverty fell from 44 per cent in 1991–2 to 21 per cent in 2010. Over the same time period, the proportion of the urban population living in extreme poverty fell from 24 per cent to 7 per cent. While other chapters in this volume have highlighted the weaknesses of official poverty and extreme poverty calculations (see Sen and Ali, 2017 in particular), there is little doubt that the official figures do not reflect accurately the extent of poverty in urban areas or, by implication, the challenges urban poverty poses. Indeed, it is true that, relatively speaking, our knowledge of urban poverty in Bangladesh lags behind our knowledge of rural poverty, and the amount of reliable and insightful data into urban poverty is significantly less.

Although we have data on the incidence of poverty by geographic region or district, this is not disaggregated for urban poverty. We know from available data that there is considerable variation in the distribution of poverty by geographic region. Thus the incidence of poverty in Kurigram in the north-west of the country is as high as 64 per cent and it is higher than 50 per cent in districts such as Barisal, Shariatpur, Chandpur, Jamalpur, and Mymensingh (BBS et al., 2010). We also know that where the incidence of poverty is high, the incidence of extreme poverty is also likely to be high. By contrast, we find relatively low incidences of extreme poverty in a number of districts, including Kushtia (with only 1 per cent), Noakhali (3 per cent), Chittagong (4 per cent), Meherpur (5 per cent), Naogan (7 per cent), Narail (8 per cent), and Gazipur (8 per cent). The data suggests a correlation between the district level of urbanization and the incidence of poverty and extreme poverty, with lower levels of poverty and extreme poverty being present in areas with higher levels of urbanization. However, this finding needs to be treated with some caution as the correlation between level of urbanization and poverty incidence is –0.2148, and with the extreme poverty incidence it is –0.2599 (our own calculation). Furthermore, some of the districts with lower incidences of poverty do not have high levels of urbanization or GDP. For example, the district of Kushtia, which is in the west, has only 1 per cent of its population living in extreme poverty but also has a low level of urbanization (only 8.19 per cent) and a GDP of US$236 per capita. A similar argument can be made for Meherpur district in the same region and Rangamati district in the south-eastern hill region.

Challenges faced by the extreme poor

In this final section, we turn our attention to some of the key challenges facing the extreme poor in urban settings in Bangladesh. In so doing we are mindful of the argument rehearsed above about the paucity of reliable and insightful data on urban extreme poverty. Consequently, here we rely on insights from urban slum populations, since these have been studied to a relatively greater extent. We are aware that the urban extreme poor do not all live in slums, and, indeed, that some slum-dwellers are not extreme poor. We hope, however, that the reflections below act as vignettes and help stimulate discussion and reflection.

The rights of the urban extreme poor

The Constitution of the People's Republic of Bangladesh allows all its citizens to move freely to any part of the country and to settle anywhere (Article 36 of the Constitution). The extreme poor enjoy this same freedom, and are therefore able to migrate and move around the country without restriction. Indeed, temporary or permanent mobility is a key part of many poor people's livelihood strategies. However, when an individual moves, they need to have a place to stay. Squatting on public or privately owned land is not legal in Bangladesh, even if the extreme poor, particularly destitute rural migrants, often adopt such practices. According to a recent government report, there are some 16,000 pavement-dwellers – or 'floating people', as they are formally defined – in different urban areas of Bangladesh (BBS, 2015). Many street-dwellers live on pavements with their family, including children, sometimes for months and even years. In many ways, these people are among the very poorest in society. Often, they end up being evicted by city authorities or other agencies of the government, and are forced to find alternative dwelling arrangements.[3]

Most of the urban extreme poor are unable to afford even the smallest habitable dwelling. They end up sheltering in privately owned slums or in squatter settlements developed on publicly owned land or, as mentioned above, they live on pavements. According to the 2005 study of slums in urban Bangladesh by the Centre for Urban Studies, 74 per cent of the 4,996 slums in Dhaka were developed on private land and the remainder on government land (CUS, 2006). Some of these settlements are huge and home to many extreme poor. For example, the Korail slum in Dhaka, which is the largest of all squatter settlements and covers an area of approximately 94 acres, accommodates nearly 100,000 people. At least a third of its population can be categorized as extreme poor. According to the NIPORT Urban Health Survey, 70 per cent of households have less than 4.6 square metres of floor space per person or less than 23.2 square metres per household (NIPORT, 2006). In privately owned slums, the proportion of extreme poor is much lower as they have to pay rents that are normally unaffordable. In the squatter settlements developed on publicly owned land, we find a mixture of owners and renters. Here, rents tend to be more affordable for the extreme poor. However, those living in squatter settlements are more vulnerable to eviction.

The Government of Bangladesh has on rare occasions arranged for the post-eviction resettlement of squatters or the extreme urban poor. The largest such resettlement occurred in January 1975, when some 75,000 people were resettled in three fringe locations of Dhaka. All those resettled were given a title of land or permission to stay. The current government has declared that it will provide permanent shelter to the extreme urban poor in the future by offering space in high-rise buildings. The formal private sector has not shown any interest in providing shelter to the extreme poor but it seems willing to enter into partnership with the government if free land and funds are made available on favourable terms. NGOs are yet to be significantly involved in the housing provision for the urban poor.[4]

Article 20 (and also Article 15) of the Bangladesh Constitution guarantees 'work' as a citizen's right. The ability to work and generate income is essential to any livelihood. However, for various reasons (including the absence of political commitment), the government cannot provide employment or work for all, nor can the formal employment sector. The advantage of securing employment in the public or formal private sector is that such employment almost always guarantees an income above the poverty line. In urban centres, the export-oriented garment industries are a major source of formal employment for around nearly 4 million people, most of whom are women and from poor backgrounds. However, in this case, many new starters have incomes below the extreme poverty line. Given the lack of opportunity in the formal sectors, the urban extreme poor turn to the informal sector to secure employment. In Bangladesh, the urban informal sector provides employment to around 60 per cent of the urban poor. In the case of the extreme poor, this figure may rise to around 80 per cent. The urban extreme poor are generally employed as manual transport workers, domestic helpers, unskilled construction workers, petty traders and itinerant vendors, and also as beggars. Their work is insecure and temporary in nature.

Although a right to recreation is not listed among the basic necessities of life in the Constitution, it is universally accepted as essential to the healthy development of children. The lack of playgrounds and open spaces, even in Dhaka, is often lamented; however, the situation for the poor and extreme poor is far worse. In Korail, for example, there is no more than an acre of multipurpose open space. The only recreation spaces are the narrow lanes within slums or the public road nearby. Both options can be dangerous and can cause serious or fatal accidents.

Article 38 of the Constitution ensures citizens the right to form associations for good reasons. The urban poor, particularly the slum-dwellers, have been able to organize some of their own associations and collective forums. Examples include Nagor Doridro Bastibashir Unnyan Songstha (NDBUS) or Association for Protecting the Rights of the Urban Poor), which was formed in 2010 with support of the Centre for Urban Studies (CUS) and URBIS, a US-based NGO. NDBUS has supported various initiatives to help safeguard the interests of its over 1 million members. However, although there are various urban associations with poor and extreme poor members, in reality the opportunity to participate in urban decision-making is highly restricted. The poor and extreme poor are very rarely consulted about development projects or service provision.

Access to urban services

The quality of urban life and living depends very much on access to transportation. Desirable systems of transportation depend on availability, affordability, speed, safety, and comfort. While citizens of small towns in Bangladesh travel mostly on foot or by manual transport such as bicycles and rickshaws, and by three- or four-wheeled shared autos, those in large cities and the megacity Dhaka depend on a wider variety of transport options, including intra-city buses, auto-rickshaws, and private cars. The recent Dhaka Structure Plan (2016–35) shows that 19.8 per cent of all trips in Dhaka are made by walking, 38.3 per cent by rickshaw, 30.0 per cent by bus, and the rest by auto-rickshaw (6.7 per cent) and private cars (5.0 per cent). The extreme poor usually walk in order to move around, and sometimes use public buses or the *tempo*, which squeezes in 12 to 14 people in a space meant for eight (RAJUK, 2015). Walking on a Dhaka street is neither safe nor comfortable. The few pavements that do exist are mostly occupied by vendors and hawkers or are rendered unusable due to poor maintenance. The urban extreme poor are also major providers of transport services to the urban middle class. In Dhaka city alone, there are more than 600,000 rickshaws (JICA and DTCA, 2015), which are pedalled by around 1 million rickshaw pullers, half of whom are extreme poor.

For survival and good health, one needs access to hygienic sanitation and safe drinking water. For the urban extreme poor who live either on pavements or in the highly congested squatter settlements or in private slums, hygienic sanitation is not easily available. The 2014 EEP/Shiree baseline report quoted by Sen and Ali (2015) shows that 14 per cent of urban extreme poor households resorted to open defecation, whereas the CUS 2005 survey of slums showed that over 60 per cent of households used pit latrines, hanging latrines, or open defecation, while only 40 per cent had access to septic tank or water-sealed latrines. On the other hand, it seems that the urban extreme poor's access to drinking water is much better. Almost 100 per cent of slum-dwellers (including the extreme poor) have access to drinking water from sources such as piped water or tube wells (NIPORT, 2006). Around 60 per cent of slum-dwellers in Dhaka also have access to gas for cooking. This, however, seems to be an anomaly because, in other cities and municipalities, the level of access to gas for slum-dwellers ranges from only 6 per cent to 24 per cent (ibid.). There seems to be a greater convergence in relation to access to electricity, with around 92 per cent of the urban poor in Dhaka and around 82 per cent of the urban poor in district municipalities enjoying access (ibid.). However, these relatively high figures mask the fact that in many squatter settlements access to electricity is ensured through informal means, with users paying intermediaries to have electrical lines illegally connected to their residences.

In terms of waste and garbage disposal within slums, nearly 60 per cent of households deposit their garbage in open spaces and only around 22 per cent of households have their garbage collected (ibid.).

Bangladesh has one of the lowest levels of literacy in Asia. In the 2011 census only 65 per cent of the population aged seven and above were found to be literate (meaning that they can read or write simple sentences and are capable of basic arithmetic). In urban areas, the rate of literacy was somewhat higher than in rural areas. In slum communities, the literacy rate was almost uniform in all cities at around 70 per cent (NIPORT, 2006). Slum children are often able to access government primary schools, madrasas,[5] or schools run by NGOs. These are normally located within or close to the slums. However, many extreme poor children in Dhaka's slums are forced to discontinue their studies at primary school level because they are expected to help bring income into the household.

The 2006 *Urban Health Survey* report by NIPORT contains very rich data about health-related issues in urban slum and non-slum households. It reports that between 74 per cent and 87 per cent of females from different age groups in slums claim to have had no 'health-related functional difficulty' in the four weeks preceding the survey; in the case of males, between 68 per cent and 81 per cent made the same claim (NIPORT, 2006). The same report provides data on the active working-age group (15–59 years of age), showing that 16.4 per cent to 19.2 per cent of urban poor women and 8.7 per cent to 11.8 per cent of males claimed to be unhealthy. Not surprisingly, those living in slums report higher levels of ill health and more cases of serious illnesses than their non-slum counterparts.

Conclusion

During the four decades since its independence, Bangladesh has experienced rapid urbanization and a phenomenal growth of the urban population. It has also achieved remarkable progress in economic development and this has helped support efforts to reduce poverty in the country. The dynamics of urban poverty and extreme poverty are different from those found in rural contexts. And although much of the poverty reduction efforts have been targeted at rural communities, the pace of poverty reduction has been greater in urban centres. The incidence of extreme poverty in urban areas decreased drastically from 21.3 per cent in 1991 to only 7.7 per cent in 2010. However, this still means that there are almost 3 million extreme poor living in urban centres. This is a matter of concern for policymakers.

Bangladesh faces the enormous challenge of managing urban growth, urban expansion, and urban poverty. The task of facing such a challenge demands vision, wise policy thinking, intelligent long-, medium-, and short-term planning, skilful implementation, efficient management, and participatory democratic governance. In less than four decades from now, Bangladesh will be an urbanized country in demographic statistical terms, but it is not clear how this 'urban profile' will look. Political and cultural realities, the threat of climate change impacts, and the crisis of governance at the national as well as the urban local level suggest high levels of insecurity and instability in the future. And yet there is a silver lining: the inclusion of urban extreme poverty and poverty reduction in the government's recent Five Year Plan means that the urban question is now centre stage in policy terms. This rhetorical commitment now needs to be followed up with impactful action.

Notes

1. These districts are Barisal, Comilla, Shariatpur, Chandpur, Barguna, Dhaka, Perojpur, and Brahmanbaria. Other districts that act as sources of rural-to-urban migration are Mymensing, Kishoreganj, Bhola, Comilla, Putuakhali, Madaripur, Jamalpur, Netrokona, Sherpur, Tangail, Barguna, Faridpur, Gaibandha, and Jhalokati.
2. Bangladesh is divided into seven divisions, 64 districts, and 483 sub-districts or *upazilas*.
3. Although there is an intuitive appeal to the argument that street-dwellers are among the poorest in society, recent work in Bangladesh reveals a far more complicated and sophisticated understanding of their lives and livelihoods (Jackman, forthcoming).
4. The only exception is an NGO called ARBAN which has built 40 flats for its beneficiary microcredit members in Dhaka. There are plans to build an additional 100 flats, and to use 60 per cent of these to house its poor members.
5. Madrasas are Islamic religious schools. In Bangladesh there are two main types: *alia* and *qawmi* madrasas. The former are controlled by government and offer a broad curriculum while the latter are owned by the private sector and tend to focus on subjects pertaining to Islamic knowledge.

References

ADB (2010) *City Cluster Economic Development: Bangladesh Study*, Manila, Asian Development Bank (ADB).

BBS (2014) *Bangladesh Population and Housing Census 2011: National Report. Volume 3: Urban Area Report*, Dhaka: Bangladesh Bureau of Statistics (BBS), Statistics and Informatics Division (SID), Ministry of Planning, Government of Bangladesh.

BBS (2015) *Preliminary Report on the Census of Slum Areas and Floating Population 2014*, Dhaka: Bangladesh Bureau of Statistics (BBS), Ministry of Planning, Government of Bangladesh.

BBS, WFP, and WB (2010) *Poverty Maps of Bangladesh*, Dhaka: Bangladesh Bureau of Statistics (BBS), United Nations World Food Programme (WFP) and World Bank (WB).

CUS (2006) *Slums of Urban Bangladesh: Mapping and Census, 2005*, Dhaka: Centre for Urban Studies (CUS).

GoB (2011) *Sixth Five Year Plan FY2011–FY2015: Accelerating Growth and Reducing Poverty*, Dhaka: General Economics Division, Planning Commission, Government of Bangladesh (GoB).

Islam, N. and Saleheen, M.U. (2006) *Rural–Urban Linkage and Migration Issue in Bangladesh. A Secondary Literature Study*, Dhaka: Centre for Urban Studies (CUS).

Jackman, D. (forthcoming) 'Living in the shade of others: order, opportunities and violence in Dhaka City', PhD thesis, University of Bath.

JICA and DTCA (2015) *The Project on the Revision and Updating of the Strategic Transport Plan for Dhaka. Urban Transport Policy (Draft)*, Dhaka: Almec Corporation, Oriental Consultants Global and Katahira & Engineers International for Japan International Cooperation Agency (JICA) and Dhaka Transport Coordination Authority (DTCA).

Mathur, O.P., Islam, N., Samanta, D. and Shafi, S.A. (2013) *Sustainable Urbanization in Bangladesh: Delving into the Urbanization-Growth-Poverty Interlinkages*, Dhaka: Centre for Urban Studies (CUS).

NIPORT (2006) *Bangladesh Urban Health Survey 2006*, Dhaka: National Institute of Population Research and Training (NIPORT), Ministry of Health and Family Welfare, Associates for Community and Population Research (ACPR).

RAJUK (2015) *Draft Dhaka Structure Plan (2016–2035)*, Dhaka: Rajdhani Unnayan Kartipakkha (RAJUK).

Sen, B. and Ali, Z. (2015) *Ending Extreme Poverty in Bangladesh during the Seventh Five Year Plan: Trends, Drivers and Polices*, Background Paper, Seventh Five Year Plan, Dhaka: Planning Commission, Government of Bangladesh.

Sen, B. and Ali, Z. (2017) 'Ending extreme poverty in Bangladesh: trends, drivers, and policies', in J. Devine, G. Wood, Z. Ali, and S. Alam (eds), *Extreme Poverty, Growth, and Inequality in Bangladesh*, Rugby: Practical Action Publishing.

UGC (2015) *41st Annual Report 2014* (in Bangla), Dhaka: University Grants Commission of Bangladesh.

About the author

Nazrul Islam is a retired Professor of Geography at the University of Dhaka, with a long-established reputation as a leading scholar on urban Bangladesh. Throughout his academic career, Professor Islam has served on numerous government committees. He was Chairman of the University Grants Commission of Bangladesh. He is currently the Honorary Chairman of the Centre for Urban Studies (CUS) in Dhaka and an Expert Member of Habitat III.

CHAPTER 9

Reforming the social security system for poverty reduction

Sadiq Ahmed

The social security system of Bangladesh is an important element of the government's strategy to fight poverty. In its current state, however, the system is severely limited in its impact, particularly for the extreme poor. Budgetary resource constraints have led to a reduction in the GDP share of public spending on social protection since 2011, while leakage and overlap across ministries remain a problem. The needs of the country are also changing due to significant demographic, economic, and social transformations. There is thus an urgent need to reform the social security system of Bangladesh. This chapter provides an analysis of possible ways forward, exploring how reforms can lead to improved and more comprehensive measures for poverty reduction.

Keywords: social protection, demographic change, reform, lifecycle, vulnerability

Introduction

Bangladesh has made impressive progress in reducing poverty. Nevertheless, there is a substantial population that remains exposed to poverty, including those who live under the poverty line[1] and those who are just above the poverty line. Evidence shows that the poor and near-poor groups cannot cope with all the downside risks and shocks they face with their own resources. Consequently, the government has initiated various social safety net programmes to help the poor and near-poor address the risks and shocks that affect their well-being.

Successive Household Income and Expenditure Surveys (HIES) suggest that the coverage of these programmes has increased over the years but that a large proportion of poor and vulnerable households are not able to access them. The same surveys show that the average benefit of safety net programmes is low and falling in real terms, there is considerable leakage of allocated funds, and a substantial percentage of beneficiary households are non-poor.

The underlying reasons for the low poverty impact of safety net programmes are numerous. The programmes have mainly emerged in a somewhat ad hoc fashion to meet the needs of an ongoing crisis resulting from exogenous shocks such as natural disasters or in response to donor initiatives. As a result,

http://dx.doi.org/10.3362/9781780449463.009

there is a high number of programmes, which often overlap with each other and are implemented by different ministries and implementation agencies. Moreover, all of the programmes have low budget allocations and are poorly evaluated and monitored, with progress being measured mainly in terms of the amount of money disbursed rather than the results achieved.

Given that the programmes are initiated in an ad hoc and reactive manner, they are not linked to any strategic policy framework, such as the commonly used lifecycle framework, and they are not sensitive to emerging future needs that might result from demographic changes. We know that Bangladesh is moving away from a primarily agrarian economy towards a more urban-based manufacturing and modern service economy. As it does so, however, the underlying social and economic risks faced by the poor and near-poor are changing. These changes require a broadening of the safety net approach to a more inclusive concept of a social security strategy that supports recipients of the schemes to engage in the labour market as well as in social insurance schemes. This vision of social security fits in much more cogently with the needs of a modern urban-based economy and aligns well with a lifecycle framework. The main objective of this chapter is therefore to identify the core elements of what might constitute a reformed national social security strategy capable of responding better to the current and future needs of poverty reduction and equity in Bangladesh.

Progress with poverty reduction, 2000–15

Bangladesh has seen a rapid decline in the rate of poverty measured in terms of the percentage of the population below the upper poverty line (UPL) (see Sen and Ali, 2017 for a fuller discussion of poverty reduction in Bangladesh). Thus the incidence of poverty declined from around 60 per cent in 1983–4 to 31.5 per cent in 2010 (BBS, 2011). Similarly, the number of extreme poor, defined as the population below the lower poverty line (LPL), fell from 40 per cent to 17.6 per cent over the same period. Projections based on the growth in gross domestic product (GDP) and poverty elasticity suggest that the reduction in poverty and extreme poverty has continued over the 2010–15 period.

Poverty reduction has declined substantially in both rural and urban areas and also across the main regions of the country (Ahmed, 2015). Along with the reduction in poverty, considerable progress has been made in enhancing human development. However, despite these achievements, Bangladesh faces considerable challenges in the future and these have implications for the country's future poverty reduction strategy as well as for decisions regarding its social security system (SSS). It is worth reiterating the scale of some of these challenges.

First, notwithstanding past progress, some 25 per cent of the population (42 million) in 2015 still lived below the poverty line. The estimated proportion of extreme poor is 12.6 per cent (21 million people).

Second, and very importantly, a sizeable population is consuming barely above the UPL. For example, according to 2010 HIES data, an additional

18.6 per cent of the population was consuming less than 1.25 times the UPL (BBS, 2011). This population is highly vulnerable: a shock such as a major illness or a natural calamity, for example, could easily see a substantial part of this population fall into poverty.

Third, the disaggregation of the poverty profile by location shows substantial variations. The incidence of poverty and extreme poverty is much higher in rural areas than in urban areas, and also much higher in the country's poorest district (Rangpur) compared with other regions. These geographic variations underscore the need to further refine the notion of extreme poverty to understand the impact of important axes of difference such as gender, age, education, assets, and employment. Only by disaggregating in this way are we able to design appropriate poverty reduction policy responses. The relevance of this is illustrated by the following findings from HIES 2010 (see also Khondker, 2014).

- At 41.7 per cent, the poverty rates in households with children aged 0–4 years are much higher than national poverty rates. When the near-poor are included, around 57 per cent of households with children aged 0–4 years can be classified as poor or vulnerable to poverty.
- The poverty rate of households with disabled members is similar to the national poverty rate (31.5 per cent), but the poverty rate of households with a severely disabled member is higher (34.7 per cent), suggesting that disability places a greater burden on households. Furthermore, if a working-age adult is disabled, the poverty rate for this group reaches almost 40 per cent.
- Some 28.2 per cent of people aged over 60 are found below the poverty line. However, when the vulnerable population is considered (1.25 × UPL), there is a substantial increase in the proportion of older people considered poor or at risk of falling into poverty.

Finally, there is growing evidence that, as a result of transformations to the economy and society, traditional forms of care for vulnerable individuals and groups are breaking down. This is common in all countries as a result of demographic changes and processes such as urbanization and migration; its impact in Bangladesh, however, is particularly relevant for discussions on social protection and welfare support.

Determinants of poverty

There are numerous studies that identify different determinants of poverty in Bangladesh. Recently, the World Bank (2013) produced a comprehensive report that focused on three key and interconnected factors: labour income, the demographic dividend, and international remittances.

Growth in employment, labour productivity, and real wages are the most important factors for sustainable reductions in poverty. Rapid GDP growth, expanding by an average of 6 per cent per annum over the 2000-10 period, has provided the main backbone for the reduction in total and extreme poverty in Bangladesh. GDP growth was associated with noticeable structural transformations that saw rapid growth in the share of industry and manufacturing and a commensurate reduction in the share of agriculture. The employment structure also changed as the employment share of industry and services expanded and that of agriculture fell (Ahmed, 2013). These trends continued during the 2010–15 period.

The slow but steady transformation of the rural economy reflects ongoing changes in production and employment structures, and the effects of the rapid growth of remittances and microcredit in the rural economy. Evidence shows that agriculture is no longer the dominant source of income in rural areas (Ahmed, 2014), and that the expansion of non-farm rural enterprises and service activities has opened up new sources of income and employment. The growth of income from non-farm sources and the rapid inflow of foreign remittances have supported the increase in demand for a range of activities in construction, housing, trade, transport, schooling, health, and other services. The expansion of the ICT network and related services along with the growth of rural electricity and rural roads have also helped reduce transaction costs between rural and urban economies, thereby facilitating better trade and higher prices for the products of the rural economy.

The growth in employment – along with increases in labour productivity, especially in agriculture – has supported rapid growth in real wages in agriculture throughout the country. Agricultural workers tend to be among the poorest, and an increase in productivity and real wages is the most sustainable way of securing a reduction in extreme poverty. Evidence shows that agricultural wages shot up considerably over the 2010–14 period, with annual increases ranging from 5.0 per cent to 14.3 per cent (Ahmed, 2014). Data also indicates that there has been a substantial narrowing of the gender gap in agricultural real wages. The ratio of female to male wage rates has narrowed from 73 per cent in 2010 to 78 per cent in 2014. This is yet another indication of a tightening of the agricultural labour market. Similarly, the spatial wage differential has also narrowed. Traditionally, the district of Rangpur has the highest level of rural poverty and lowest daily agricultural wages: the wage gap between Rangpur and the national average was as high as 30 per cent in 2010. This gap has progressively narrowed; in 2014 it stood at 17 per cent (ibid.).

Remittance inflows from migrant workers also grew rapidly between 2000 and 2015, and some 60 per cent of these remittances accrue to the rural economy. Remittances have lowered poverty in a number of ways. First, the migration of rural workers to international work destinations has helped tighten the rural labour market, thereby supporting the growth of real wages. Second, income transfers from remittances have directly supported poverty reduction by increasing the income and consumption of the rural poor. Third, and very importantly, the massive inflow of remittance income into the rural economy has supported the expansion of housing, construction, trade, and other services. These in turn have provided a diversified employment base for rural workers and increased their income base.

Many rural and urban poor are self-employed, and access to credit is an important determinant of income opportunities for these people. Additionally, access to credit allows a smoothing of consumption that supports people, especially in times of crisis. Bangladesh is famous globally for pioneering the growth of the microcredit industry and continues to develop innovative services. New financial instruments based on ICT (mobile banking), for example, are slowly changing the access of the poor and extreme poor to financial services in both rural and urban areas.

Current social security programmes in Bangladesh

The evolution of social security programmes

Bangladesh has a long history of formal social safety net programmes, which has shaped the nature of the current SSS. At the time of independence in 1971, the main social security scheme in place was the government pension. It was complemented by a provident fund that acted as a savings vehicle for government and formal private sector employees, providing them with a lump sum amount on retirement. In response to the 1974 famine and the floods of the 1980s, new schemes were developed for poorer families. These were mainly public works and other food aid programmes, which relied on foreign development assistance. In the 1990s, the government began to introduce a range of schemes that addressed risks across the lifecycle, such as school stipend programmes and allowances for the elderly, people with disabilities, and widows. At the same time, throughout the 1990s, there were significant donor investments in various NGO programmes that provided a range of social services, including social protection.

There has also been a gradual increase in the proportion of transfers provided as cash rather than as food, with cash mainly provided through lifecycle programmes. By the mid-2000s, foreign food aid had been mostly withdrawn and had been replaced by food transfers funded from taxation. This was accompanied by an important increase in small schemes implemented by both NGOs and the government that included some element of social security. Reflecting the government's commitment to social security provision, budgetary allocations grew in absolute terms and as a share of GDP. Thus the allocation for social security programmes (SSPs) increased from 1.3 per cent of GDP in 1998 to 2.5 per cent in 2011. However, since then, this figure has declined; in 2015, SSP spending stood at 1.7 per cent of GDP. Although this level of funding is modest by international standards, when measured against the government's tight budget situation it represents a significant commitment accounting for 10 per cent of total government spending.

Bangladesh's current SSS is complex: there are 95 programmes under the system that are financed through the budget and administered by as many as 30 line ministries or implementing agencies. There is no formal mechanism for sharing information among these implementing ministries or agencies.

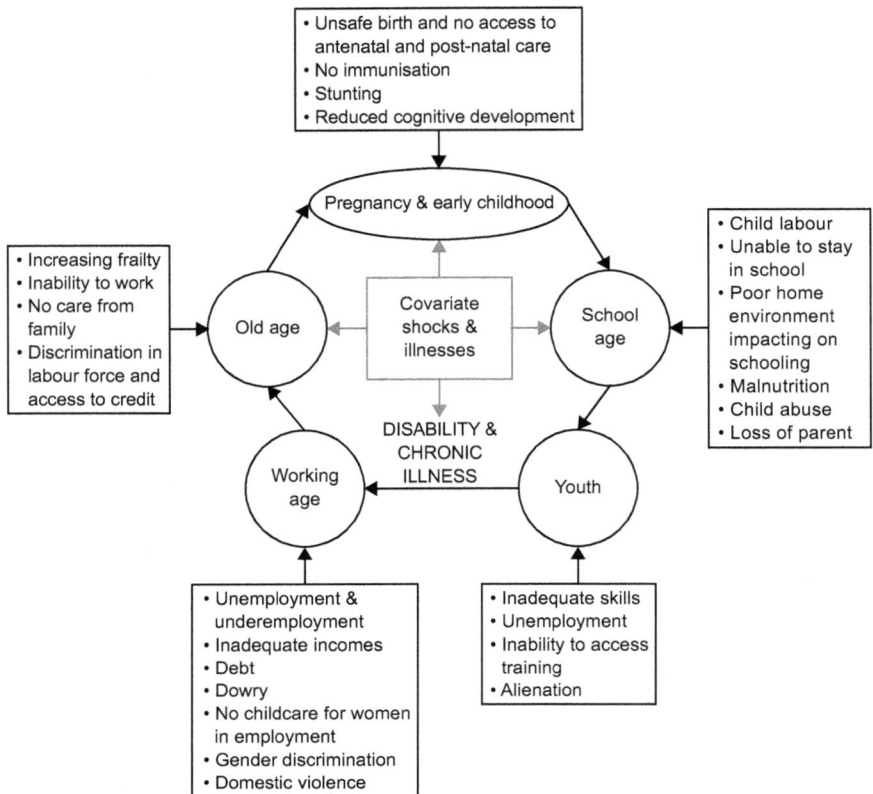

Figure 9.1 Lifecycle risks
Source: Adapted from Kidds et al. (2014).

As a result, there are serious overlaps between the various programmes in terms of programme content and coverage. Furthermore, about 58 per cent of programmes have annual budgets of less than 500 m (US$6.3 m) Bangladeshi Taka (BDT) and collectively they account for only 4 per cent of the government's total social security spending (2013 figures). On the other hand, the top 10 programmes account for 69 per cent of the total SSP budget. Programmes with small budgets tend to be less efficient and struggle to make lasting changes in the lives of their beneficiaries.

A strategic approach to looking at the structure of the current portfolio of programmes is to classify them in the context of a lifecycle framework. The underlying rationale of this framework is that poor and vulnerable people face shocks and challenges at different stages of the lifecycle (Figure 9.1). If risks are not addressed in time, they can have lifelong negative impacts. For example, if the special healthcare needs of a mother during pregnancy or delivery or childcare needs during infancy (age 0–2) are not properly addressed, they can easily jeopardize the infant's well-being for their entire life.

Similarly, vulnerabilities faced by the elderly can be much more challenging and are different from those faced by a poor person during the working-age cycle. An SSS that recognizes these differences in risk at different stages of the lifecycle and seeks to address them is likely to provide a more effective support system.

Many existing social programmes in Bangladesh align well with the lifecycle framework but there are also major concerns and weaknesses. The following are often cited: much of the social security budget is spent on government pensions and general-purpose food distribution schemes; programmes to mitigate risks in pregnancy and early childhood and those relating to disability are limited in both beneficiary coverage and financing; the average benefit of the old-age allowance programme (excluding the government pension) is very low and many poor older people are excluded; the disability benefits and vulnerable women's programmes suffer from low coverage and low average benefits. We could cite many other examples.

The impact of social security programmes on poverty

At the national level, the impact of SSP spending can be assessed through three key indicators: the reduction of hunger, the impact on poverty, and the impact in lowering the depth of poverty.

One major achievement of Bangladesh, especially since the famine of 1974, is its sharp reduction in the incidence of hunger-based poverty. The 2013 report on progress against the millennium development goals shows that the percentage of those suffering from hunger fell from 34.6 per cent in 1990 to 16.8 per cent in 2012 (GoB, 2014). In terms of absolute numbers, this represents a fall from 37 million people to 25 million. A combination of good agricultural development, especially in the area of food grain production, along with a strong food security focus in the social security strategy contributed to this achievement.

The impact of SSPs on poverty reduction is shown in Table 9.1. The simulation results are based on the HIES 2010 data that reports on 30 of the 95 SSPs. In the absence of SSP spending, the data indicates that the poverty rate would have been about 33 per cent, which is 1.5 percentage points higher than the recorded

Table 9.1 Poverty impact of current SSP spending

Simulations	Poverty rate (headcount index)	Depth of poverty	Poverty gap
HIES 2010 outcome	31.5	6.5	21.0
Outcome without SSP	33.0	7.4	22.5
Outcome with SSP benefits concentrated on the extreme poor	32.0	5.8	18.2
Outcome with SSP benefits targeted to the poor	29.0	6.0	20.7

Source: HIES 2010 and simulations.

level. The depth of poverty would also have been higher. If perfect targeting to the extreme poor were possible, it would have lifted many from extreme poverty, but the transfer amount would not have been adequate to lift them over the UPL. With perfect targeting to the poor group based on the UPL, the incidence of poverty would have been reduced to 29 per cent, which is 2.5 percentage points better than the final reported level.

These simulations are indicative of the inefficiencies present in the way benefits of SSPs are currently distributed. While perfect targeting may not be a practicable proposition, the performance gap in terms of poverty reduction impact is significant enough to suggest that a more efficient system is needed. With improved programme design and better implementation, the poverty impact of SSPs would be significantly stronger.

An important question is how much of the poor and vulnerable population is covered by social security provisions. Simulations again based on the 2010 HIES indicate that 57 per cent of the extreme poor and 66 per cent of poor households did not have access to any SSPs. If the target is broadened to include vulnerable populations (i.e. the near-poor), the excluded share of households increases to 69 per cent. When this result is considered alongside the fact that most of the large SSPs have low average benefits anyway, it is clear that the future challenges for the social security agenda are substantial.

Another important policy consideration concerns the geographical coverage or reach of the SSPs. The 2010 HIES shows that 30.12 per cent of rural households were covered by different SSPs, compared with only 9.42 per cent of urban households. The rural–urban gap holds for all divisions. However, one positive aspect of the spatial dimension is that the coverage of SSPs is higher in the poorer divisions of Rangpur, Barisal, and Khulna than it is in better-off divisions such as Dhaka, Chittagong, and Sylhet.

Issues and challenges for social security reform

The brief review above of the present SSS suggests a number of important issues and challenges that will need to be addressed in any future reform. These include the following:

- SSPs need to be consolidated into a smaller number of programmes and be allocated higher budgets. Furthermore, they should be implemented by fewer agencies and mechanisms to support greater coordination across agencies. These measures alone would immediately yield significant efficiency gains by lowering administrative costs and reducing leakages.
- Programmes for addressing pregnancy, early childhood, and old-age risks in particular have low coverage and low levels of funding. Similarly, programmes for addressing disability challenges are very small. This means that the lifecycle approach, highlighted above, has serious gaps.

- The ageing population in Bangladesh is gradually increasing and many traditional care practices are either breaking down or are not reliable. The country's population is also migrating much more from rural areas to urban ones, and the growth of cities continues unabated. The SSS needs reforming if it is to address these changes.
- The SSS is currently dominated by programmes relating to food security and rural employment in terms of both beneficiary participation and funding. Evidence suggests that the incidence of hunger and food poverty is decreasing while the labour market in agriculture is tightening, as reflected in growing agricultural real wages. In view of these changes, the nature of poverty and the poverty risk profile are also changing. This requires a careful review of the relevance and adequacy of the current SSPs.
- Many of the SSPs focus on addressing risks faced by the rural poor. Any future SSS needs to position itself so that it can engage directly with the evolving economic transformation in Bangladesh in which both the GDP and employment shares of the rural economy are declining and both the urban economy and the size of the urban population are growing. The lack of urban focus in the current SSPs indicates a social security strategy that is inadequate if not outdated.
- Although the employment market is still dominated by informal employment, the share of organized manufacturing and services is growing. In 2015, Bangladesh crossed the World Bank-defined income threshold of a low-income economy. As the economy grows further and the share of modern manufacturing and organized services grows, the SSS will have to change dramatically. An SSS agenda for a middle-income economy differs vastly from that of a low-income country.
- The very low coverage of the poor and vulnerable suggests that, even with efficiency improvements in the use of funds, the current level of funding will not be adequate for the social security needs of a middle-income country. This is especially true when we consider that the current level of funding includes 0.5 per cent of GDP set aside for civil service pensions, which, of course, do not benefit the poor.
- The simulations above indicate that there is significant scope to improve the effectiveness of the present SSS in terms of poverty impact. Ineffectiveness is a widely held criticism of the current suite of SSPs. A careful approach to programme design and beneficiary selection will therefore be an important challenge for any future national SSS.
- A major shortcoming of the present SSS is the absence of a robust and transparent monitoring and evaluation (M&E) system. In fact, the lack of a results-based M&E system is in part the reason why Bangladesh has launched and retained such a large number of programmes. A results-based M&E can play an important role in helping the government strengthen and improve its SSS, and in providing evidence that can inform decisions about programme retention or closure.

Proposed reform strategy for social security[2]

The proposed reforms build on the past rich experience of Bangladesh and seek to streamline and strengthen the existing safety net programmes with a view to better addressing the lifecycle risks faced by the poor and vulnerable, and achieving better results for the money spent. They also broaden the scope of social security from the narrow safety net concept to include employment policies and social insurance in order to address the emerging needs of a middle-income Bangladesh in 2016 and beyond. By broadening the scope and coverage and by improving programme design, the reformed SSS will help lower income inequality and contribute to higher growth by strengthening human development. The long-term objective should be to move towards building an SSS that is available to all Bangladeshis who are in need of support, provides them with a guaranteed minimum income, and also includes a comprehensive safety net for those who suffer shocks and crises that may push them into poverty. For the medium term, the aim should be to build the foundations of a progressive and inclusive system. This should focus on expanding core schemes to the extreme poor and to the most vulnerable in society, including mothers and their children, the youth, the elderly, and people with disabilities. Programme delivery could be improved by using advanced management systems, and services should be extended to urban areas. A social insurance system could be initiated to enable people to invest in their own security.

Programme consolidation along the lifecycle risks

The SSS needs to be reformed around a lifecycle approach by consolidating programmes in a small number of priority schemes. The aim is to identify high-priority schemes and make the system more inclusive by incorporating a higher proportion of poor and vulnerable people. This can be achieved by gradually increasing the coverage of priority schemes and ensuring that selection processes give priority to the inclusion of poor and vulnerable families. The benefits should be non-discriminatory and available to all poor and vulnerable people who satisfy the criteria relating to lifecycle or disability. The consolidated five core lifecycle programmes are described below. These five programmes are based on the major lifecycle risks faced in Bangladesh. The value of benefits is derived by comparing benefits in countries at similar income levels (Kidds et al., 2014). These values are indicative and are used to estimate cost and affordability. To prevent the value of transfers from falling, all cash transfers provided through the lifecycle-based core schemes below should be indexed to inflation.

Programmes for children

The strategy advocates two core programmes for children:

- A child grant of BDT800 per month for children of poor and vulnerable families up to the age of four. This could be limited to a maximum of two children per family to avoid incentives for larger families.

- A school stipend of BDT240 per month for all children from poor and vulnerable households going to primary and secondary school.

Children will also have access to the disability benefit, the school meals programme, the orphans programme, and legal provision to ensure that abandoned children receive financial support from the responsible parent.

- Supply-side interventions relating to immunization, childcare, health and nutrition, water supply and sanitation outreach should be strengthened.

Programmes for the working age

The proposed strategy consists of the following:

- Strengthening education and training programmes to motivate the youth to complete education, and to enable the working youth and the older workforce to acquire required skills.
- Implementing a strengthened workfare programme for the unemployed poor. The government should build on the ongoing reforms of the workfare programmes by converting food-based programmes into cash-based approaches and consolidating these fragmented schemes into one workfare programme within the employment generation programme for the poor.
- Introducing legislation to provide unemployment, sickness, maternity, and accident insurance as a part of the National Social Insurance Scheme (NSIS), explained in more detail below.
- Implementing a programme of financial support to vulnerable women and facilitating their participation in the labour market. Under the strategy, women would be entitled to the citizen's pension and the disability benefit if applicable. Additionally, in recognition of the special difficulties faced by vulnerable working-age women, the strategy advocates a consolidated income transfer under the reformed Vulnerable Women's Benefit, which would provide BDT800 per month to this group.
- Expanding the Maternal Health Voucher Scheme administered by the Ministry of Health and Family Welfare and a range of policy measures to facilitate the entry of women into the labour market. These include the continuation of training provided under the ongoing Vulnerable Group Development scheme, the provision of childcare facilities in all government offices and in the formal private sector, as well as maternity insurance through the NSIS.

Comprehensive pension system for the elderly

This reform programme has four components:

- The citizen's pension at the rate of BDT800 per month for citizens who are aged 60 years and above and belong to the poor and vulnerable population.

- Based on political economy considerations, the government service pension should continue with no changes at this time.
- An NSIS that makes it obligatory for all private enterprises in the formal sector to offer a contributory pensions programme for all employees. The NSIS should provide pensions as well as address other contingencies such as disability, sickness, unemployment, and maternity.
- A review of options to facilitate the development of private voluntary pensions (PVPs), which would be open to all citizens irrespective of occupation or formality of employment.

The citizen's pension and the government service pension should be funded through the government's budget, while the NSIS and the PVP should be funded through employer and employee contributions.

Programmes for people with disabilities

The proposed support strategy for the disabled consists of two elements:

- A disability benefit of BDT800 per month for children suffering from disability.
- A disability benefit of BDT800 per month for working-age people suffering from disability.

Selection and targeting challenges

Since the safety nets will be financed through the national budget and resources are limited, it is imperative that the selection criteria ensure that resources are channelled to the poor and vulnerable groups. How can this be achieved? The strategy proposes a combination of income and other criteria to reflect the risks faced by the poor and vulnerable population at different stages of the lifecycle. The application of the income criteria presents a major challenge since reliable income data is not available. As a substitute, a proxy means test (PMT) is often used, even if it is well known that the test suffers from significant exclusion errors. The selection challenge is illustrated in Figure 9.2, which shows the cumulative per capita consumption distribution in Bangladesh based on the 2010 HIES. The figure clearly indicates that the consumption distribution curve (note that the y axis reports on Taka per month) is heavily concentrated around the Bangladesh National Poverty Line (BNPL). Thus, in 2010, 80 per cent of the population consumed 2 times below the poverty line, close to 70 per cent consumed less than 1.5 times the poverty line, and 50 per cent of the population consumed less than 1.25 times the poverty line. This suggests that the size of the population that is both poor and vulnerable on income grounds is large. By focusing on only the poor, therefore, social safety net programmes risk missing the vulnerable population that is concentrated around the poverty line and risks falling below that line due to shocks.

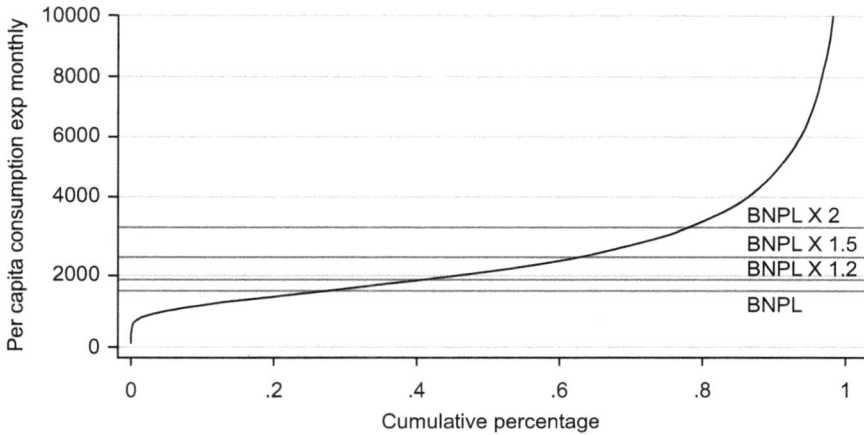

Figure 9.2 Cumulative distribution of per capita consumption
Source: HIES 2010.

A related and important question is how successfully a PMT will identify the poor. Since the PMT methodology is based on projecting income based on measurable proxy variables, there are understandably large prediction errors resulting from, inter alia, sampling and measurement errors. These errors include both exclusion errors (excluding the poor) and inclusion errors (including the non-poor). Empirical work shows that these errors are large in cases of relatively small coverage but that they fall in cases of relatively higher coverage. Thus, using a somewhat higher cut-off point for determining income eligibility will considerably reduce the exclusion risk, thereby including many more poor people. Consequently, a good strategy would adopt an income cut-off point of 1.25 times the poverty line. This is a relatively small increase in the income cut-off that will significantly reduce exclusion risk and also ensure that highly vulnerable populations are included in safety net programmes. It is, of course, well established that the income criterion is but one variable, and arguably an imperfect one. Other criteria such as gender, age, physical disability, and marital status therefore need to be used to prioritize and narrow the actual recipients of transfer payments.

Qualifying the agenda

The agenda outlined above needs to be complemented with a number of qualifying considerations, which are rehearsed below.

First, without health financing reforms and adequate supply-side interventions in health, education, water supply, and sanitation, cash transfers from the lifecycle schemes alone will not achieve the desired results. The Government of Bangladesh has already adopted a long-term comprehensive health financing reform strategy, which needs to be fully implemented.

Additionally, efforts to strengthen the provision of healthcare, nutrition, water supply and sanitation, and education will have to continue.

Second, the Government of Bangladesh should gradually convert all food-based transfer programmes that are part of SSPs into cash transfers. The strategy proposes that all workfare-based food programmes should be converted into one consolidated cash-based workfare programme under the World Bank-supported Employment Guarantee Programme for the Poorest. The transfer of food during disasters will continue as a disaster management response under the management of the Ministry of Disaster Management and Relief. The only food programme that might continue under the social security framework is the Open Market Sales (OMS) managed by the Ministry of Food. However, the scope of the OMS could be expanded as necessary to tackle hunger and food affordability issues as appropriate. The OMS should remain self-targeted as it is at present.

Third, certain existing SSPs should be strengthened, including the government's programmes to address climate change and disaster prevention, agricultural research, embankment and reforestation programmes, and disaster preparedness. The value of these programmes is that they are already making important inroads into lowering the vulnerability of the population to climate change and natural disasters. Longer-term programmes such as the planned Delta Plan can be of further benefit in this regard.[3] In the case of freedom fighters, this group has social security priority from a political economy point of view. As such, the ongoing schemes to support the freedom fighters and their families should continue under a consolidated freedom fighters' benefit programme.

Fourth, programmes need to reach both the urban population and socially excluded groups. At present, the focus of safety net schemes is the rural poor. There is an important need to bring more of the poor and vulnerable population living in urban areas under the umbrella of social security. Accordingly, steps should be taken to ensure that the priority social security schemes for the elderly, children, vulnerable women, and people with disabilities are expanded so that urban residents have equal access. It is also important to note that new proposals to modernize the SSS, such as the childcare proposals and the NSIS, will initially benefit mostly urban residents owing to the location of formal economic activities. In such cases, special efforts should be made to expand these benefits to the rural population. This is a longer-term agenda and the government should review experiences of countries such as Brazil and Mexico to determine how the scope of social insurance schemes can be expanded for the rural population.

Fifth, a range of socially excluded groups exists that face various forms of social discrimination based on religion, ethnicity, profession, or illness. It is important that the government ensures that social welfare provision helps eliminate these forms of socio-economic discrimination through legislative and other affirmative policies. The government should also ensure that these groups have the same access as the rest of the population to all SSPs and to all publicly provided basic services in education, health, nutrition, population planning, water supply, and sanitation. These two strands of public policy are the best way to support the well-being of these groups. From an administrative point of view, special efforts will be needed to reach many of the members of these groups. This will involve sensitizing the staff of social security agencies as well as relying on local government and NGOs to help identify potential beneficiaries. An effective grievance-redressing mechanism will also be helpful to bring members of these excluded populations into the social security network.

Financing and delivering the social security system

The financing of the reformed SSS should be based on cost-sharing arrangements between the government and the private sector. The tax-financed component is just one part of the financing package; the other – dealing with social insurance and employment-based regulations – should be largely financed by the private sector. A fundamental policy question, however, focuses on whether the tax-financed component of the reformed programme is affordable in terms of available budgetary resources. An illustrative costing exercise suggests that the proposed reform can be implemented and paid for with available resources. Two tasks then emerge: the first is to tailor the average benefits of the reformed programmes to fit the available resources (2.2 per cent of GDP), and the second is to implement the revised programme over a period of three to five years in line with the resource envelope. The principled position is that spending on social protection should expand over time as Bangladesh is able to mobilize more resources.

Administrative problems and weak governance in the implementation of SSPs are linked. Establishing good institutional arrangements for administering well-designed SSPs will help reduce leakage levels. A review of past experience suggests that there are a number of areas that need to be reformed, such as:

- establishing vastly simplified institutional arrangements that allow proper planning, implementation, and M&E of the SSS;
- professionalizing staff so that there is a group of public servants with expertise in the delivery of social security schemes at both national and local levels;
- introducing a more effective means to identify beneficiaries of social security schemes;
- upgrading management information systems (MISs) so that they are able to underpin the effective and efficient delivery of transfers and promote cross-governmental coordination and monitoring of performance;
- strengthening payment mechanisms to minimize leakage and using the SSS to promote financial inclusion, particularly among poor and vulnerable families;

- establishing an effective grievance and complaints system so that all citizens are able to appeal decisions on selection and can notify the competent authorities about instances of misconduct and failures in the delivery of the promised benefits.

Drawing on good international practice (Kidds et al., 2014), the government should establish a coordinating ministry and a specialized agency to simplify and coordinate programme delivery. This will involve a significant transformation in how Bangladesh delivers its SSS, and is intimately linked to initiatives to build a professionally MS competent social security staff and to modernize MISs across all SSPs. One possible way forward would be to convert the existing Ministry of Social Welfare into a significantly strengthened Ministry of Social Development (MSD), through which SSPs could be coordinated. Under the auspices of the MSD, a National Social Security Agency (NSSA) could be created with responsibility for the delivery of all SSPs. The NSSA could incorporate the current Department of Social Services in the Ministry of Social Welfare and become a semi-autonomous institution. The NSSA could also work closely with local government institutions (LGIs) and NGOs. The LGIs would be instrumental in helping identify potential beneficiaries, resolving disputes, and helping conduct M&E exercises. The LGIs could also work with line ministries in the delivery of programmes that are outside the remit of the NSSA.

The government should continue – and, where necessary, deepen – its partnership with NGOs in the area of delivering social security services. Specific areas in which NGOs could be helpful include the piloting of innovative ideas for possible scaling up; identifying potential beneficiaries, especially those who are hard to reach; and helping redress grievances and disputes relating to programme implementation. Since these administrative changes are far-reaching, the full implementation of reforms will take time and so it is important that, in the interim, the current programmes and benefits should be administered by those currently responsible for their delivery.

The efficient administration of social security schemes also requires that high-quality MISs are in place. A number of developing countries have shown that it is possible to establish effective MISs using advanced technologies. One option for Bangladesh would be to establish a form of national single registry based on a network of independent but interlinked scheme-specific MISs. This could use the database from the national identity system and focus on building scheme-specific MISs that communicate with each other and deliver comprehensive information across government. The MSD could take the lead in establishing the single registry in coordination with other relevant ministries.

A further key reform that should be introduced is an initiative to transform the government-to-person (G2P) payment systems so that they promote financial inclusivity and prevent leakages. The government has already improved the cash delivery systems in some SSPs so that transfers are delivered through financial institutions. The next step is to move to this full G2P system. The rapid growth of mobile phone services in rural Bangladesh potentially offers an efficient way in which this could be administered.

Given the increases in expenditure proposed for core SSPs, it is imperative to ensure that transfers go to the right people. However, identifying the right people is a challenge faced by many developing countries, particularly when using poverty-based selection processes. Recently, the Bangladesh Bureau of Statistics (BBS) launched an initiative to establish a Bangladesh poverty database using the PMT scorecard approach. In view of the limitations of the PMT approach outlined above, a combination of PMT, support from local government, and support from NGOs could be employed to better identify poor and vulnerable beneficiaries. More specifically, the PMT scorecard should be used only when it is triangulated with or endorsed by local communities. It is impossible, however, to always make the correct decision when identifying recipients of social security services. Therefore, the government should develop a nationwide complaints and grievance mechanism aimed at resolving disputes relating to social security benefits fairly and in accordance with agreed provisions.

Finally, a more sophisticated M&E system is needed to improve delivery mechanisms, document results, better inform policymakers about the effectiveness of alternative approaches, and mobilize political support for sustainability and expansion of the programmes. M&E activities can be divided into three parts. First, implementing ministries or agencies should monitor the progress of their respective programmes and prepare regular evidence- and results-based reports. Second, the government's Implementation Monitoring and Evaluation Department should assess the implementation of individual projects and programmes. Finally, the Planning Commission should prepare a results framework using specific indicators and evaluate it in a holistic approach. The Planning Commission should also be responsible for overall coordination of the M&E framework and dissemination of the evaluation results.

The availability of reliable data and its timeliness are crucial for policymaking and impact evaluation, and this calls for increasing the efficiency of the statistical system. The M&E of the SSS should rely in large part on regular surveys undertaken by the BBS, such as the HIES, augmented by panel surveys and qualitative approaches. The capacity of the BBS should be further strengthened to enable it to conduct general surveys, tailored surveys, and censuses to produce the quality data required for conducting M&E. Critically, the findings of any M&E must be shared with beneficiaries and used for policy decisions. One step towards achieving this could be to put all M&E results on the website of the MSD as well as on the website of the Planning Commission. All evaluation reports would be shared with the cabinet and the responsible parliamentary standing committee. The MSD should then be responsible for reporting to the cabinet and the parliamentary standing committee any actions taken in response to the findings of evaluation reports.

Table 9.2 Poverty impact of the redefined lifecycle programmes

Simulation type	Headcount poverty (%)	Depth of poverty (%)
No SSPs	33.0	7.4
Using 2010 SSPs reported in HIES	31.5	6.5
Using National Social Security Strategy (NSSS) lifecycle programmes	28.3	4.8

Source: NSSS simulations using 2010 HIES data.

Poverty impact of the reformed SSS

Reforms are only useful if they lead to better outcomes. While the real test of a reformed SSS will be in its actual implementation, the simulation results of the likely poverty impact of the redefined lifecycle programmes are reported in Table 9.2. The predictions suggest that the restructured programmes are likely to result in significantly better poverty outcomes when compared with the present programmes. The improved outcomes reflect minimized leakages and wastage, reduced administration costs, and better defined and higher average values of the SSS going to the poorest and most vulnerable.

Conclusion

Owing to growing resource constraints, the GDP share of public spending on social protection is declining in Bangladesh. And yet, with demographic and other socio-economic changes, new challenges are emerging for the SSS. The need for an effective SSS is crucial to Bangladesh's future shared prosperity. However, there are considerable problems with the present SSS that must be addressed through major reform. The reforms proposed in this chapter, if implemented well, will go a long way to strengthen the poverty impact of the SSS. The effectiveness of the reforms must be monitored and evaluated at regular intervals and necessary changes made to ensure the best use of limited public resources.

Notes

1. Bangladesh uses two poverty lines: the upper poverty line (UPL) and the lower poverty line (LPL). People whose consumption falls below the UPL are defined as poor; people whose consumption falls below the LPL are regarded as extreme poor. Both figures are calculated using the 'cost of basic needs' approach, which calculates the minimum per capita expenditure required to meet basic food and non-food needs. The difference between the two lines reflects differences in calorific intake.
2. I am grateful to Stephen Kidds for contributions and inputs that have influenced this section.
3. See <www.bangladeshdeltaplan2100.org>.

References

Ahmed, S. (2013) *Employment, Productivity, Real Wages and Labour Markets in Bangladesh*, Dhaka: Policy Research Institute of Bangladesh.

Ahmed, S. (2014) *The Dynamics of Rural Development and Agricultural Wages in Bangladesh*, Dhaka: Policy Research Institute of Bangladesh.

Ahmed, S. (2015) *Reforming the Social Security System for Poverty Reduction in Bangladesh*, Dhaka: Policy Research Institute of Bangladesh.

BBS (2011) *Summary Report of the Household Income and Expenditure Survey 2010*, Dhaka: Bangladesh Bureau of Statistics (BBS), Ministry of Planning.

GoB (2014) *Bangladesh National Social Security Strategy*, Dhaka: General Economics Division, Planning Commission, Government of Bangladesh.

Khondker, B. (2014) *Poverty, Vulnerability and Inequality in Bangladesh*, Background Paper prepared for the Bangladesh National Social Security Strategy, Dhaka: General Economics Division, Ministry of Planning.

Kidds, S., Bazlul, K., Khan, N. and Ahsan, T. (2014) *Building a Social Protection System to Address the Demographic Challenges Faced by Bangladesh*, Background Paper prepared for the Bangladesh National Social Security Strategy, Dhaka: General Economics Division, Ministry of Planning.

Sen, B. and Ali, Z. (2017) 'Ending extreme poverty in Bangladesh: trends, drivers, and policies', in J. Devine, G. Wood, Z. Ali, and S. Alam (eds), *Extreme Poverty, Growth, and Inequality in Bangladesh*, Rugby: Practical Action Publishing.

World Bank (2013) *Bangladesh Poverty Assessment*, Washington, DC: World Bank.

About the author

Dr Sadiq Ahmed is Vice Chairman of the Policy Research Institute, Bangladesh. He obtained his PhD from the University of Boston. He has had a distinguished career with the World Bank, including as country director for Afghanistan and Pakistan, and as chief economist for the South Asia region. A development economist by training, he has published widely on topics including the private sector, poverty reduction, fiscal policy, trade, and governance.

CHAPTER 10
Conclusion: sharing the well

Zulfiqar Ali and Geof D. Wood

This chapter advances the case for the adoption of a 'universal basic income' approach in Bangladesh, rooted in a rights-based framework. It is argued that this is a feasible, affordable, and cost-effective means of eradicating extreme poverty. This challenges the dominant ideology underlying existing approaches to poverty reduction and social protection, and in particular the method of micro-targeting.

Keywords: universal basic income, social security, social safety net, lifecycle intervention

Why should the eradication of extreme poverty get priority attention?

It is now beyond doubt that Bangladesh has made noticeable progress in reducing poverty (both moderate and extreme) and in achieving social progress. Bangladesh's progress is faster than its neighbours. However, the challenge to eradicate extreme poverty remains significant.

Why should the eradication of extreme poverty get priority attention? First, despite the good progress in reducing extreme poverty over the past several years, over 20 million people still live in extreme, long-term poverty in Bangladesh. Also, those who have been able to escape extreme poverty and are either moderately poor or moderately non-poor can fall back into extreme poverty due to the various hazards and shocks they face. Moreover, there are some communities and groups living on the margins that are largely excluded from mainstream economic and social activities. They include, among others, ethnic minorities, persons with disabilities, sex workers, transgender people, street children, dying occupational groups, and people forced to live in ecologically fragile areas (Ali and Mujeri, 2016). A large majority of people in these groups and communities are still forced to live in extreme poverty over generations.

Second, there are deprivations that are faced not only by the extreme poor but also by the moderate and non-poor, but when the extreme poor experience them, there are greater negative multiplier effects upon their lives. Natural hazards, health shocks, and lack of access to public healthcare facilities are examples in this respect. And the extreme poor are much more vulnerable to these than other groups of people.

Third, a good proportion of those living in extreme poverty do not have any other option but to live in life-threatening conditions. Consider people

http://dx.doi.org/10.3362/9781780449463.010

living on pavements or next to railway lines under a mere polyethylene roof, living in remote coastal areas or on the slope of hills with a high risk of landslides, and living without proper housing or clothing or suffering from severe ill health or malnutrition, and without two full meals a day. This can also be called 'the ugly face of extreme poverty', and it should never be tolerated in any welfare-oriented society. The state, as the ultimate duty-bearer, must try to assist them to overcome these desperate conditions within the shortest possible time. In this respect, the Government of Bangladesh's (GoB's) seventh Five Year Plan period should be the period during which the country frees itself from this ugly face of poverty. The first aim of the sustainable development goals, to which Bangladesh is also a signatory, is to eradicate extreme poverty by 2030. As Bangladesh has had some success in achieving poverty reduction during the millennium development goal (MDG) period, it can reasonably have the ambition as a leading developing country to eradicate all forms of extreme poverty well ahead of 2030.

Fourth, Bangladesh has recently graduated into the league of the World Bank's lower middle-income countries, where there are as many as 51 countries at the moment. However, the level of social progress and improvements in human capital development are not similar in these countries. There are some lower middle-income countries that have been in this group for quite some time, but their levels of poverty, inequality, and deprivation are still pervasive. Nigeria, Pakistan, and even India are examples of this.

Can Bangladesh do it?

Now, the question is: can Bangladesh eradicate extreme poverty? The recent history of progress supports the answer: yes! The pace of poverty and extreme poverty reduction has increased in recent years. While the poverty reduction rate was below 1 percentage point per year during the 1980s, it was about 1 percentage point per year during the 1990s and more than 1 (about 1.7) during the 2000s (BBS, 2011). Favourable structural changes can also be observed within the composition of poverty groups. The proportion of extreme poor people among the total poor has declined over the years. Furthermore, Bangladesh's social progress and achievement on MDGs is significant:

- The prevalence of underweight children under five years of age has gone down from 66 per cent in 1990 to 57 per cent in 2000 and 31.9 per cent in 2013, against the MDG target of 33 per cent for 2015.
- Net enrolment in primary education has gone up from 60.5 per cent in 1990 to 85.5 per cent in 2000 and 97.7 per cent in 2014, against the MDG target of 100 per cent for 2015.
- The ratio of girls to boys in secondary education has moved from 0.52 in 1990 to 1.06 in 2000 and 1.14 in 2013, against the MDG target of 1.00 for 2015.

- Under-five mortality (per 1,000 live births) has also gone down, from 146 in 1990 to 84 in 2000 and 41 in 2013, against the MDG target of 48 for 2015.

There are also signs of convergence in economic and social progress among different geographic regions of the country. The earlier lagging regions are now catching up and hence spatial inequality is decreasing, which indicates that those living in more vulnerable areas are now having a proportionately greater share of the social-economic benefits the country is producing (Sen et al., 2014). All these factors give us confidence that Bangladesh can emerge as a lower middle-income country while leaving no one behind.

Challenges lie ahead

However, we should also acknowledge that the pathways for achieving this goal will not be smooth. There are clear challenges that lie ahead. First, the remaining extreme poor will be the most difficult group to assist because the factors underpinning their poverty are complex and stubborn. Second, the impact of economic growth on extreme poverty reduction is unlikely to be the same in the future. This is because the growth elasticity of poverty reduction has been calculated based on the past record of relatively stable income inequality. If income inequality rises, the impact of growth on poverty reduction will also be lower. Finally, the growth elasticity of poverty reduction is estimated on the assumption that the poor and the extreme poor are a homogeneous group. This is clearly not the case and there are significant differences between the poor and the extreme poor and different conditions of extreme poverty within the extreme poor group.

The way forward: improving present strategies

Given the above, what then has to be done in order to expedite the reduction of extreme poverty in Bangladesh? This concluding chapter observes the following:

1. Bangladesh has examples of micro-successes on effectively tackling extreme poverty. There have been quite a few successful targeted livelihood programmes that have helped diverse extreme poor groups to overcome their adverse conditions. For example, under the Economic Empowerment of the Poorest (EEP) programme, over 1 million extreme poor people 'graduated' from extreme poverty during the 2010–15 period.[1] Targeted livelihood programmes of this kind could be scaled up.
2. Hazards and shocks play an important role in shaping the pace of extreme poverty reduction. Hazards and shocks make poor people poorer and the extreme poor destitute. This is why preventing asset erosion should also be given equal priority alongside asset generation (Marsden and Wood, 2011). Risk reduction and hazard prevention for

the poor and the poorest are therefore important in order to achieve quicker declines in both moderate and extreme poverty.

3. Bangladesh is currently implementing around 100 social safety net programmes, accounting for more than 2 per cent of gross domestic product (GDP) annually. However, only about 13 of these are core poverty-focused programmes, and these account for only 0.77 per cent of GDP. Moreover, the monthly allowances for most of these schemes is less than US$4 per month (PPRC, 2012). These need to be reviewed to identify the programmes that cater to the needs of the poorest of the poor. In 2015, the GoB prepared a national social security strategy (NSSS) with the vision to build an inclusive social security system that tackles poverty and inequality and contributes to broader human development, employment, and economic growth. The goal over the next five years is to 'progress towards a more inclusive form of social security that effectively tackles lifecycle risks, prioritizing the poorest and most vulnerable members of society' (GoB, 2015). This signals a move from a social protection strategy built around a highly imperfect targeting approach to a lifecycle intervention approach.

4. There needs to be more investment in the poorest to develop their human capital. Despite the fact that Bangladesh has made good progress in human development and social indicators, approximately 23 per cent of children of primary school age remain out of school, 6 per cent of children aged 10–14 years are engaged in child labour, and 29 per cent of females get married before the age of 15 (BIDS et al., 2013). A large majority of these children belong to the poor and the poorest households. Hence, it is essential to take appropriate steps to help the poor and the poorest send their children to school and keep them there up to secondary level and to ensure easily accessible and better healthcare facilities for them. This also relates to tackling the intergenerational transmission of poverty.

5. Developing more market entry points for the extreme poor is also essential. Because of limited capacity, the poorest and the vulnerable have limited access to existing markets. If they cannot integrate into existing or new markets, they will not be able to progress further, and whatever progress they have been able to make may not be sustained. Helping to develop and facilitate market access is therefore crucial for sustainable graduation out of extreme poverty.

6. Finally, steps need to be taken to help the poorest raise their voice effectively so that they are heard by the policymakers and the elites in order to have effective empowerment leading to the enactment of their rights and entitlements.

No room for complacency

In addition to these incremental options, this chapter offers further ideas about how to approach social policy in Bangladesh. Should we target the poor and the poorest only, or each and every citizen in the country? Should we take the lifecycle approach to social protection or the universal basic income (UBI) approach? Can the latter policy be afforded in the country? These are discussed in some detail below.

In addressing extreme poverty, Devine and Wood (2017) have argued for a new political settlement around social policy in the country, under the conditions of a projected shift for the country towards upper middle-income status and the prospect of seriously extending the domestic revenue base. The neoliberal agenda – exclusively focused on entrepreneurialism, employment generation, and market entry – has not realized early hopes of poverty reduction, and is being replaced by arguments for blended strategies based on a pre-neoliberal understanding that the extreme poor are the least able to rely on markets for their livelihoods due to a complex interlocking of constraints that work against them.

An important context for this discussion is that the present claims for poverty reduction in the country are inflated, especially if vulnerability is taken into account, but also if the income poverty lines are adjusted only a little upwards to reflect more realistically acceptable standards of living.[2] Ahmed (2017) argues that multiplying the upper poverty line by 1.25 would define nearly 50 per cent of the population as poor with high vulnerability. Multiplying by 1.5 would define 80 per cent of the population as poor or with significant vulnerability. Under such conditions, it makes little sense to target 70 to 80 per cent of the population for specific asset transfers either for market entry or for social protection. Indeed, it would make better sense to invert present social protection logic and target the top 20 to 30 per cent for tax purposes in a new politics of distribution. Could that case ever be made for Bangladesh?

The limitations of Western social policy as a guide

Let us therefore return to the implications of the oft-repeated claim for imminent middle-income status. For some observers in Bangladesh, the claim for middle-income status is purely arithmetical and potentially misleading. The doubts about its implications are reinforced by also questioning the claims for poverty reduction when different, and perhaps more realistic, thresholds are introduced to differentiate the poor and vulnerable from some concept of the middle class. If we add that we cannot assume a range of improvements in social practices, including access to justice and entitlements accompanying the arithmetical middle-income status, then we have to conclude that significant challenges remain to lift millions out of poverty and achieve inclusive social cohesion in society.

This may not be a popular view with either government and donors, which have possible vested interests in overstating the middle-income claim. But the implied pessimism makes the argument for a new political settlement even more urgent, because 'business as usual' under these arithmetical conditions is clearly inadequate to the task of extreme poverty reduction. 'Business as usual' is responsible for high levels of inequality, with a present Gini coefficient of

0.47, reflecting strong question marks over the prospects of economic growth alone reducing poverty significantly through trickle-down assumptions.

Our driver for a new political settlement has, so far, been a combination of the moral and the pragmatic. For both drivers, rising inequality in the context of economic growth prompts an agenda of redistribution as the route to extreme poverty reduction and also fairness. The moral case for a new political settlement draws upon inclusive aspects of Bengali culture and identity as well as more universal notions of collective well-being as the basis for individual well-being. The pragmatic case is that continuing poverty amid palpable rising inequality is simply not sustainable politically, as relative deprivations are more easily perceived and converted into political challenge.

The thinking behind social protection in Bangladesh is complicated and reflects specific aspects of the recent history of social protection as well as more universal welfare regime thinking derived from Western social policy. We need to deconstruct this further. Let us deal with universal welfare regime thinking first. Although there are variations in welfare capitalism (Esping-Andersen, 1990), a single principle of partial de-commodification guides them all. As capitalism matures to the point where labour is just a commodity, so livelihoods themselves become a commodity function, vulnerable to the volatility of dynamic and competitive capitalism in which sectors and regions rise and fall in their fortunes. People need to have their livelihoods insulated to a greater or lesser extent, depending upon precise regime type, from sole dependency on the valorization of labour as a commodity. In other words, thanks to Polanyi (1944), it is unacceptable morally and pragmatically to expose people's livelihoods entirely to their labour market status, in terms of both income claims and the security of that income.

Social policy has been based on this essential principle, as a de-commodifying reaction to the actual or potential failure of the commodity – labour – to deliver present basic livelihoods. Decent work regulation, social insurance, sickness benefits, disability benefits, old age pensions, and many more categories are all part of the repertoire of social protection, including safety nets. These have one feature in common: welfare payments defined in relation to the failure of labour markets to underpin family welfare and to protect households from either idiosyncratic or systemic poverty. Welfare regimes, in their varied forms, essentially exist to mop up the needs of those unable to survive on wages alone.

However, this discourse about social protection also reflects over-simple and Western-centric thinking about economic growth and capitalist development. It assumes a steady progression to near full employment with the related assumption that labour market employment can account for most people's livelihoods, leaving any notion of public welfare in the role of residual support and a minor charge upon the national budget. It also assumes a steady progression towards the organized labour sector, supported by regulatory frameworks arising from socially progressive states. At this point it is worth recalling those estimations that 85 per cent of labour activity in Bangladesh is located in the informal sector. This linear account of growth needs to be challenged in order to reset the discourse about the role of social protection in a broader, blended policy framework.

First, the agrarian transition in Bangladesh is by no means completed, with much economic activity in the countryside remaining in agriculture that is not fully commoditized. This includes small-scale subsistence agriculture supported by horticulture, alongside more market-oriented cereal production (mainly rice), which is not grown commercially but is integrated into market sales through the purchase for cash of fixed and variable inputs. This means that, although rising real wage rates in agriculture account significantly for poverty reduction (World Bank, 2013), under-valorised labour (especially that of women) is widespread in family production and reproduction. At the same time, there is an expansion of agricultural services, with valorized labour at different skill levels absorbed in both manual and technical operations. The picture is further complicated because individuals as well as families combine valorized and under-valorized labour functions across these sectors. So some of their time and their livelihood contribution is commoditized and some is not. Given internal family dependency ratios, this means that significant proportions of rural family members work in the non-commoditized part of the workforce, where in-kind work contributions to livelihoods are inherently difficult to monetize and thus assess for value against a monetized poverty line. And it is often the poorest and the most vulnerable people who depend on these various and precarious food- or in-kind-earning, bonded-labour opportunities.

We can then add the further complication that levels of actual or attributed valorization are subject to negatively interlocked markets, linking monetary wage rates to credit, to land access, and to in-kind employment of family members (i.e. domestic service). All of this depresses potential wage returns. So we have to acknowledge that labour is far from fully commoditized, making any social policy strategy of de-commoditizing labour markets through social insurance and protection theoretically premature. And since such a strategy relies essentially on means testing to fill the livelihood gap left by inadequately paid wages, then the requirement for impartial state capacity to determine that gap fairly becomes an issue.

Second, once we add migration (internal as well as external), then we have to consider the commodity aspect of those employment relations (i.e. the real subsumption of labour under capital) alongside the social and poverty function of remittances. Rates of urbanization in the larger cities generally exceed the capacity for incoming labour to be formally absorbed in the organized sector. Garment manufacturing, construction, infrastructure, and some services (domestic and transport, for example) absorb most of the wage labour, but there are significant casual incomes gained in informal petty services, manufacturing, and trading markets. Being casual and non-regulated, those incomes are highly volatile seasonally, and are acutely affected by political insecurity.

Is the full employment assumption for targeted social protection realistic?

The key question that arises from the characteristics of transition in Bangladesh, and in many other countries (including in Europe), is whether there will ever be realistic circumstances again in which a model of near full employment is possible. For example, economic growth in India over recent decades has occurred without generating similar rates of employment increases in its most dynamic and productive sectors (Luce, 2006). Indeed, the strongest growth sectors, such as garment manufacturing, mining, and car production, have also been shedding labour per unit of output as technology-induced productivity rises. So the idea of near full employment is being undermined globally, not least in rich economies, by casualization, part-time working, and zero hours contracts, a phenomenon represented by the concept of the 'precariat' (Standing, 2011).

In societies with recent agrarian pasts, the incomplete path of commoditization indicates a large reserve army of labour that acts as a depressor on wage levels in the organized sector, especially in the relatively unskilled services sector. In the UK, over the last decade or so, the instrument of giving tax credits to working individuals has recognized these conditions and has acted as a subsidy and further disincentive for employers to pay what would otherwise be market rates. This has been the nearest the UK has reached in terms of a universal social protection instrument for the working-age population, recognizing redistribution as a necessary condition for the reproduction of social cohesion. It is now being contested by anti-welfare zealots who deceitfully maintain a faith in the market – especially in the labour market, but also in the financial market – to regain its primary contribution to adequate livelihoods. Living wage legislation will be easily subverted by short-term contracts. If we consider that it is unrealistic to expect labour markets to deliver livelihoods, it is equally inappropriate to conceive of social protection as residuality, as is presently the case in most contemporary welfare regimes.

This broad ideological fiction about employment-derived livelihoods has also underpinned an increasingly dubious discourse about rights to entitlements. This is a labelling point about establishing a categorical distinction between the deserving and undeserving poor with respect to their inclinations to work, whenever they can, regardless of reward. Indeed, tax credits in the UK have implicitly focused on the 'deserving' poor, with tax credits as the more secure, less stigmatized entitlement compared with other benefits for those out of work. In other words, the basis of a secure right to state-supported livelihoods is contingent upon participation in labour markets that then subvert the actual value of that right when activated, while the right for others outside the labour market (idiosyncratically or systemically) is understood more as institutionalized charity for the feckless, entailing dependency and loss of dignity.

But the ultimate immorality in unequal societies is to impose the fiction that work opportunities are available at adequate levels of valorization as an argument against redistributive taxation. Indeed, the estimates for Bangladesh are that 2 million new entrants annually to the labour force need to be absorbed. Failure to absorb them will certainly lead to many problematic social and political consequences, threatening the integrity of the state. However, regardless of prevailing conditions, the neoliberal fictional view of the world maintains that individuals are solely responsible for their own livelihoods so that the route to poverty reduction can feature only in a market landscape.

Supporting the lifecycle

The recently promulgated NSSS in Bangladesh (GoB, 2015) has taken the debate forward through a clear commitment to the lifecycle as a basis for intervention. It seeks to use the lifecycle as the core concept for reforming the current plethora of instruments under a social protection umbrella. This approach undoubtedly offers a core rationale for blended policy, drawing in a wider range of government support for livelihoods than is available from pensions and social safety nets calibrated to labour market failure. The approach thus embraces maternal and child nutrition support, preparation for labour market entry through skills acquisition and vocational training, social safety nets, pensions for the elderly, and benefits for those unable to work through physical or mental disability or morbidity. The NSSS sets out a two-stage reform programme: up to 2025, and from 2026 onwards The strategic intention in the first stage is to streamline the present array of social protection instruments around the lifecycle support principle; at present, these instruments involve many ministries and departments. The second stage then focuses on bringing the new array of instruments predominantly under the responsibility of a restructured Ministry of Social Welfare, with other ministries playing clearly defined support roles. The intention and ambition are laudable within present paradigm thinking (i.e. full employment for the working-age population), but our core question is whether the paradigm fits the conditions and challenges that lie ahead.

Rethinking social protection and distribution in Bangladesh: the case for sharing the well through UBI

So, can we imagine a settlement that does not start from the 'employment default' position? That is the key challenge offered by Ferguson in a recent book, *Give a Man a Fish* (2015). Consider this quotation from a recent letter to the *Guardian* in the UK, in the context of tax credit reform:

> But what if, instead of regarding this (i.e. £30bn of tax credits) as a burden, we envisage it as the first stage in the construction of a citizens' income? In a globalised economy, with huge disparities of wage levels, an overall surplus of labour and an oncoming tsunami of automation,

it's unlikely that pushing up minimum wage rates or strengthening trade unions – desirable though both are – will on their own bring about an acceptable degree of economic justice. Following the moral logic of economic equality would begin the necessary process of sweeping away the whole tired discourse of handout, subsidy, incentives, deserving and undeserving. (Richard Middleton, 28 October 2015)

This is an effective summary of Ferguson's core argument, especially the reference to citizens' income. Ferguson rejects the notion of employment as the main route to livelihoods, so connecting welfare to work must be seen as an ideological deceit in the modern age. He contests the idea that what poor people need is the means to work (either training for the labour market or assets that will generate self-employment) when there is no prospect of even near full employment. Although he makes this observation globally, his own empirical context is Southern Africa, a context to which we return presently. He also refers to the evidence of inequality, arguing that certain classes (and races) have disproportionately extracted rents from the natural resource endowments that belong to all citizens. In this sense, then, people are 'owed' fair shares of national wealth rather than required to seek handouts from that national wealth. While differential rewards can be accepted to a degree as a return on risk-taking investment and effort, such rewards should not include rents derived from monopoly pricing of either commodities or labour. Being 'owed' a fair share becomes synonymous with having a basic income as an entitlement rather than a 'handout', whose existence and amount can be decided, varied, and targeted by others, reflecting ideology about residuality as well as interpreting labour market conditions.

Ferguson is keen to remove 'dependency' from the debate. In other words, why should poor people have to feel dependent upon others for their livelihoods and accept social inferiority and loss of dignity as the price? In other words, why should they have to make Faustian bargains (Wood, 2003) that postpone rights and cement dependency? But also, payments should not be withheld by powerholders in society on the grounds that they encourage dependency, as if the poor are unfairly stealing from the wealth of others and constitute an undeserving burden. Furthermore, as citizens, the poor should not be incentivized to accept exploitative wages by reducing payments to below subsistence levels and making people grovel for scraps. How can political equality be based on such economic inequality and dependency?

Ferguson thus develops an argument for 'rightful shares'. In doing so, he is also critiquing some of the discourse about rights. Rights to work, food, housing, education opportunities, health, and so on exist in unequal societies only if others are prepared to perform the correlative duties to uphold those rights and make the claims derived from them a reality. He refers to a seminar about rights to housing, which all the participants supported until late in the meeting an old man stood up and said he did not want a right to a house! He appeared to break the consensus in the room. After sharp intakes of breath and a pause throughout the room, he went on to say that he wanted a house, not a 'right' to a house. In other words, the abstract claim was no good to him if there was no prospect of honouring it. The same applies to work and employment.

Ferguson then proceeds to illustrate the partial action on his core argument through the basic income grant (BIG) schemes in universal operation in Namibia, and some tentative pilots in South Africa itself. UBIs are received by everyone (monthly amounts are credited to an adult's smart card, enabling withdrawals via ATMs). Such incomes are 'basic' in that they are calculated to sustain subsistence and limited other requirements. They do not provide anything lavish. But, for the poor, they offer security and a platform on which other incomes, if earned or transferred, can be used not just for present, immediate short-term needs but for longer-term security to enable improvement and/or insurance against family-level hazards. Obviously, for the poor, such basic incomes have huge significance, while for the richer families that receive them such incomes are a minor part of their income portfolio (rather like state pensions in the UK when compared with occupational pensions accrued over many years, and, of course, all regarded as amalgamated income for income tax purposes). So the state gets basic incomes back in tax from richer families who 'don't need them' without having to engage in the expensive business of targeting and means testing, while upholding the principle of citizens' income and rightful shares. By creating security, the BIG for poor people has strong implications for changing their time preference behaviour, which is the core indicator of real graduation and resilience.

Applying Ferguson's 'rightful shares' argument to Bangladesh

So how might these arguments translate to the Bangladesh context? It is true that some aspects of social protection in Bangladesh have not based entitlements on status within the labour market, but on other criteria. And, in a sense, these other criteria open up the door to a different way of thinking about a political settlement. Let us take the example of freedom fighters. Leaving aside the problem of verification, claimants of freedom fighter status during the liberation struggle receive a stipend from the GoB. This, in effect, is saying that this category of people have a 'citizen+' status and thus have an entitlement to a benefit. This is irrespective of any disabilities arising from injuries that may have been sustained. It is therefore unrelated to any capacity to operate in the labour market. There is, therefore, no principle of residuality being applied.

The argument for a UBI in Bangladesh can be supported by an acknowledgement of the costs, risks, and logistics currently associated with the micro-targeting obsession. There is a core problem of targeting the extreme poor in order to focus on the eradication of extreme poverty. To date, many of the extreme poor eradication programmes have felt obliged to target households very precisely, irrespective of the poor neighbours and communities around them whose situations are not so dissimilar. This inter-household similarity is reinforced by acknowledging the churning of fortunes between the moderate and extreme poor, and between the poor and non-poor vulnerable, requiring dynamic rather than static understanding. Not only is targeting information costly, in identification and selection terms it can be arbitrarily preferential and basically corrupt. It can also function to separate the targeted households from the support of non-targeted ones (Marsden and Wood, 2011). We have argued above that, under the socio-economic conditions of Bangladesh, neither the state nor the market alone support the livelihoods of the poor and poorest. Neighbours and micro-communities, most likely connected by kin, are crucial in coping with many crises. Relationships are important, and excessive targeting can hurt or even sever these.

A new settlement therefore needs to be more realistic in its understanding of the socio-economic dynamics of poverty in the contexts in which it is experienced. Rather than being based on a false premise about employment-based access to livelihoods and well-being, leading to exclusive social policy based on residuality, it needs to recognize the revised facts of widespread poverty and vulnerability amid a churning population alongside a pattern of inequality that is concentrating wealth and income among rent-seeking and tax-avoiding elites. Of course, there remains the practical question of what would entice these elites into a new, more inclusive politics of redistribution. Our answer is the threat posed to social cohesion, and thus ultimately elite interests, by the present politics of distribution in terms of political volatility and millenarianism.

However, many observers may contest the introduction of this paradigm shift in social protection thinking towards a 'citizens' income' in Bangladesh on the grounds of overall economic conditions and low GDP levels, mass poverty, inadequate natural resource endowments, weak governance, and constrained public budgets. But Bangladesh does have some other counter-forces that are conducive to a paradigm shift.

It is worth recalling that a key economic argument in the liberation discourse for an independent Bangladesh was that West Pakistan and its Punjabi, capital-owning elites were disproportionate rent-takers upon the key foreign exchange earner for joint Pakistan – namely, the jute grown in East Pakistan. Such earnings were recycled into other growth sectors in West Pakistan, with East Pakistan underdeveloped as a consequence. This was the region's equivalent of apartheid. So the language movements and regionally discriminatory army and civil service recruitment (with substantial implications for rent capture), together with this core economic argument about resource and value-added diversion, established the basis for an East Bengali citizenship, a nationalist basis for confronting the causes of underdevelopment. With such a history, surely the idea of a resulting citizens' income is not so strange to contemplate? The liberation was fought on the notion of a dispossessed citizenship.

Let us take this a step further. Jute may have declined as a key export and source of wealth creation in the liberated Bangladesh. But there are other national endowments akin to the mineral resources found in Southern Africa. The most obvious endowments are gas and oil. Although there has been exploration and some extraction since before liberation in the Bay of Bengal as well as in the delta, there is huge unrealized potential. Bangladesh is estimated to be the seventh largest producer of natural gas in Asia. Geologists believe that the country's maritime exclusive economic zone holds one of the largest oil and gas reserves in the Asia-Pacific region. Gas supplies meet 56 per cent of domestic energy demand, although the country remains a net importer of crude oil and petroleum products at present. To date, protectionism and lack of technical capacity have impeded Bangladesh's potential to be a major global hydrocarbon producer.

There is clearly the potential with these resources to transform the country into a strong middle-income one. But who should gain from the exploitation of this endowment? Its intrinsic value belongs to all citizens of the country. All have a rightful share in Ferguson's language. We can only hope that the under-exploitation of these resources to date reflects a conscious link between protectionism and technical capacity. Clearly, there is a danger that this national resource could be significantly lost to its citizens through the rents accruing to the large multinationals for their investment capital and technical ability. There are also other dangers of internal capture and pollution, which arise when considering the Nigerian experience. In many ways, therefore, the idea of rightful shares needs to be accepted into the social protection and poverty reduction discourse in Bangladesh before further and comprehensive exploitation of this endowment, to ensure its contribution to UBIs in the country.

There are other, perhaps less obvious, citizen resources in Bangladesh that are covered by the principle of being owed a stake in the revenue from such sources. Groundwater, for example, which significantly irrigates the late winter *boro* rice crop, has transformed the aggregate food security of the country, while a large proportion of the population remains hungry. These aquifers are a national citizens' resource. Three decades ago, the country launched the landless irrigation initiative in which landless groups supplied irrigation to farmers through shallow tube wells (Wood, 1999). This separated the principle of land ownership from water ownership, thus allowing a broader part of the population to gain from the exploitation of groundwater. With a little ingenuity, the same principle can be applied to surface water management for both irrigation and flood protection, with a broader group of locally poor citizens owning the infrastructure constructed by their hands which provides the 'service' of flood protection through maintained embankments. The present government wishes to emphasize the value of surface water in overall water management (as reported in the *Daily Star*, 27 October 2015) and thus this opportunity can be extended up to a national principle.

Closely connected to water are fish – both in the waterways and *beels* (wetlands with static water) of the delta and in the maritime space. Ferguson writes about hunting, and the social and moral requirement of the hunter to share his captured meat with the community where the game was killed. In the complex pond ownership settings of Bangladesh, the netted catch from ponds needs to be shared (in proportion) with those who have acknowledged rightful shares to the product of the pond. It is not difficult to apply this principle nationally, especially for common pool sources of fish – obviously via taxes and redistributed revenues. The citizen claim is valid. Unfortunately, we currently have many examples of common pool and common property resources being converted into private ones: for example, the shrimp production intrusion into mangroves. This constitutes a process of enclosure that removes the commons from its citizens.

We could elaborate on other examples to make the general point about citizens being owed basic incomes as a function of rightful shares rather than being supplicants dependent upon the institutionalized philanthropy of the limited-access state, dominated by rent-seeking elites, determined by factionalism, and characterized by systemic discrimination, often by gender and ethnicity. However, the proposition about rightful shares is not just dependent upon the presence of obvious large-scale resource endowments. More profoundly, the notion of rightful shares relates to participation in the economic growth and rising national wealth of the country from wherever it comes. When we consider the poverty elasticity of economic growth, we assume the link to be either via labour/employment/wages or via returns on capital invested. And that link is inherently volatile and uncertain. But the argument about rightful shares, by privileging citizen over worker, posits a more elastic link between growth and basic incomes, mediated through the concept of a citizen's income.

Resourcing three alternative approaches

We organize the remaining discussion in this conclusion around resourcing these three strategic choices for social protection: a continuation of the present targeted income supplement or cash transfer approach; the lifecycle intervention approach proposed in the NSSS; and a more radical UBI approach. The resourcing assumptions are indicated below:

- Under a targeted approach, we initially propose to target the extreme poor only. This is because this is the group that suffers from multiple deprivations and a large majority of them are also compelled to live in inhuman conditions. Under this approach, all the extreme poor households will have to be properly targeted and provided with an adequate income supplement or cash transfer so that they have access to the minimum required food and other basic necessities. The idea behind this approach is to help the extreme poor 'graduate' from their condition of poverty.

- Under lifecycle-based interventions, citizens, especially the poor and the poorest, will be provided with necessary support at different stages of their life. This is more or less the case in the country at present, although it is not well organized or effectively coordinated. Under this approach, health and nutritional support at early stages, education and skills development to support labour market entry, and social safety net support for various vulnerable groups are provided.
- Under the UBI approach, each and every citizen in the country will be provided with a basic income each month, every month. For the poor and the poorest, it will enable them to meet some basic necessities that they otherwise could not. This approach also treats all citizens equally. This will require no targeting and hence transaction costs are reduced. However, the total resource requirement will be higher for this than for the other approaches.

Now, let us review the necessary resource requirements under these alternative approaches for social protection.

Individual or household? And how much?

Let us first discuss what amount should be given to citizens and whether it should be per person or per household. According to the latest Household Income and Expenditure Survey (HIES) conducted by BBS in 2010, the lower poverty line (LPL) income for rural areas was estimated at about 1,278 Bangladeshi Taka (BDT) per person per month. According to the same survey, average per capita monthly expenditure[3] for the extreme poor was estimated at BDT1,065. Taking the approximate rates of inflation in Bangladesh during 2010–15, the estimated LPL income and average per capita monthly income of the extreme poor comes to BDT1,725 and 1,438 respectively. Hence, the difference between these two (i.e. the LPL income and average per capita income of the extreme poor) comes to BDT287, which can be considered the allowance to be given to each person per month. The justification for this amount as a per capita monthly allowance is that, on average, this is the per capita shortfall for extreme poor people to reach the LPL income level.

However, there is also inequality within extreme poor households. While some are able to earn close to the poverty line income, others can earn only a very small amount. Hence, the above amount (BDT287 per person per month) will not be able to help approximately 50 per cent of the extreme poor to meet the minimum income requirement. In this scenario, it may be appropriate, for example, to consider doubling the basic amount to BDT574. If a targeted approach is adopted, then it may be valuable to consider targeting the extreme poor with a payment of at least 50 per cent of the LPL income (i.e. BDT863 per person per month). More ambitiously, one might also consider paying the full amount equivalent to the LPL income (i.e. BDT1,725) as a way of covering all extreme poor households.

A further question is whether to give payments to individuals or households. Although, in Bangladesh, the household is the centre of all economic and social activities and is thus considered to be the primary unit of analysis in most economic interventions and policy considerations, our view is that it is best to give payments to individuals. This is because intra-household equity and the empowerment of each member of the household are closely related to distributing benefits to each member separately. Of course, in most cases, these payments will contribute to a common pot for the household, and decisions on expenditure will mainly be decided by the head of that household, who, in the majority of cases, is a male adult. Nonetheless, receiving benefits in an individual's name or account would give each household member a status and a degree of voice in the household.

Resource requirements under a UBI approach

The resource requirements under a UBI approach are presented in Tables 10.1 and 10.2. If we consider BDT287 as the amount to be given to each and every citizen in the country per month, then it would cost 3.64 per cent of GDP and 18.67 per cent of the national budget in total (Table 10.1). But if we consider BDT574 per person per month, the equivalent figure would be 7.27 per cent of GDP and 37.35 per cent of the national budget (Table 10.2). So, we are talking about a total expenditure of between 4 per cent and 7 per cent of GDP. This, we argue, is affordable.

The estimations above assume universal coverage. In both tables we provide alternative estimates against different population target levels, ranging from 13 per cent to 80 per cent (the former is the official estimation of extreme poverty prevalence and the latter has been calculated by Ahmed (2017) to include the extreme poor, poor, and vulnerable non-poor). Table 10.1 shows that the total expenditure required would be between 0.5 per cent and 2.9 per cent of GDP per person per month with the lower BDT287 payment; and between 0.9 per cent and 5.8 per cent of GDP for the higher payment of BDT574. If we target only the poor (26 per cent of the population) or only the extreme poor (13 per cent of the population) and use the same payments, it would cost 0.5 per cent to 1 per cent of GDP (option 1) or 0.9 per cent to 1.9 per cent of GDP (option 2).

Resource requirements if we target the extreme poor only and give them adequate support

Both tables also give estimates of resource requirements if we target only the extreme poor and offer adequate support to bring them out of extreme poverty. Two alternative provisions have been thought about here: half of the LPL income equivalent, and the full poverty line income equivalent. The tables shows that, no matter which provision we adopt, we could adequately cover all the extreme poor in the country with an expenditure that does not exceed 3 per cent of GDP.

Table 10.1 Resource requirements for UBI and other alternative social protection measures: option 1

Percentage of people to be covered	No. of people to be covered (million)	Amount to be given (BDT per person per month)	Total amount required (million BDT per year)	Total amount as a % of GDP	Total amount as a % of the national budget
100	160	287	551,040	3.64	18.67
80	128	287	440,832	2.91	14.94
68	108.8	287	374,707	2.47	12.70
50	80	287	275,520	1.82	9.34
26	41.6	287	143,270	0.95	4.85
13	20.8	287	71,635	0.47	2.43

Table 10.2 Resource requirements for UBI and other alternative social protection measures: option 2

Percentage of people to be covered	No. of people to be covered (million)	Amount to be given (BDT per person per month)	Total amount required (million BDT per year)	Total amount as a % of GDP	Total amount as a % of the national budget
100	160	574	1,102,080	7.27	37.35
80	128	574	881,664	5.82	29.88
68	108.8	574	749,414	4.94	25.40
50	80	574	551,040	3.64	18.67
26	41.6	574	286,541	1.89	9.71
13	20.8	574	143,270	0.95	4.85

Two further observations are worth considering. First, while one might argue that targeting and identifying each and every extreme poor household in the country would be a challenge, we should be ready to meet this challenge if we are committed to Bangladesh being free from extreme poverty within the shortest time possible. In fact, the GoB has already taken an initiative to identify and track all moderate and extreme poor households. With the introduction of digital national identification and the rapid expansion of mobile phones and internet connectivity, the challenge of tracking the poor and extreme poor is made less difficult. Second, if we target the extreme poor, our estimate shows that the total number of extreme poor people will decline by 6 per cent plus 1 incremental per cent per year from now on, assuming a population growth rate of 1.6 per cent and an extreme poverty reduction rate of about 1 percentage point per year. This means that, if we target the extreme poor only, the resource requirements would also decline by about 6 per cent per year.

Resource requirements under a lifecycle approach

Under the lifecycle approach, the country is spending over 2 per cent of GDP on social protection programmes. Some have reduced this figure to 0.7 per cent if we look only at poverty-focused social protection interventions. It is widely accepted that the social protection programmes need to be reviewed so that the lifecycle approach is properly supported. Initial calculations indicate an investment of at least 3 per cent of GDP for poverty-focused social protection interventions. The drawback of the lifecycle approach is that it is information-heavy, requiring a complex tracking infrastructure to identify the micro-shifts in the basis of entitlements as a household moves through its lifecycle stages.

Conclusion

The post-liberation history of Bangladesh, in social policy terms, has actually been an optimistic one. Despite continuous political upheavals involving periods of military rule alternating with democratically elected governments, alongside poor governance, corruption, disruptions, and violence, there has been steady progress from a low base in development and social outcome indicators, more recently those associated with the MDGs. In this limited sense, the country has displayed remarkable resilience. If recent positive trends in these indicators are projected forward, then further reductions in poverty should be expected. But reduction is different from permanent eradication. Several core challenges or worries remain: that recent achievements have focused on the 'easier to reach' poor; that poverty responses to growth are becoming more inelastic; that inequality (incomes and wealth) may be increasing rather than decreasing; that estimates of poverty are over-optimistic through using unrealistically low poverty line thresholds; that corruption and rent seeking remain widespread alongside poor governance and accountability; that revenue raising continues to rely on regressive rather than progressive taxation, and that there is widespread evasion and avoidance; that the structure of the economy cannot absorb the annual rate of new entrants to the labour market; that further disruption and violence arising from militancy and extremism are possible; and that reaching middle-income status does not automatically solve these challenges.

This concluding chapter argues that it is not unreasonable to be optimistic in Bangladesh about poverty eradication. There are inherent features in the Bengali identity, emphasizing the unity of a mutually caring citizenship in the past struggles with Pakistan, which are still relevant today. These features can be more actively promoted as the socio-cultural basis for building more progressive and inclusive political settlements. The desirable political settlement has to recognize that the livelihoods of the majority of people in the country cannot rely solely upon the neoliberal mantra of being successful in the labour or petty business market, and that the politics of redistribution have to embrace more inclusion through social protection derived from public revenues. In this way, inequality can be 'compensated for' through taxation and a redistributive welfare strategy.

The chapter has examined three versions of that welfare strategy: the present paradigm of targeting, but cleaned up and enhanced; the lifecycle strategy proposed in the NSSS; and a paradigm shift towards the principle of a citizens' income through the mechanism of a UBI. Each of these options is priced, and is shown to be affordable when set against the risks of failing to eradicate extreme and moderate poverty – even vulnerability – in terms of political stability. And we put on the agenda the notion that targeting should be more about 'targeting for tax than for receipt of income', given the skewed distribution of income and wealth in the country.

Is Bangladesh ready to show the world again that a populous country can innovate for the benefit of all of its people?

Notes

1.   The term 'graduation' remains highly problematic and the discourse has now shifted much more towards resilience.
2.   There is currently a global move, led by the World Bank, to adjust poverty lines upwards to $1.90 purchasing power parity (PPP), which, if adopted, will change claims for poverty reduction worldwide and therefore in Bangladesh.
3.   Expenditure, rather than income, is considered here as the poverty line because it is considered a better approximation of households' actual income status.

References

Ahmed, S. (2017) 'Reforming the social security system for poverty reduction', in J. Devine, G. Wood, Z. Ali, and S. Alam (eds), *Extreme Poverty, Growth, and Inequality in Bangladesh*, Rugby: Practical Action Publishing.

Ali, Z. and Mujeri, M.K. (2016) *Revisiting Extreme Poverty and Marginality in Bangladesh: How Successful are the Policies and Programs in Reaching the Extreme Poor?*, Working Paper 30, Dhaka: EEP/Shiree, <www.shiree.org/wp-content/uploads/2012/02/30-Working-Paper-30-Ali-Mujeri.pdf> [accessed 1 November 2015].

BBS (2011) *Report of the Household Income & Expenditure Survey 2010*, Dhaka: Bangladesh Bureau of Statistics (BBS), Government of Bangladesh.

BIDS, BBS and UNICEF (2013) *Child Equity Atlas: Pockets of Social Deprivation in Bangladesh*, Dhaka: Bangladesh Institute of Development Studies (BIDS), Bangladesh Bureau of Statistics (BBS), and UNICEF.

Devine, J. and Wood, G. (2017) 'Leaving no one behind in Bangladesh: the case for a new political settlement', in J. Devine, G. Wood, Z. Ali, and S. Alam (eds), *Extreme Poverty, Growth, and Inequality in Bangladesh*, Rugby: Practical Action Publishing.

Esping-Andersen, G. (1990) *The Three Worlds of Welfare Capitalism*, Princeton, NJ: Princeton University Press.

Ferguson, J. (2015) *Give a Man a Fish: Reflections on the New Politics of Distribution*, Durham, NC: Duke University Press.

GoB (2015) *National Social Security Strategy (NSSS) of Bangladesh*, Dhaka: General Economics Division, Planning Commission, Government of Bangladesh.

Luce, E. (2006) *In Spite of the Gods: The Rise of Modern India*, London: Little, Brown.

Marsden, H. and Wood, G. (2011) *Dilemmas of Reaching the Poorest: Learning So Far from Shiree's Experiences of Targeting the Extreme Poor*, Working Paper 1, Dhaka: EEP/Shiree, <www.shiree.org/wp-content/uploads/2014/10/1-Reaching-the-poorest.pdf> [accessed 1 November 2015].

Polanyi, K. (1944) *The Great Transformation*, Boston, MA: Beacon Press.

PPRC (2012) *Social Safety Nets in Bangladesh (Volume 2): Ground Realities and Policy Changes*, Dhaka: Power and Participation Research Centre (PPRC) and United Nations Development Programme (UNDP).

Sen, A., Yunus, M. and Ali, Z. (2014) *Regional Inequality in Bangladesh in the 2000s: Re-visiting the East–West Divide Debate*, BIDS-REF Study Series 14-01, Dhaka: Bangladesh Institute of Development Studies (BIDS).

Standing, G. (2011) *The Precariat: The New Dangerous Class*, London: Bloomsbury Publishing.

Wood, G. (1999) 'Contesting water in Bangladesh: knowledge, rights and governance', *Journal of International Development* 11(5): 731–54.

Wood, G. (2003) 'Staying secure, staying poor: the "Faustian bargain"', *World Development* 31(3): 455–71.

World Bank (2013) 'Poverty assessment: assessing a decade of progress in reducing poverty, 2000–2010', Bangladesh Development Series Paper 31, Dhaka: World Bank.

About the authors

Dr Zulfiqar Ali is a Senior Research Fellow at the Bangladesh Institute of Development Studies (BIDS). From July 2014 to September 2016, he was seconded to EEP/Shiree as Head of Research and Advocacy. Dr Ali's expertise lies in the economics of inequality and poverty; human and social development; food security; natural resources and environmental economics. He recently co-authored the background paper on extreme poverty for the seventh Five Year Plan of Bangladesh.

Geof D. Wood is Emeritus Professor at the University of Bath. A sociologist by training, he has over 40 years of research experience in South Asia, particularly Bangladesh, working on issues ranging from agrarian change, extreme poverty, and social mobilization to urban livelihoods, governance, and political settlements. He is also interested in and has written on the application of social policy concepts to thinking about welfare and development in poorer countries.

Index

Page numbers in *italics* refer to figures and tables.

agricultural commercialization and employment generation 109–11, 122–3
  access to agricultural inputs and labour costs 117–18
  access to credit 115, 119, 121
  agricultural value chain 110–12
  changing village context (2007–13) 112–15
  crop production 115–16
  disposition of sales 114–15
  land and cropping patterns 113–14
  non-farm economy 114
  performance of farm households 115–18
  storage and cold storage capacity 114–15, 116–17, 120–2
  traders and employees 118–20
  wages 114
agricultural credit 77, 115, 119, 121
agricultural wage labour market 18, 94
agricultural wages 17–18, 91, 92–3, 114, 144
agriculture 4–5, 167
  and hunger-based poverty 147, 149
  and rural non-farm sector 15, 93–4, 114, 144
agro-processors 115
assets
  and liabilities 38
  strengthening 44–5
  women's 62–3

Bangladesh 1–3
  changes in structure and values 3–6
Bangladesh Bank 76–7, 82, 84
Bangladesh Bureau of Statistics (BBS) 5, 40, 51, 63, 72, 92, 126, 129, 131, 134, 142–3, 157, 162
  see also Household Income and Expenditure Survey (HIES)
basic income grant (BIG) schemes 171
BRAC: CFPR/TUP programme 22, 24, 75

capability approach 42–3
CARE: SHOUHARDO programme 22
cash transfers vs food aid programmes 145, 154
Char Livelihoods Programme (CLP) 22, 24
children
  investment in 164
  maternal and childcare needs 146
  poverty rates of households with 143
  social security programmes for 150–1
  urban conditions 135, 137
'chronic poverty' vs extreme poverty 37–8
chronic seasonal distress (*monga*) 17
citizen's rights 134–6
cold storage capacity 114–15, 116–17, 120–2
contract farming 115
credit access 74–5
  agricultural 77, 115, 119, 121
  microfinance institutions (MFIs)/ microcredit system 72–3, 75, 77, 81–2, 83, 145

disabled people
  poverty rates of households with 143
  social security programmes for 152
dowry issues 56–7, 58, 63, 64–5

Economic Empowerment of the Poorest (EEP/Shiree) programme 23, 24, 55, 75, 163
education 15, 164
elderly people
  poverty rates of households with 143
  social security programmes for 151–2
employment
  full employment assumption for social protection 168–9
  self-employment 145
  urban 18, 135
  women 61–2, 65–6
  see also agricultural commercialization and employment generation; labour market
extreme poverty 11
  contemporary profile 14–16
  cost and effectiveness of programmes 23–4
  drivers of improvements 17–19
  growth elasticity of extreme poverty 19–20, 22, 42
  growth and poverty trap 11–12
  'knot effects' 39
  need for 'mini big push' 12, 20, 26–7
  policy implications 24–6
  proxy means test (PMT) 152, 153, 157

reduction trends 13–14
    scaling up successful pro-poor interventions 20–4, 25
    spatial dimensions: ecology, deprivation, and income poverty 16–17
    zero extreme poverty 12–13, 20

female-headed households 52, 63–6
feminization of poverty *see* guardianship and feminization of poverty
financial access 71–2, 84–5
    competitive system 82
    efficient services and relevant products 80–1
    ICT/digital services 73, 77, 78–9, 80, 145
    key issues 73–7
    learning from MFIs and informal markets 81–2
    partnerships between formal and quasi formal institutions 81
    policy framework: challenges and opportunities 77–9
    recent policies for improving 76–7
    targeting issues 82–3
    transaction costs of borrowing 75–6, 82
    see also credit access
Five Year Plan 1–2, 5–6, 20, 89, 115, 138, 162
food aid programmes vs cash transfers 145, 154
food/hunger-related poverty 147, 149
'freedom from' and 'freedom to' distinction in welfare policy 35, 41, 42, 43–4

garment industry 18, 135
gas and oil resources 173
GDP
    agricultural share 109
    growth 143–4
    growth scenarios 19–20, 22
    social security 26, 145, 155, 158, 164
    urban sector 131–2
geographic/spatial considerations 16–17, 40
governance shocks 25–6
government-to-person (G2P) payment systems 156–7
'group mobilization and individual entrepreneurship' (GMIE) 41–2
growth elasticity of extreme poverty 19–20, 22, 42
growth and poverty trap 11–12
growth-inducing institutional/structural transformation 18–19, 26–7, 143–4
guardianship and feminization of poverty 51–2, 66–7
    community support 66
    coping alone 65–6
    costs and benefits of time 57–8
    dowry issues 56–7, 58, 63, 64–5
    female-headed households 52, 63–6

    intersectionality 54–5, 62
    life trajectories 58, 59, 60
    male guardianship requirement 55–6
    marriage and mobility 56–61
    'material' marital games 56–7
    paid work 61–2, 65–6
    property rights and assets 62–3
    widowhood and separation 63–5

health
    children's 135
    maternal and childcare needs 146
    Maternal Health Voucher Scheme 151
    shocks/illness 25, 39
    urban slum vs non-slum households 137
    urban water and sanitation 136–7
Household Income and Expenditure Survey (HIES) 92, 99, 101–5, 133, 141, 142–3, 147–8, 152, 153, 175
household vs individual payments 175–6
hunger/food poverty 147, 149

ICT
    digital/mobile financial services 73, 77, 78–9, 80, 145
    network expansion 144
illness/health shocks 25, 39
income poverty
    and non-income poverty 16–17
inheritance practices 62–3
institutional responsibility matrix (IRM) 34, 35–6, 40–1, 42
'institutional voids' 53, 54
institutional/structural transformation 18–19, 26–7, 143–4
insurance programmes 83–4
    National Social Insurance Scheme (NSIS) 151, 152
intensity of extreme poverty 39
intergenerational poverty 42, 164
intersectionality 54–5, 62

labour market
    agricultural wage 18, 94
    de-commodification/valorization 32, 33, 166–7
    institutions 19
land
    ownership 15, 94, 113, 116
    tenancy 18–19, 94
    urban squatter settlements and slums 134–5
landlessness 113
'leaving no one behind' 1–2, 3, 6
'Lewis's tipping point' 93
liabilities of extreme poverty 38
liberation and post-liberation era 4–5, 172
lifecycle approach
    risks 145, 146–7
    social security programmes 150–2, 158, 169, 178

literacy rates 137
local-level dynamics and planning *see* regional poverty
lower poverty line (LPL)/upper poverty line (UPL) 95, 96–7, 101–5, 142–3 148, 165

macro-economic context 25
marginalized/socially excluded groups 16
    social security reform agenda 154–5
    women 58–61, 63–6
marriage *see* guardianship and feminization of poverty
mechanization of agriculture 117–18
microfinance institutions (MFIs)/microcredit system 72–3, 75, 77, 81–2, 83, 145
middle-income country (MIC) status, significance of 31–2, 165–6
migration
    domestic and international 18, 94, 167
    rural-urban 15, 128–9
    and urbanization 127–9
Millennium Development Goals (MDGs) 12–13, 162
'mini big push', need for 12, 20, 26–7
Ministry of Social Development (MSD) 156, 157
mobile financial services (MFS) 77, 78, 145
mobile networks operators (MNOs) 80
monitoring and evaluation (M&E) system 149, 157

national consensus building 46
National Social Insurance Scheme (NSIS) 151, 152
national-level and regional level analysis 89–90

pavement-dwellers ('floating people') 134
pensions 151–2
Planning Commission 106, 114, 157
    Five Year Plan 1–2, 5–6, 20, 89, 115, 138, 162
political representation 17, 44
political settlement 31, 46, 165
    development state to social policy regime 32–5
    drivers and dimensions of debate 43–5
    institutional responsibility matrix (IRM) 34, 35–6, 40–1, 42
    significance of contrast between extreme and moderate poor 37–40
    significance of middle-income country (MIC) status 31–2, 165–6
potato production *see* agricultural commercialization and employment generation
'poverty effects' 38, 39
poverty threshold 5

property rights and assets 62–3
proxy means test (PMT) 152, 153, 157
purdah norms 56, 61

regional poverty and real wages 89–92
    association between poverty and real wages 101–5
    increase in rural real wages 92–4
    policy recommendations 105–6
    poverty dynamics at sub-district level 94–9
    variations in real wages 99–100
remittances 18, 144
rice crops 114
rice prices 92–4, 95, 99, 101–5
'rightful shares' argument 170–4
rural economy
    growth 109–10
    non-farm sector 15, 93–4, 114, 144
    and social security provision 149
Rural Employment Opportunities for Public Assets (REOPA) 22
rural wages
    agricultural 17–18, 91, 92–3, 114, 144
    agricultural value chain 120, 121–2
    increase in 92–4
rural-urban gap in social security provision 148, 154
rural-urban migration 15, 128–9

safety net programmes *see* social protection; social security system reform
sanitation, urban 136–7
self-employment 145
self-interest and well-being regimes 43–5
sharing the well
    full employment assumption for social protection 168–9
    future challenges 163
    improving present strategies 163–4
    lifecycle model *see* lifecycle approach
    limitations of Western social policy as guide 165–7
    metaphor 1–5, 44
    prioritizing eradication of extreme poverty 161–2
    recent trends 162–3
    resourcing alternative approaches 174–8
    rethinking social protection and distribution 169–71
    'rightful shares' argument 171–4
shocks
    prevention and mitigation 27, 163–4
    types and impacts 25–6
SHOUHARDO programme 22
slums/squatter settlements 134–7
'smart economics' 54
social capital 36–7
social isolation 39–40

social protection
  current programmes 26
  financial inclusion and safety net
    programmes 83
  pre-capitalist period 3–4
  see also sharing the well
social security system reform 141–2,
    158, 164
  determinants of poverty 143–5
  evolution of programmes 145–7
  financing and delivering 155–7
  impact on poverty 147–8, 158
  issues and challenges 148–9
  progress with poverty reduction (2000–15)
    142–3
  proposed strategy 150–2
  qualifying agenda 153–8
  selection and targeting 152–3
socially excluded groups *see* marginalized
  groups
spatial/geographic considerations 16–17, 40
squatter settlements/slums 134–7
successful poverty eradication programmes
  20–4, 25
sustained eradication of extreme poverty
  1–6
systemic vs idiosyncratic forms of poverty 38

targeting
  financial access 82–3
  resource requirements 176–7
  social security system reform 152–3
Targeting the Ultra-Poor (TUP) programme
  22, 24, 75
tax credit reform 169–70
tax revenues 45
'threshold effects' 15, 16
transaction costs of borrowing 75–6, 82
transportation, urban 136

universal basic income (UBI) 169–72, 173,
  175, 176, 177

upper poverty line (UPL)/lower poverty line
  (LPL) 95, 96–7, 101–5, 142–3, 148, 165
urban employment 18, 135
Urban Partnerships for Poverty Reduction
  (UPPR) programme 22–3
urbanization 125, 137–8
  access to services 136–7
  challenges faced by extreme poor 133–7
  citizen's rights 134–6
  current and future profiles 129–32
  and extreme poverty 132–3
  and migration 127–9
  recent trends 126, 127

wages *see* regional poverty and real wages;
  rural wages
water
  resources 173–4
  and sanitation, urban 136–7
well-being regimes model 33–5
  institutional responsibility matrix (IRM)
    34, 35–6, 40–1, 42
Western social policy, limitations of 165–7
women
  female-headed households 52, 63–6
  garment industry workers 18, 135
  wage rate and rural labour
    participation 114
  see also guardianship and feminization
    of poverty
working age, social security programmes
  for 151
World Bank 51, 54, 64, 79, 90, 91, 109, 167
  determinants of poverty 143
  Employment Guarantee Programme for
    the Poorest 154
  financial inclusion data 73
  lower middle-income classification 31,
    149, 162
World Food Programme (WFP) 92

zero extreme poverty 12–13, 20